Christian Living

Passion for Christ
New Beginnings

By Lori Ann Moeszinger

Memoir
The Secrets of Prayer
When Death Knocked at My Door

Autobiography
Total Surrender: My Story
and Your Blueprint for a Meaningful Life

Christian Living
Passion for Christ: New Beginnings

The Living Waters Series
Faith On Trial: The Startling Reality of Genuine Belief
Drenched in Faith: The Transformative Act of Water Baptism
Spirit Filled Life: The Unseen Force of Divine Power
The Bible Unbound: Trust, Translation, and Transformation
Prophets and Pulpits: Discerning Truth in the House of God
Beyond the Tithe: The Transformative Power of Generous Faith
Heart of Abundance: The Journey to Radical Giving and Receiving
Heaven's Reach: Drawing the Unbelieving into the Fold
Breaking Silence: The Charge to Uphold the Faith Out Loud
Beyond the Final Breath: The Christian's Voyage into Eternity

Christian Living
In Sacred Conversation: The New Testament Prayer Guide

Christian Living

Passion for Christ
New Beginnings

By

Lori Ann Moeszinger

THE RIDGE

PUBLISHING GROUP

The Ridge Publishing Group
Coeur d'Alene, Idaho, U.S.A.

Library of Congress Control Number: 2024916247

Passion for Christ: New Beginnings by Lori Ann Moeszinger

ISBN: 978-1-956905-07-6 (e-book)
ISBN: 978-1-956905-08-3 (softcover)

1. Religion / Christian Living / General. 2. Religion / Christian Living / Spiritual Growth. 3. Religion / Christian Life / Inspirational. 4. Religion / Christian Life / Personal Growth. 5. Religion / Christian Living / Social Issues. I. Title.

First Edition: August 2024

Printed in the United States of America

Contents

"Passion for Christ: New Beginnings" invites readers to rediscover the transformative power of faith. This book opens the door to a renewed understanding of devotion, exploring the foundational truths of Christianity with fresh insights and heartfelt sincerity. Whether you are at the start of your spiritual journey or seeking to deepen your faith, this book offers guidance, inspiration, and a renewed sense of connection with Christ.

Join Our Community

Dive deeper into your faith and join a community of like-minded believers by connecting with us across multiple platforms:

- **Facebook Page**: Follow us at Guardians of Biblical Truth to stay updated with inspirational content and community discussions.
- **Facebook Group**: Join our closed group, Guardians of Biblical Truth Forum, for more personal interactions, where you can share, discuss, and grow in your understanding of biblical truths.
- **Blog**: Visit our blog at Jesus-Says.com for thoughtful posts, devotionals, and biblical interpretations aimed at nurturing your spiritual growth.
- **Social Media**: Connect with us on X, Instagram, and Pinterest @NNSBible to get daily inspirations and engage with a community that values deep, scriptural truths.

We look forward to connecting with you and growing together in faith!

Acknowledgments

THANK YOU, GOD, OUR HEAVENLY FATHER, it's because of You, I've become a passionate student of your Holy Scriptures.

I have always desired a deeper understanding of the Bible and a deeper knowledge of God Himself. But it wasn't until I began studying the Holy Bible—King James Version: translated out of the original languages (Hebrew and Greek); with the previous translations diligently compared and revised, conformable to the edition of 1611, commonly known as the Authorized or King James Version—given to me (50-something years ago) by my parents for my ninth birthday, and other study aids, that I found the fulfillment of those desires.

I am immediately grateful to my husband, Eric, for the opportunity to take on this task, which has shaped my life these past few years. Thanks to Eric for taking the extra time in feedback—despite all the pain and frustration it caused us both—the result is a new appreciation and instruction for a life reflecting God's will. Eric's acceptance has made this book a serious contribution towards reaching eternal life with the Lord. Thanks also to Eric for an intellectual comradeship like no other in my life. Our minds continually challenge and build on each other's ideas about God, which have made my work on this book so much stronger because of our dialog.

To my parents, Charles (RIP) and JoAnn: words cannot express how much I love and appreciate you. When life got tough you were always there for Michael, Daniel, Joseph, and me. Thank you for your sacrifice. I love you eternally.

To my sons: Matthew, John, and Jared. To Matthew who was responsible for the beginning of my life and its true journey, I am forever eternally grateful. To John and his beautiful extended family, life would not be the same without your love and easiness. Thank you all for enriching our lives again and again. To Jared, thank you for your honest reflection and for inspiring me to be better, purer, and more awake. I am truly blessed to have you in my life. My sons are the precious jewels of my life, and they illuminate every breath I take through their very existence.

To my teachers; to Pastor Paul D. Van Noy: thank you for your guidance and wisdom. To Pastor Steve Cioccolanti: thank you for your leadership, creative passion, and our friendship. I appreciate you. To Evangelist Tiff Shuttlesworth: thank you for giving me an ear. You came through for me in a moment when I needed it most. I'm grateful for our partnership and thankful for your presence in my life.

And finally, I want to tell you how honored and blessed I am to be serving our Heavenly Father. Thank you, God, for the desire, the energy, the determination, and the enthusiasm You have placed in my spirit. I am fully devoted to You because You first have been fully devoted to me!

Dear reader, may this book, "Passion for Christ: New Beginnings," speak deep into your soul with promise and possibility—because if you've always wanted a deeper relationship with our Lord Jesus Christ, and if you enjoy a great read; then this is a perfect book for you.

Thank you for accepting this invitation . . .

Christian Living

Passion for Christ
New Beginnings

Introduction

What Does It Mean to Be a Real Christian?

Welcome to "Passion for Christ: New Beginnings," the cornerstone of the prequel to The Living Water series, where we embark on a journey to quench the thirst of the soul with clear, life-giving flow of divine truth. This is not just a book; it is a pilgrimage, a soul-searching voyage into the heart of what it means to live fully and passionately for Christ.

In these pages, you will find the gateway to a transformative path. Each chapter stands as a beacon, illuminating a key aspect of spiritual life, designed to guide you through the stages of deepening your relationship with God. This book serves as a primer, an overview of the spiritual landmarks that will be explored in-depth in the books to come. But make no mistake—each chapter is a complete reflection of essential truths, inviting you to begin to renew your walk with Christ.

And so, welcome, beloved in Christ, to the threshold of discovery and the embrace of the family of God. In Part One: Child of God, we will embark upon the first half of our spiritual journey together, exploring what it means to be born anew into the kingdom of heaven. This section is dedicated to the foundational experiences that define our identity in Christ.

1. **"Awakened Souls: The Journey to Salvation"** opens the doors to understanding what it truly means to be saved, to comprehend the miraculous birth of one's faith. It sets the stage for everything that follows, inviting you to surrender to the call of grace.

2. As you turn the page to **"Submerged in Faith: The Power of Water Baptism,"** we plunge into the sacred waters of commitment, exploring the profound significance of full immersion baptism as not just a symbol but a declaration of a life reborn.

3. The journey continues with **"Breath of the Divine: Embracing the Holy Spirit,"** where we seek the indwelling presence that empowers and comforts believers, encouraging us to live in the fullness of God's Spirit.

4. In **"Daily Bread: The Habit of Bible Reading,"** we discover the sustenance of daily scripture, nourishing our spirits and renewing our minds, as manna for the modern soul.

5. **"Home in His Word: Finding Your Place in a Bible-believing Community"** extends the invitation to join hands with fellow pilgrims, to grow within the vibrant body of a church that stands firmly on the scriptures.

Part One is about rooting yourself in the identity that has been bestowed upon you by grace. It is about grounding your life in the practices that will enable you to grow as a Child of God—cherished, nurtured, and eternally loved.

Embarking on Part Two: Ambassador for God, you are called to step beyond the warm embrace of spiritual infancy into the purposeful stride of maturity in faith. In these chapters, you will explore how to manifest the love and wisdom of God through your actions and interactions with the world.

6. With **"Seeds of Generosity: The Joy of Tithing and Supporting Ministry,"** we explore the blessings of giving, delving into how our contributions can support the local church and evangelistic missions.

7. **"The Giver's Path: Cultivating a Philanthropic Heart"** encourages us to embrace generosity not just as an act but as a way of life, opening our hands and hearts to reflect God's own generosity.

8. In **"Intercessory Love: Praying for Those Yet to Believe,"** we engage in the soul-stirring practice of intercession, carrying the hope of salvation to our unsaved loved ones through fervent prayer.

9. **"Voices of Hope: The Call to Share Your Faith"** is a clarion call to witness, to share the good news with boldness and love, igniting the flame of faith in others as we articulate our own belief.

10. Lastly, **"Designed for Forever: Living with Eternity in Mind"** elevates our perspective, encouraging us to live not for the fleeting moments but for the eternal promises that beckon beyond the horizon of our earthly existence.

Part Two is about living out your divine commission with every breath, every action, and every encounter. It is a call to be salt and light, to represent the kingdom of heaven on Earth, and to carry the banner of Christ's love and salvation to all corners of the world.

Together, these parts offer a holistic view of the Christian experience: understanding your identity as a Child of God and embracing your mission as an Ambassador for Christ. May your heart be stirred, your spirit be equipped, and your faith be emboldened as you journey through "Passion for Christ: New Beginnings."

Welcome to your new beginning.

"Passion for Christ: New Beginnings" is your invitation to set out on this spiritual odyssey, a comprehensive primer for the rich explorations to come in The Living Waters series. May you be refreshed, renewed, and deeply nourished by the faith you will encounter within.

Invitation

After reading this far, I thank you. With that said, I never start a book without giving an opportunity for people to get right with God. It is really inescapable, the fact that the Bible does teach eternity—once we are born, we live forever. There really is a heaven. There really is a hell. And the Bible tells us that we are going to spend eternity in one of these two places. The choice is ours. God has already made His choice. God loves us. He sent His only Son, Jesus Christ, to die on a cross for the forgiveness of our sins.

> "For God so loved the world, that He gave His only begotten Son, Jesus Christ, that whosoever believes in Him should not perish (die) but have everlasting life" (John 3:16).

Because God is holy, we need to be holy through Jesus Christ; He will never change, He is immutable, unchangeable. He is in the total state of sinless perfection in everything that He does. But you and I are not holy. By nature, we are sinful and selfish. And because we are sinful and selfish, we are separated from a holy God. But God told us, we were created in His image, and it is His desire to redeem us to right relationship with Him. Therefore, Jesus is the bridge between the holiness of God and the unholiness of humanity. And the Bible also tells us that the only way to break the curse of sin and to find right relationship with God is through Jesus Christ.

> "Jesus says unto him, I am the way, the truth, and the life: no man comes unto the Father, but by Me" (John 14:6).

The Gospel

The word "gospel" in the Greek original text means "good news of the kingdom of God." In Christianity, the term "good news" refers to the story of Jesus Christ's birth, ministry, death, and resurrection. Jesus Christ, the Son of God, died for our sins and rose again, eternally triumphant over His enemies—so that there is now no condemnation for those who believe but only everlasting joy. Wherefore the fullness of the gospel is in God Himself—enjoyed by His redeemed people.

Through the death, the ministry, the burial, and the resurrection of Jesus Christ, you and I not only have power over sin, but we have power over sickness, disease, and infirmity—yesterday, today, and forever. The same seven ways Jesus healed in the New Testament are still available to every believer today. Jesus Christ is still the great physician, and no weapon formed against His children shall prosper in the name of the Lord Jesus Christ.

> "But He was wounded for our transgressions (sins), He was bruised for our iniquities (immoral behavior): the chastisement (punishment) of our peace was upon Him; and with His stripes (the marks on His back from His beating) we are healed" (Isaiah 53:5).

"Who His own self bore our sins in His own body on the tree (cross), that we being dead to sins, should live unto righteousness: by whose stripes you are healed" (1 Peter 2:24).

Making Peace with God

How do you make peace with God?

You have to do two things:

First, you must believe in the gospel—the teaching and revelation of Christ. The gospel, just as the Scripture says: (1) Jesus Christ, God the Father's only Son, lived on this Earth, (2) died on a cross for the forgiveness of our sins, (3) was buried, (4) was raised from the dead on the third day, (5) stayed on this Earth for 40 days before ascending to heaven, (6) promised to return, and (7) we are saved by faith alone in Christ alone—this is called the doctrine of salvation.

Second, you must receive Christ by doing three things: (1) Recognize and admit your sins. The Bible says, "For all have sinned, and come short of the glory of God" (Romans 3:23). (2) Repent of your sins. Jesus said, "No, I tell you; but unless you repent, you will all likewise perish (die)" (Luke 13:3). Repentance means you recognize your sins; you admit your life is headed in the wrong direction, and now you must be willing to turn your back on sin and turn your heart to Christ. (3) Receive Jesus Christ as your personal Lord and Savior. Commit your heart to Him by faith—in childlike faith; showing the good qualities that children have, such as trusting people, being honest and enthusiastic, expressing a childlike innocence or quality.

"The Lord is not slack concerning His promise, as some men count slackness; but is longsuffering toward us, not willing that any should perish (die), but that all should come to repentance" (2 Peter 3:9).

That word "men" in the Greek is generic; it means "men and women." Therefore, if you have never recognized and repented of your sins (changed your carnal ways). If you've never had a relationship with God. Or perhaps, you are backslidden or away from God or you've wandered. The Bible says, "I will heal your backsliding, I will love them freely: for My anger is turned away from him" (Hosea 14:4). You can come home to your heavenly Father today, and He will love you, and forgive you, and cleanse you, and strengthen you to be what He's called you to be.

It isn't by accident that you are reading this book. I believe the Lord by His leading and His mercy brought us together. And so, I want to ask you to pray the prayer of salvation—also called the prayer of faith and sometimes called the sinner's prayer—to make peace with God. Just, with a sincere heart, pray the prayer of salvation out loud in childlike faith and make a commitment right now.

Why out loud? Because Christ did everything publicly.

> "For whosoever shall be ashamed of Me and of My words, of him shall the Son of Man be ashamed, when He comes in the glory of His Father with His holy angels" (Luke 9:26; also in Mark 8:38).

And after you've done that, go to our Publisher Website at https://www.RidgePublishingGroup.com, and click on "Subscribe" to receive our monthly New Beginnings Newsletter sent directly to your inbox. Also, on our website, you will find this book, Passion for Christ: New Beginnings, available for free in PDF format. The e-book and print book versions are both available for purchase at Amazon.com. Follow us on our Amazon Author Central page and learn more about next steps in your walk with God as we upload more Bible-based books. Why? Because this isn't the end of what God's going to do in your life, just the beginning.

"Go therefore and make disciples of all nations, baptizing them in the name of the Father and of the Son and of the Holy Spirit, teaching them to observe all that I have commanded you. And behold, I am with you always, to the end of the age" (Matthew 28:19-20).

With a sincere heart, just pray this, out loud:

"Heavenly Father, today as I was reading the Bible, you were speaking to me. I want to be right with God. I recognize my sins and I ask for forgiveness. I believe Jesus Christ is your Son. I believe that He died on the cross as payment for sin and rose again as the hope of the world. And I recognize that Jesus is the only salvation and the only Savior available. In childlike faith, I trust in the Lord Jesus from this day forward. I repent of my sins, and I trust in the blood that was shed on the cross for the forgiveness of my sins. Cleanse me; my mind, my body, and my spirit. Come into my heart. And I vow this day, I will live for you all the days of my life. Guide my life and help me to do your will. Fill me with the Holy Spirit and give me the power to be what you want me to be. Be my Lord and Savior. According to the Bible which cannot lie, all who call upon the name of the Lord, shall be saved. Today, I'm saved. I'm forgiven. I'm delivered. I'm healed. The curse of sin and sickness and lack in my life are now broken. And I have become the righteousness of God through Jesus Christ. And I'll never be the same. I pray this in Jesus Christ's precious name. Amen."

The Bible said either your Father is God, or your father is the devil. And the Bible said that the power of sin and Satan comes to steal, and to kill, and to destroy. But Jesus said:

"The thief comes not, but for to steal, and to kill, and to destroy; I come that they might have life, and that they might have it more abundantly" (John 10:10).

Jesus is the master of life. And if you want to walk in the life of forgiveness and have that relationship with God the Father, you can begin that today. All you have to do is pray the prayer of salvation to make peace with God—in doing so, you become a born again Christian.

"Therefore if any man be in Christ, he is a new creature: old things are passed away; behold, all things become new" (2 Corinthians 5:17).

"Total Surrender: My Story and Your Blueprint for a Meaningful Life" is not just an autobiography about my call with God. It is a clarion call (a call to something that is hard to ignore). It is a wakeup call to all of humanity to choose God before it's too late. And get prepared for the second coming of Jesus Christ, our Lord and Savior—time is near, He is knocking at the door:

"Behold, I stand at the door and knock. If anyone hears My voice and opens the door, I will come in to him and eat with him, and he with Me" (Revelation 3:20).

When you know God and understand the wisdom of the Bible, it will change you! This is our calling—our true purpose in life. Let the Lord into your life; He has a plan . . . when you do that, amazing things start to happen: You'll become passionate about God. You'll begin to crave to think and speak in line with Jesus' ways. You'll start to see yourself the way Christ sees you. You'll habitually tune into the Holy Spirit, who lives within those in Christ, to check for a sense of peace in your choices. And then miracles begin to happen . . .

PART ONE

Child of God

CHAPTER ONE

Awakened Souls:
The Journey to Salvation

"Therefore, if anyone is in Christ, he is a new creation. The old has passed away; behold, the new has come."

—2 CORINTHIANS 5:17 ESV

In the quiet moments of self-reflection, a whisper calls to the depths of our being—a whisper that longs to be a shout, resonating with the truths we've been searching for, perhaps without even knowing it. This is the whisper of salvation, a call to awakening the soul to a life it has not yet known but for which it has always yearned.

This chapter is an exploration of that divine call and the profound journey of responding to it. It's a journey that begins with an echo in the heart and leads to a crescendo of transformation that reverberates through every aspect of life.

The journey to salvation is the most epic adventure a human being can embark upon. It is fraught with challenges and saturated with the ultimate discovery of truth. This path is not for the faint of heart. It is for those who dare to confront the reality of their existence, who are brave enough to face the shadow of their imperfections, and who are bold enough to reach out for a grace that is extended by a hand unseen.

As you step into the pages of this chapter, prepare to navigate through the stages of this life-changing voyage. From the unsettling realizing of our own separation from the divine to the exhilarating acceptance of God's unfathomable grace, each topic is a milestone on the road to a transformed life.

We'll traverse the terrain of conviction, where the weight of our humanity becomes palpably clear. We'll then turn the corner to witness the vast horizon of God's love and the great invitation extended through the gospel of Christ. Together, we'll walk through the doorway of repentance and confession, where burdens are lifted, and freedom is found.

In the embrace of grace, we discover the essence of faith—unmerited, unwavering, and life-altering. This faith assures us of our salvation, not through our own merit but through the promise of God's word, sealing our hearts with an eternal hope.

As the initial steps of growth are taken, discipleship begins. It is here that the journey truly unfolds, revealing the splendor of a life lived not just in Christ but for Christ.

And as we emerge, living the transformed life, we'll find that our very existence is a testament to the power of an awakened soul—a beacon of the transformative journey of salvation.

So open your heart, dear reader. The journey begins here, and the destination is nothing less than eternity itself. Welcome to the awakening. Welcome to the journey to salvation.

Recognizing the Call

In the stillness of our days and the chaos of our nights, there is a voice that whispers to the depths of our spirits, a siren call that pulls us towards something greater than ourselves. It's a stirring, a yearning for understanding, for purpose, for a connection that transcends the material world we see. This is the inception of a divine quest—recognizing the call to salvation.

"For he has set eternity in the human heart . . ." (Ecclesiastes 3:11b NIV). Within each of us lies this seed of eternity, a divine fingerprint that marks us for more than just the sum of our earthly experiences. It's the innate sense that we were created for more than we can see, touch, or fully comprehend.

As we meander through life's winding pathways, we often overlook this call, mistaking it for a hollow echo of unfulfilled dreams or unmet desires. Yet, the truth remains steadfast, calling out to us in moments. Of silence and solace, in the beauty of creation, and often in the middle of our turmoil. It beckons us to lift our gaze from the temporal and set our sights on the eternal.

"The wind blows where it wishes, and you hear its sound, but you cannot tell where it comes from or where it goes. So it is with everyone born of the Spirit" (John 3:8, NKJV). Just like the wind, the Spirit's call can be gentle or it can be as forceful as a gale, but it is always there, moving, reaching out to our hearts with a call to awaken.

To recognize this call is to open oneself to the possibility of a deeper truth—the truth of a loving God who calls out to His children, who reaches across the chasm of separation with a lifeline forged in the sacrifice of His Son. It's to hear Jesus' own words echo across the centuries, "Come to me, all you who are weary and burdened, and I will give you rest" (Matthew 11:28 NIV).

Acknowledging this call isn't about audibly hearing a voice; it's about sensing a pull on your soul that urges you to seek, to knock, to ask about the essence of life itself (Matthew 7:7). It's about an intrinsic knowledge that there must be more than what meets the eye—a knowledge that leads you to the doorstep of faith.

Recognizing the call to salvation is the first step on the most epic journey you will ever embark upon. It is a personal awakening, where the heart begins to see what the eyes cannot. It's the point where our narrative intersects with the divine story, where our history collides with His story, and the journey to salvation begins.

This section invites you to explore that call—a call to redemption, to a new birth, to a life where you are no longer defined by your past but by your future in Christ. For "if anyone is in Christ, he is a new creation; old things have passed away; behold, all things have become new" (2 Corinthians 5:17, NKJV).

So listen closely. Do you hear it? The call is there, woven into the fabric of your being, a tapestry of whispers and longings, inviting you to step into the grand adventure of salvation.

———

The Whisper in the Marketplace

Meet Jacob, a 34-year-old market analyst, who wears the same silver cross necklace under his crisp, white shirts—a remnant of a faith he once knew. Every day, he battles dragons of deadlines and the constant roar of the stock market. The sword he wields is his analytical prowess, cutting through data, but it cannot slay the growing sense of emptiness within him. At night, the glow of his multiple screens cannot illuminate the questions that haunt him—questions of purpose, of eternity, of peace.

Jacob lies awake, the silence of his apartment amplifying the disquiet in his soul. He's successful by all accounts, but success has become a dragon breathing down his neck, threatening to consume his peace with its fiery breath. The cross around his neck feels heavier with each passing day, a symbol of a battle between who he is and who he feels called to be.

It's a Wednesday, like any other, but as Jacob walks through the bustling city to his high-rise office, a street musician's melody cuts through the cacophony of the crowd. The tune is familiar—a hymn from his childhood. In that moment, there's a palpable shift. The clamor of the city fades into a backdrop as the song stirs something long dormant within him. It's the whisper of something greater, a call to a higher battle, one for his very soul.

The musician's fingers gracefully dance over the strings of an old, worn guitar, the wood weathered like the lines on the man's face. The hymn, "Amazing Grace," hovers in the air, and with it, a tranquility that Jacob hasn't felt in years. The silver cross under his shirt suddenly feels cool against his skin, a weighty reminder of a path he once walked. As he pauses to listen, the notes seem to be speaking directly to him, reigniting the embers of a faith long neglected. The dragon he's been fighting is within him, and the sword—it isn't his job, his keen mind, or even the necklace he wears. It's the rekindling of his faith, the recognition of his need for salvation, for the Christ who calls him back to life.

In that hymn, in the midst of the city's chaos, Jacob realizes the solution isn't in fighting harder, but in surrendering to the call that's been chasing him down—the call to come home, to be renewed, to slay the true dragon with a mightier sword: the power of a revitalized faith.

And in this, there lies a message for us all: that sometimes, the greatest battles are won through a whisper, calling us to lay down our weary arms and be led by a still, small voice into victory that's already been won.

The State of Separation

In the tapestry of human existence, there's a thread that runs counter to the vibrant colors of life, a somber strand that weaves through every heart and story. This is the state of separation, an intrinsic recognition that we, in our human condition, stand at a distance from the divine holiness of God.

"For all have sinned and fallen short of the glory of God" (Romans 3:23 NIV). Sin, this pervasive force, has etched a chasm deep and daunting. It's not merely an action but a state of being that tarnishes our thoughts, our deeds, our very essence. The awareness of this rift is like the chill of winter that creeps into our bones, a coldness that speaks of isolation and disconnection.

Yet, in this state of separation, there is a stark beauty, a piercing truth that illuminates our desperate need for redemption. Like a lighthouse beam that cuts through the fog, our realization of this divide is the first glimmer of hope—because only in knowing our lostness can we seek to be found.

"But your iniquities have made a separation between you and your God, and your sins have hidden His face from you so that He does not hear" (Isaiah 59:2, ESV). The scriptures lay bare the heart of our plight; our transgressions are barriers that obscure the warmth of God's presence. It's an echo of a paradise lost, a memory of Eden that haunts our collective conscience.

In this state of separation, we find the mirror of the law, reflecting our imperfections and the impossibility of reaching God's perfection on our own. It's as if we are standing on one cliff face, with God on the opposite, and no matter how hard we strive, the gap is insurmountable by our own efforts. This is the human quandary, the soul's dilemma.

But do not let your heart be troubled. For while "the wages of sin is death," there is a promise that follows, a lifeline thrown across the great divide: "but the gift of God is eternal life in Christ Jesus our Lord" (Romans 6:23 NIV). The narrative does not end at the recognition of our separation; it merely begins.

This section invites you to journey through the valleys of this separation to grasp the full scope of what it means to be reconciled to God. It's not just about understanding the vastness of the gulf but about coming to know the One who bridges it. In the midst of this exploration, we confront our frailty, our brokenness, and our need. But more than that, we encounter the profound love of a Creator who did not leave us in our state of exile but provided a way back to Him.

In the gravity of our state of separation, we are poised to discover the magnitude of God's intervention through Jesus. "For God so loved the world that He gave His only Son, that whosoever believes in Him should not perish but have eternal life" (John 3:16, ESV).

So let us tread this ground with reverence, knowing that in the acknowledgment of our separation lies the seed of our salvation, the beginning of our journey back to the heart of God, where our souls find their truest home.

The Bridge Over Troubled Waters

Emma is a 42-year-old art teacher with laugh lines that tell a story of joy, and eyes that hint at a deeper, unresolved struggle. She adorns herself with a scarf every day, a tapestry of brilliant hues that mirrors her love for art but contrasts the internal monochrome of her spirit. A creative soul, she paints scenes of harmony, yet her life's canvas bears the blot of dissonance. The dragon she faces is not in her studio but within her—a deep-seated feeling of disconnection from something essential, something sacred.

Night after night, Emma sits on the balcony of her city apartment, gazing at the stars that seem to speak in silent whispers of a grand design, of a Creator's touch she once felt part of. In the quiet of the night, her heart wrestles with the weight of something akin to homesickness, a yearning for a place she's never seen but somehow remembers. It's the feeling of separation from God that haunts her, the invisible yet palpable wall between her and the divine presence that once brought peace to her soul.

It's a rainy Thursday evening, and as Emma wipes her paint-stained hands on her apron, her gaze settles on an old, tattered Bible—a relic from her childhood. The moment feels charged with an inexplicable urgency. As she opens it, the scent of musty pages fills the air, and a passage catches her eye: "For I am convinced that neither death nor life . . . will be able to separate us from the love of God that is in Christ Jesus our Lord" (Romans 8:38–39 NIV). The walls seem to stand still, the rain's rhythm pauses, and for a heartbeat, the distance between her and God feels like it might just be all illusion.

The Bible's leather cover is worn, the edges frayed, much like Emma's resolve. But as her fingers trace the verses, the texture of the paper whispers promises of restoration. The rain against the window sings a harmony with the words, and the room feels hallowed, a sanctuary in a world of chaos. In that moment, with the simple act of opening a book and allowing the ancient words to seep into her heart, Emma discovers the bridge that spans the chasm—faith. It's the realization that her artwork, her love of beauty, is not just a profession but a calling, a way to express the divine connection she has been seeking.

Emma's scarf, now soaked with the tears of a profound epiphany, becomes her banner of truth. And through her story, we find a reflection of our own journey—the understanding that the path to God is not built by our hands but has been laid before us, waiting for the moment we choose to step forward, to cross the divide. It's a reminder that the deepest value lies not in the art we create or the success we achieve but in the reconciliation with the One who has painted the stars, the One who calls us home.

Confronting Conviction

There is a moment in every believer's journey where the quiet whisper of the Holy Spirit becomes a resounding echo in the chambers of the soul. It's an encounter that brings us face-to-face with a piercing truth: the gravity of our sin and the stunning realization of our desperate need for redemption.

"And when He comes, He will convict the world concerning sin and righteousness and judgment" (John 16:8, ESV). The Holy Spirit, our divine advocate, does not come to condemn but to lovingly convict, to gently nudge our conscience until we awaken to the stark contrast between our earthly deeds and God's heavenly standards.

As a sculptor chisels away at the marble to reveal the form within, the Spirit works within us, revealing the blemishes of our character, the wayward impulses of our hearts. This confrontation is not to shame us but to shine a light on the truth that we cannot save ourselves. It's an invitation to transformation, a call to turn from our wayward paths and find solace in the open arms of grace.

"Search me, O God, and know my heart! Try me and know my thoughts! And see if there be any grievous way in me, and lead me in the way everlasting!" (Psalm 139:23–24, ESV). David's psalm is not just a plea but a bold request to be known fully—even the darkest corners of his heart—and to be guided back into harmony with God.

Confronting conviction is not about wallowing in guilt but about embracing the catalyst for change. It's about seeing the sin for what it is—a barrier to fullness of life—and recognizing that we are not left to overcome it alone. "If we confess our sins, He is faithful and just to forgive us our sins and to cleanse us from all unrighteousness" (1 John 1:19, ESV). This promise is the essence of hope, the assurance that though our sins may be like scarlet, they shall be as white as snow (Isaiah 1:18).

In the heat of this conviction, we may feel the weight of our missteps, the cost of our mistakes. Yet, it's here, in the crucible of our own self-awareness, that we discover the depth of God's love for us. For the Lord does not bring us to this place of realization to abandon us but to rebuild us, to reshape us into His image, and to prepare us to receive the fullness of His mercy.

So let us walk through this section with open hearts, allowing the Holy Spirit to do the intricate work of conviction. Let us trust in the process that strips away the old to make way for the new. In the embrace of conviction, we find the path to true repentance and the sweet assurance that we are being made whole, not by our might but by the power of the Spirit that works within us.

The Quiet Revelation

Meet Michael, a 35-year-old software developer, whose sharp mind is adept at untangling complex codes but struggles to decode the unrest in his soul. Always in a neatly pressed suit, he's the embodiment of professionalism with a reputation for his analytic mind, yet he faces a conundrum that logic alone cannot resolve. The dragon he battles is not a glitch in his programming but an inner turmoil, a conviction that beckons him to confront the flaws in his character's code—his pride, his selfishness, and his neglect of the spiritual.

Michael lies awake, the green glow of the digital click casting a ghostly hue in his minimalist bedroom. He's haunted by a recurring dream where he stands before a mirror that reflects not his face, but his innermost being—and the reflection is far from the image he's meticulously crafted for the world. The emotions are a cocktail of anxiety and a profound sense of lacking, a dissonance between who he is and who he's meant to be.

During a routine coffee break at work, Michael overhears a conversation about grace and redemption. It's a narrative foreign to his usual podcasts and tech forums, yet it resonates with a part of him that's been long neglected. That evening, as he dusts off an old Bible from a forgotten corner of his bookshelf, his heart thuds with an unfamiliar anticipation. The moment his eyes scan the words "for all have sinned and fallen short of the glory of God" (Romans 3:23 NIV), it's as if the code of his soul is finally compiling without errors. There's a deafening silence in his spirit, signifying a shift, a pivotal explosion of clarity.

The Bible's leather cover is cold but quickly warms to his touch, the pages are stiff but yield to his fingers. As he reads, his well-structured world, the binary of right and wrong, blurs into a spectrum of grace he never accounted for. The reflection in his nightly dreams begins to shift—the image softens, becomes more humane, more real. In this moment, Michael comprehends the value of his faith not as religious artifact but as a transformative force, a tool not just for moral navigation but for personal rebirth.

Through Michael's story, we're invited to see our reflection—not just in a mirror but through the lens of divine scrutiny. We are called not to fear the revelation but to welcome it, for in the confrontation with our deepest convictions, we discover not just the problem but the path to redemption. And in this narrative, we find the courage to lay down our own swords, our defenses, and allow the Spirit to slay the dragons within, leading us into a freedom that rewrites the codes of our existence.

The Great Invitation

In the midst of our deepest struggles and most profound convictions, there emerges a beckoning, a call that resonates through the noise to everyday life. It's an invitation not of this world, yet for every soul within it. This is the Great Invitation, extended to each of us, whispering of love unfathomable, sacrifice unimaginable, and life unending.

"For God so loved the world, that He gave His only Son, that whoever believes in Him should not perish but have eternal life" (John 3:16, ESV). At the heart of this invitation is the narrative of Jesus Christ—God in flesh, walking among us, teaching us, loving us, dying for us, and triumphantly conquering death itself in His resurrection. It's a story that turns every notion of worldly power and wisdom on its head.

The life of Jesus, depicted in the gospels, is more than a historical account; it's the unfolding of God's plan for humanity's redemption. His teachings, parables, and actions were not just for the people of His day, but for us here and now. "I am the way, and the truth, and the life. No one comes to the Father except through Me" (John 14:6, ESV).

Through His words, we find the path; through His truth, we gain clarity; and in His life, we discover our purpose.

Jesus' death on the cross, a moment of profound agony, was also one of unmatched love. In His crucifixion, we see the weight of our transgressions and the depth of God's grace intersect. "But God demonstrates His own love for us in this: While we were still sinners, Christ died for us" (Romans 5:8 NIV). His stretched arms were an open invitation, a bridge built over the chasm of sin, allowing us to walk into reconciliation with God.

And yet, the story didn't end in death. The resurrection is our beacon of hope, the confirmation of Jesus' promise, and the cornerstone of our faith. "He is not here; He has risen, just as He said" (Matthew 28:6 NIV). The empty tomb is God's exclamation point to the world that death is not the end, and in Christ, a new beginning is always possible.

This Great Invitation is offered freely to all. It's an invitation to shed the old self, to be born anew in the spirit of love and truth. "Therefore, if anyone is in Christ, the new creation has come: The old has gone, the new is here!" (2 Corinthians 5:17 NIV). It's an invitation to join a story much greater than our own, to become part of a family that spans the breadth of time and space, united by the Spirit that whispers this truth into every seeking heart.

As we explore this section, let's open our hearts to the profound simplicity and transformative power of the gospel. The Great Invitation awaits your response. Will you step into the embrace of God's eternal narrative? Will you accept the call to a life reborn in Christ? The journey is not always easy, the road not always smooth, but the destination is a place of everlasting love, and the way is lit by the One who calls us each by name.

The Great Invitation

In a bustling city, amid the cacophony of countless lives intersecting, there was a man named Kirk, age 35, a corporate lawyer by profession. His days were a blur of contracts and courtroom battles, a modern-day knight in tailored suits instead of armor. His dragon was not a literal beast of fire, but an inner turmoil, a void no victory in court could fill, a sense of purposelessness that whispered relentlessly in the quiet hours of the night.

Kirk's authentic emotion was not fear but an aching emptiness. Despite his success, something crucial was missing. There was a hunger for something deeper, a thirst that the finest wines from his collection couldn't quench. The accolades, the corner office with a view, the sound of "Sir" from his associates, it all felt hallow.

Then came the moment, unremarkable to any observer but earth-shattering for him. It was a simple scene—on a rainy Tuesday evening, while waiting for the pedestrian signal, he noticed a street musician playing a soulful melody on a worn violin. The music pierced through the noise, and for a moment, Kirk was transported. The busy street faded, and in that silence, he felt a stirring in his soul, awakening. It was as if the melody was speaking directly to him, inviting him to a life where success was measured not by wealth but by something infinitely richer.

The specific details of that moment were forever etched in his memory—the rhythmic tapping of raindrops on his umbrella, the faint smell of wet asphalt, the soothing melody of the violine playing "How Great Thou Art." Kirk couldn't have articulated it then, but that experience was a prelude to an encounter with the Great Invitation, a call to explore the life and teachings of Jesus Christ.

As he embarked on this journey, the gospel became the sword with which he could slay his personal dragons. The stories of Jesus—His compassion, His sacrifice, His resurrection—offered Kirk a new narrative for his life, one in which he could find the meaning that had eluded him. The message of salvation and hope found in Christ, wasn't merely a set of beliefs or doctrines; it was a transformative experience, offering redemption, purpose, and a new beginning.

As Kirk's story unfolded, he became more than a character in his narrative; he became a beacon for others facing similar dragons. The life of this modern-day knight was profoundly altered by the Great Invitation, and his story, rich with emotion, a moment of clarity, and poignant details, resonates with those yearning for a call to something greater than themselves. It says to the audience, "I have been where you are, I understand, and there is hope."

Repentance and Confession

In the narrative of faith, repentance and confession emerge not as mere rituals, but as the deeply personal and transformative steps on the pathway to spiritual freedom. It's in this profound act of turning—turning away from the past, from sin, and towards a future illuminated by grace—that we find the true heart of repentance.

Picture a prodigal son moment (Luke 15:18), as we journey alongside those who've realized that their steps have led them away from home, away from the presence of the Father. The narrative is familiar to any who have felt the sting of regret—of choices made, paths taken, and words spoken in haste. "For all have sinned and fallen short of the glory of God," (Romans 3:23) the Scripture gently reminds us, not to condemn but to open the door to redemption.

As the soul acknowledges its wanderings, a whisper of divine promise calls it back: "If we confess our sins, He is faithful and just and will forgive us our sins and purify us from all unrighteousness" (1 John

1:9). Herein lies the invitation to cast off the weight of past missteps, to speak aloud the truths of a heart in need. This confession is not an end but a beginning—a first step on a renewed journey.

Repentance is a turning of the heart, illustrated by the prophet Joel's cry to "rend your heart and not your garments" (Joel 2:13). It is in the quiet surrender, where the external trappings of religiosity fall away, that a soul stands bare and humbled, yet hopeful before its Maker. In this sacred space, the narrative weaves a tale of repentance that is both intimate and universal.

The act of voicing confession, of laying bare one's faults before the throne of mercy, becomes not a chorus of despair but a sign of hope. As the psalmist proclaims, "The sacrifices of God are a broken spirit; a broken and contrite heart, O God, you will not despise" (Psalm 51:17). In these words, we find a portrait of a soul restored, a life set back on course by the gentle hands of forgiveness.

Thus, repentance and confession become not only a tale of turning from sin but also an enduring testimony of turning to God's unfailing forgiveness and grace. Each story interlaced with the eternal truths of the Scriptures becomes a beacon to all who seek to leave the shadows behind, stepping into the warmth of God's everlasting light.

The Path to Liberation

In the heart of a teeming metropolis, Susan, a 42-year-old nurse, faced her dragon every night. Her dragon wasn't a fearsome beast breathing fire but the creeping shadows of her own past mistakes that seemed to darken her world. Despite the white uniform she donned—a symbol of purity and healing—she couldn't cleanse her conscience of the guilt that had been accumulating like the silent buildup of dust in an abandoned room.

Susan's authentic emotion was remorse. A kind and dedicated nurse, she saved lives at the hospital, but back at home, she couldn't save herself from the regret that gnawed at her during the long, sleepless nights. It wasn't one monumental misstep but a series of small, seemingly insignificant choices that spiraled into a sense of personal failure. No amount of accolades could mute the inner voice that whispered accusations in her ears.

The moment of change was subtle yet significant. During a routine shift, she washed her hands at the sink, the water spiraling down the drain like her spiraling thoughts. But as she looked up, she met the gaze of a patient in the reflection of the mirror—a woman who had just received forgiveness from a family she had wronged. The patient's eyes were bright with unshed tears, but her smile was free and unburdened. Susan felt a profound shift within her. It was as if she was seeing the patient's soul lightened from the weight of guilt through the power of forgiveness.

The specific details of that moment—the coolness of the water on her hands, the flickering fluorescent light above, the distant sound of a beeping heart monitor—forever marked the turning point in Susan's life. It was her encounter with the deep, personal meaning of repentance and confession. She realized then that the way forward wasn't to hide from her guilt but to face it, to voice it, and to find release.

Returning home, Susan sought the solace of the Bible, and the verses she once found cliché now held a profound truth. "Repent, then, and turn to God, so that your sins may be wiped out," Acts 3:19 beckoned. She understood that her profession was her sword, her calling to heal, but it was through the acts of repentance and confession that she would slay her personal dragons.

Through repentance and confession, Susan's life was not just changed; it was transformed. Her journey became a testament to the promise of Psalm 32:5, "I acknowledged my sin to you, and I did not cover my iniquity." Her story resonated with anyone haunted by the shadows of their past, offering hope that through repentance and confession, there's a path to forgiveness and a new beginning.

Susan's story, laden with authentic emotion, a pivotal moment of realization, and the tangible details of her life, tells others, "I understand the burden of guilt, but there is a way to redemption, and it is open to all." It's a story that says to the audience. "This could be you, and the peace found in this journey can also be yours.

Embracing Grace

Imagine a stage where the spotlight cuts through the darkness, centering on a lone figure. This is David, a seasoned teacher, who spent his life guiding others through the labyrinth of knowledge, yet found himself lost in his own search for peace. His dragon was the relentless pursuit of perfection, a chase for a flawlessness that always danced just beyond his reach.

David's emotion was one of weariness, his spirit fatigued by the unyielding effort to earn an elusive approval from the world, and perhaps, from a higher power he felt he had failed. Every accolade in his distinguished career was overshadowed by an internal ledger of faults and failures that no amount of human achievement could balance.

But then, amidst the cacophony of his striving, came a moment of extraordinary silence. It was during a quiet morning, the sun casting a warm glow over his pile of ungraded papers, that David stumbled upon a passage: "For by grace you have been saved through faith. And this is not your own doing; it is the gift of God" (Ephesians 2:8). The words struck a chord in him, an illuminating note that resonated with the core of his being.

The specific details of this revelation—the soft rustling of leaves outside his office window, the comforting scent of a well-loved book, the gentle timbre of the morning—created a scene of profound simplicity and clarity. It was in this stillness that David encountered the breathtaking beauty of grace. It wasn't something to be earned like the accolades on his wall; it was a gift, waiting to be accepted.

Grace became David's silent anthem, the rhythm that soothed the disquiet of his soul. His teachings began to weave in the narrative of this grace—a transformative and unmerited favor that had the power to liberate and renew. "For it is by grace you have been saved," echoed in his heart, a divine whisper that no scholarly achievement could match in understanding or reward.

David's embrace of grace told a story that reached into the classrooms and homes, touching the lives of those who, like, him, had been chasing their own dragons of perfection and self-reliance. The verses that once felt like ancient text now became the most contemporary truth he had known. "Therefore, since we have been justified by faith, we have peace with God through our Lord Jesus Christ. Through Him, we have also obtained access by faith into this grace in which we stand, and we rejoice in hope of the glory of God." (Romans 5:1–2).

His journey to embracing grace rewrote his internal ledger, not with his own deeds, but with the boundless, saving grace of Christ. It is a narrative that invites others into this dance of grace—a dance where steps are not judged, and every fall is met with a loving hand that lifts and steadies. David's story, his moment of revelation, resonate with those weary from their own efforts, whispering the liberating truth, "You are understood, you are loved, and grace is here for you."

The Birth of Faith

Envision a crossroads, not of roads and signposts, but of destinies and decision. Here stands Anna, a diligent nurse, whose life has been a testament to service. The corridors of the hospital have known her steadfast stride, the rooms have felt her tender touch, yet her heart harbors an unrest, a seeking for something that the sterility of the words could not cleanse or heal.

Anna's dragon is doubt, a specter that casts long shadows over her many acts of kindness, a question that lingers in the afterglow of her daily sacrifices. "Is this all there is?" becomes her silent mantra, a refrain that follows her through the long nights and demanding days.

It is in a moment of exhaustion, her defenses worn and her spirit pliable, that Anna finds herself in the chapel beneath the hum of fluorescent lights. The Bible in the chapel is old and worn, much like the many souls who have sought its comfort. Her fingers, still careful from years of practice, open to a passage that seems to have been waiting just for her: "Truly, truly, I say to you, unless one is born again he cannot see the kingdom of God" (John 3:3).

The specific details of this encounter—the cool touch of the wooden pew, the flickering of a candle's flame, the quiet assurance in the chapel's hush—become the backdrop for a rebirth. The concept of being "born again" was not alien to her; she has witnessed the first breaths of many new lives in her line of work. But now, it beckons to her as a personal genesis, an intimate awakening to a faith that is vibrant and alive.

Anna's birth of faith is not a loud declaration but a soft yielding, gentle release of the doubts that have long encased her heart.

"Therefore, if anyone is in Christ, he is a new creation. The old has passed away; behold, the new has come" (2 Corinthians 5:17). With these words, the seed of faith takes root in her soul, and she senses the stirrings of a spiritual renaissance.

This new birth is not marked by the cries of a newborn, but by the silent lifting of a burden, the feeling of being held in arms far stronger than her own. Anna's commitment to trust Christ for salvation becomes a wellspring of hope and a fountain of new purpose. Her service in the hospital gains a deeper dimension, infused with a love that flows from an inexhaustible source.

Her story, this birth of faith, becomes a testament to the transforming power of belief. As Anna walks the halls, her steps are lighter, her smile brighter, for within her beats the heart of one reborn. To those who observe her, both colleagues and patients alike, she is a living epistle, embodying the promise that "whosoever believes in Him may have eternal life" (John 3:15).

Anna's journey, her moment of divine commitment, whispers to all who cross her path, "There is more to life, more to you. Faith is born in a moment but lasts an eternity. Come, be born again into a living hope."

The Assurance of Salvation

Within in the tapestry of faith, there exists a golden thread that binds the believer to the heart of the divine—a sure and steadfast assurance that one's salvation is as certain as the dawn. Meet Thomas, a seasoned sailor, whose life upon the waves has taught him to read the stars and trust the compass, yet his heart has often wavered like a ship tossed by tempests when it comes to the certainty of his spiritual voyage.

For Thomas, salvation had often seemed like a distant shore, its reality shrouded in the mist of his doubts and fears. The ocean of his heart was awash with questions: "Is my faith strong enough? Am I truly saved?" These were the gales that threatened to capsize his peace of mind.

But as Thomas sat one evening on the deck of his vessel, the sea around him a mirror to the heavens above, he found solace in a passage from the Bible he'd carried with him like a life raft: "I write these things to you who believe in the name of the Son of God so that you may know that you have eternal life" (1 John 5:13). This wasn't just an ancient text; it was a beacon, a lighthouse that pierced through the fog of his uncertainty.

Specific details from that night—the salty tang of the sea air, the creaking of the ship, the serene expanse of the starlit sky—became etched in his memory as the moment when assurance solidified within him. These words were not a flimsy parchment of hope but a solid declaration, as tangible as the timbers of his ship.

The promises of God, he realized, were the stars by which he could navigate his faith. "For God so loved the world, that He gave His only Son, that whoever believes in Him should not perish but have eternal life" (John 3:16). This promise became his North Star, unwavering, constant, guiding him to the safe harbor of God's embrace.

With this assurance, the storms of doubt could rage, but Thomas's heart remained moored to the Rock of Ages. "And this is the promise that he made to us—eternal life" (1 John 2:25). The assurance of his salvation became the compass by which he set his course, the anchor he could drop in any storm, finding peace in the midst tumult.

The story of Thomas, the sailor whose faith found its footing on the promises of Scripture, speaks to every heart that yearns for certainty amidst life's undulating seas. His tale becomes a testament to the assurance that is available to all who believe—a pledge from the Divine that stands firmer than the earth, deeper than the ocean, and more enduring than the sky above.

To those who listen, Thomas's life whispers the eternal truth, "Your salvation is secured not by the strength of your grip on God, but by His unrelenting hold on you. Fear not, for your anchor holds, and it is grounded firm and deep in the Savior's love."

Initial Growth and Discipleship

In the sacred dance of life with the Divine, the initial steps of faith are both a rite of passage and a joyful declaration of a new way of living. Consider the story of Brit, a young artist whose canvas had long been painted with questions and searching strokes. Her conversion was like the first splash of brilliant color on a once-muted palette, vibrant with the hues of hope and renewal.

Her journey began at the waters of baptism, an outward symbol of an inward grace. As she was immersed, it was not just the water that enveloped her but a sense of dying to the old self, as Paul described: "We were therefore buried with him through baptism into death in order that, just as Christ was raised from the dead through the glory of the Father, we too may live a new life" (Romans 6:4). Rising from the water, Brit felt the weight of her past washed away, her life a blank canvas upon which grace could now paint.

Joining a community, faith was the next step in her spiritual odyssey. Brit found herself woven into the tapestry of a church family, a place where "every joint supplies" and "every part works properly," making the body grow so that it builds itself up in love (Ephesians 4:16). In this fellowship, her faith found both expression and encouragement, her story interlacing with others, creating a mosaic of shared belief and mutual support.

The adventure of discipleship unfolded before her like a path through an explored forest. With the Bible as her map and the Holy Spirit as her compass, Brit began to navigate the terrain of her new life. "Your word is a lamp for my feet, a light on my path" (Psalm 119:105), she would recall, finding direction and comfort in the Scriptures, her every step illuminated by its wisdom.

Discipleship meant more than learning; it was a process of becoming—of being "transformed by the renewing of your mind" (Romans 12:2). It involved planting the seeds of God's Word deep in her heart and tending to them diligently, so they might bear fruit in every season of her life. It was in these moments of growth, through service and study, prayer and perseverance, that Brit's faith began to flourish, spreading roots deep into the fertile soil of God's truth.

As Brit's story unfolded, her initial growth in faith became a testament to the transformative power of discipleship. Each act of obedience, each step in her journey, was a stroke of the Master's brush on the canvas of her life, revealing the masterpiece that God intended her to be.

For all who witness her walk, Brit's life serves as a vivid portrayal of beginning anew in Christ. Her story invites others to take those initial steps of baptism, fellowship, and discipleship, and join in the divine dance, growing in the grace and knowledge of our Lord and Savior Jesus Christ (2 Peter 3:18). It's a story of a life transformed, a spiritual journey that resonates with the promise of what is to come for all who follow the path of growth in faith.

Living the Transformed Life

Imagine if you will, the metamorphosis of a caterpillar to a butterfly—a transformation so radical that it hardly seems possible. Now, picture this in the life of Eric, a once self-proclaimed skeptic, who, upon embracing faith in Christ, began to experience a revolution of the heart and mind that altered the trajectory of his life.

This new life Eric stepped into wasn't merely a polished version of the old; it was as if he had stepped out of the shadows and into the brilliance of the sun for the first time. His priorities shifted from chasing fleeting pleasures to seeking eternal treasures. "But seek first His kingdom and His righteousness, and all these things will be given to you as well" (Matthew 6:33), became the compass by which he navigated his daily decisions.

The lifestyle changes in Eric were evident to all who knew him. Gone were the weekends lost to the pursuit of the next thrill, replaced by moments spent in community service and fellowship. His time, once his most guarded possession, became a gift he offered freely, living out the command to "love your neighbor as yourself" (Mark 12:31). He found joy in simplicity and purpose in serving, his life a testament to the beatitudes he now held dear.

But perhaps the most striking change was the newfound passion with which Eric approached God's mission. The Great Commission, "Therefore go and make disciples of all nations" (Matthew 28:19–20), echoed not as a distant command but as a personal calling. His conversations, once dominated by business and banter, now often turned to matters of faith and hope. His heart, once indifferent to the spiritual plight of others, now ached to share the love that had so freely been given to him.

Eric's journey was not without its valleys. There were days when the old self would whisper doubts and temptations, seeking to reclaim lost territory. Yet, these moments of struggle were met with the armor of God and the support of his spiritual family, allowing him to "stand firm against the schemes of the devil" (Ephesians 6:11).

His was a life marked by the fruits of the Spirit: love, joy, peace, forbearance, kindness, goodness, faithfulness, gentleness, and self-control (Galatians 5:22–23). Each aspect of this fruit manifesting in his daily walk was a reflection of the One he now followed, a visible display of an inward grace that transformed not just the mind, but the soul.

Living the transformed life for Eric meant that every day was a canvas upon which God's grace painted a story of redemption. His existence became a living epistle, known and read by all who encountered him, a real-time narrative of what it means to be "a new creation; the old has gone, the new has come!" (2 Corinthians 5:17).

For those watching Eric's transformation, it served as an invitation to reconsider the possibilities of a life surrendered to the Creator's touch. It showed that the journey with Christ is not just about reaching a destination but about becoming someone new along the way, someone whose life sings the melody of salvation and whose story echoes through eternity.

CHAPTER TWO

Submerged in Faith:
The Power of Water Baptism

"Therefore we were buried with Him through baptism into death, that just as Christ was raised from the dead by the glory of the Father, even so we also should walk in newness of life."

—ROMANS 6:4 NIV

Welcome to the waters' edge, where ancient practice meets personal transformation, and a simple element becomes the threshold of a profound journey. In this chapter, we will wade into the depths of one of Christianity's most sacred rites, a symbol so potent that it has weathered millennia and still evokes awe and wonder in the hearts of believers.

Baptism, a practice the predates the very walls of the church, is as rich in history as it is in meaning. It is here, in the gentle embrace of water, that countless souls have found the beginning of their story in Christ. We trace the ripples back to where they began, understanding how this tradition has anchored the faith to their historical roots while continuing to signify a transformative experience of rebirth and dedication.

From the dusty banks of the Jordan River where Jesus Himself was baptized, to the modern sanctuaries where individuals today take the plunge, baptism is a thread that weaves through the tapestry of faith. It stands as a command, a vow, an act, an aftermath, and a journey—each phase a chapter in the believer's spiritual narrative.

As we turn the pages of this chapter, we will immerse ourselves not just in the waters of baptism but in the waters of understanding, exploring the deep connections between the ancient ritual and the eternal truth it symbolizes. Join us on this enlightening path as we dive into the historical, spiritual, and personal dimensions of baptism—the sacred act that has marked the lives of millions, a holy splash that echoes the heartbeat of heaven.

Prepare to be submerged, not only in the literal sense but in the knowledge and beauty of a faith that declares through this simple act an extraordinary truth: old life has ended; a new life has begun. Welcome to the transformative waters of baptism.

The Historical Roots of Baptism

The ritual of baptism isn't a mere dot on the timeline of Christian customs; it is a rich tapestry interwoven with strands of ancient traditions, sacred rites, and divine commandments. To understand baptism is to delve into the legacy that predates the church bell's ring and reaches back to the flowing rivers where Jewish purification rites cleansed more than just the flesh.

Within the sacred texts, we glimpse its precursors: the ceremonial washings in Judaism, the mikvah, where one emerged refreshed and renewed (Leviticus 16:4). These practices set the stage for a more profound spiritual cleansing, one that John the Baptist heralded as he stood waist-deep in the Jordan River, calling for repentance and preparing the way for the One who would "baptize with the Holy Spirit" (Mark 1:8).

The waters of baptism found their significance not just in the acts of the prophets but in the ministry of Christ. Jesus Himself was baptized by John the Baptist, not as a confession of sin, but as a model for all believers and a symbolic inauguration of His messianic mission (Matthew 3:13–17). As He emerged from the water, heaven itself bore witness to this holy ordinance, with the Spirit descending like a dove and a voice from above proclaiming, "This is My Son, whom I love; with Him I am well pleased."

The early church embraced baptism as a foundational act, a rite that signified one's death to sin and resurrection to a life in Christ, as instructed by the Lord before His ascension: "Go therefore and make disciples of all the nations, baptizing them in the name of the Father, and of the Son, and of the Holy Spirit" (Matthew 28:19). This mandate wove baptism into the very fabric of Christian identity.

As we trace the ripples of baptism back through time, we recognize that this sacred act is far more than a historical footnote. It is a covenantal sign, a bridge linking the faithful across generations, an eternal bond that speaks of purification, commitment, and a profound entrance into the family of God. Through baptism, believers across ages have stepped into the waters of history, joining the great cloud of witnesses who have emerged reborn, their lives a testament to the enduring power of this divine sacrament.

Embracing the Waters of Heritage

In the heart of a sprawling metropolis, where skyscrapers stretched to the heavens and the din of daily life never waned, there lived a young woman name Erica. At 26, she was a burgeoning artist, her canvas often a mirror to the tumult within. In her compact studio apartment adorned with splashes of vibrant color and the scent of oil paints, a silent battle raged. Her dragon? A yearning for belonging that not even her most passionate creations could satisfy.

Erica's authentic emotion was a profound longing, a searching that kept her pacing the floorboards into the early hours. Amid her success, with her art showcased in local cafes and whispered about in hushed, reverent tones, there was an unshakable sense of being adrift, untethered from any sense of deeper history or legacy.

The moment that changed everything was as delicate as the stroke of a paintbrush. It happened on a visit to her grandmother, when an old family Bible was opened to a page long forgotten, revealing a lineage of faith that traced back generations. There, listed in meticulous handwriting, were the dates of baptism for her ancestors, a spiritual genealogy that she never knew existed.

This discovery was her moment of silent explosion, the stirring of waters long still. Each detail of that day became etched in her mind: the musty smell of ancient pages, the warmth of her grandmother's hand on her shoulder, the afternoon sun casting long shadows across the wooden floor, and the realization that her own name was missing from this sacred register.

Baptism, the product of this story, became not just an abstract concept but a bridge to her own heritage, a way to immerse herself in the continuum of a faith that had silently shaped her very being. It wasn't the water that held the power, but rather what it represented—

a washing away of the isolation, a rebirth into a family that stretched beyond the confines of time and place.

Choosing to be baptized, Erica stepped into the same waters that had embraced her forebears, feeling the weight of her loneliness dissolve into a current of connection. As she rose from the baptismal pool, it was not just the drops of water that clung to her but a newfound sense of identity, a lineage reclaimed.

Erica's story, rich with the details of her artistic life and her longing for belonging, whispers to the audience, "I am you. I've felt the void, the search for something more. And in this water, this ancient practice, I found my place in a story much larger than my own."

The Significance of Water in Spiritual Rituals

Water, in its ceaseless flow, carries a profound significance that transcends cultures, borders, and spiritual beliefs. It is the essence of life, the pulse of the earth, and a universal symbol for purification, rebirth, and renewal. In the Christian faith, water baptism is more than a mere rite; it's a sacrament steeped in deep spiritual symbolism, drawing from ancient currents of religious tradition.

The narrative of water as a purifying force begins in the very opening of the Bible, "the Spirit of God was hovering over the waters" (Genesis 1:2). Here water is the stage upon which creation unfolds, the substrate from which life springs forth. It's as if the waters themselves were the first witness to the divine mystery of life, an element both common and yet holy.

Across various cultures, water is revered as a cleanser of not just the body but the soul. In the rich tapestry of Hinduism, the Ganges River is considered sacred, a means to purify one's sins through its sanctifying waters. This reverence for water echoes in the Christian rite of baptism, which signifies the washing away of sin, as proclaimed by the apostle Paul: "He saved us through the washing of rebirth and renewal by the Holy Spirit" (Titus 3:5).

In the crystalline narrative of baptism, we are invited to consider the transformative power of water. Jesus Himself was baptized in the Jordan, sanctifying the waters for all who would follow. As the Gospel of John recounts: "Jesus answered, 'Very truly I tell you, no one can enter the kingdom of God unless they are born of water and the Spirit'" (John 3:5). This profound declaration ties the act of baptism to the journey of spiritual awakening, setting a precedent that has flowed through the ages.

The Christian baptism, viewed through this universal lens, becomes a river that connects us to the very heart of spiritual practice. It is both a personal and communal act, one that mirrors the many traditions where the water serves as a threshold to the sacred. To step into these waters is to join a myriad of believers in a shared act of faith, to be submerged in the legacy of those who have found in water a symbol of hope and a promise of new life.

This section of our spiritual exploration invites you to wade into the depths of water's symbolism, to understand how a simple element can carry the weight of such profound spiritual truth. It beckons us to reflect on the potency of water in rituals of faith and how, through the act of baptism, we tap into the enduring narrative of renewal that water has always represented.

———

A River of Renewal

In the stillness of a small town, there lived a woman named Sophia, 32, a librarian with a love for ancient texts and a curious, searching spirit. She wore a pendant of lapis lazuli around her neck, a symbol of truth and enlightenment her grandmother had given her. Sophia's dragon was not a beast of scales and fire, but a restlessness of the soul, an ache for a connection to something transcendent that she felt was missing from her life.

By day, she was surrounded by stories of heroes and myths, of knights and their valiant deeds. But as dusk fell and the library's lights dimmed, Sophia would find herself haunted by an authentic emotion— a profound longing for transformation and purpose that her quiet existence in the library could not satisfy.

The pivotal moment came on a cool autumn evening, as a light rain whispered against the library windows. Sophia was archiving a donated collection when she came across an ancient-looking manuscript on spiritual rituals. The text spoke of water as a metaphor for rebirth and purification, present in countless traditions, but it was the passage on Christian baptism that caused the air around her to still—as if in that very moment, the very essence of the library shifted, welcoming a sacred silence.

It detailed a believer's journey through water baptism, a physical and spiritual immersion that was both a closing of one chapter and an opening of another, a tangible expression of inner change. As she turned the brittle pages, each specific detail painted a picture so vivid that Sophia could almost feel the cool touch of the water on her skin, and hear the collective breath of witnesses to this holy act.

The story resonated with her, stirring the waters of her own spirit. It wasn't just the act of baptism that moved her—it was the value, the profound transformation promised in that plunge beneath the surface. It spoke of dying to the old self, emerging renewed, connected to a lineage of faith that spanned the ages.

Sophia's heart raced as she read how the early Christians viewed baptism as a profound solution to the universal problem of spiritual estrangement, a bridge to the divine. In that moment, the water of baptism became more than a ritual; it became the sword with which she could slay her own dragons of doubt and disconnection.

As she closed the manuscript, Sophia realized that her life had shifted. the pendant on her chest seemed to glow warmer, as if in approval of the truth she had uncovered. This ancient practice could be the path she had been seeking, the journey she was yearning to embark upon. With a newfound resolve, she decided to explore this act of faith, to see if perhaps her story too could be interwoven with the timeless tapestry of rebirth that water baptism represented.

This narrative of transformation through the sacred waters spoke not just to Sophia, but to all who seek a renewal of spirit, echoing the deep-seated yearnings of countless souls before her. It's not merely about the water; it's about what the water allows one to become— reborn, renewed, and profoundly connected to a faith that has quenched the spiritual thirst of generations.

―――――――

Jesus and the Baptism Command

In the narrative of faith, there are moments so potent that they ripple through time, touching the lives of countless individuals across millennia. Among these is a scene of divine humility and heavenly proclamation: the baptism of Jesus by John the Baptist.

Imagine the Jordan River, its waters gently flowing, the reeds whispering with the secrets of the ages. Crowds have gathered, drawn by the call of a wild prophet clothed in camel's hair, his voice thundering with the urgency of repentance. Then, amidst this scene of anticipation and awe, Jesus Himself steps forward. In this moment, heaven touches earth, as John, recognizing the One before him, lowers Jesus into the watery depths and rises Him into the open skies.

The heavens part and the Spirit descends like a dove, while a voice from above declares, "This is my Son, whom I love; with Him I am well pleased" (Matthew 3:17). It is a celestial endorsement, an anointing for the ministry that would change the course of history.

Yet, this act is more than a mere precursor to Jesus' earthly ministry; it is an archetype for all believers. Fast forward to the closing chapter of Jesus' sojourn on earth. The resurrected Christ stands with His disciples, delivering what would become known as the Great Commission: "Therefore go and make disciples of all nations, baptizing them in the name of the Father, and of the Son, and of the Holy Spirit, and teaching them to obey everything I have commanded you" (Matthew 28:19–20). Here, baptism is not just a symbolic act; it is a directive, a calling that echoes the validation of Jesus' own baptism.

The call to baptize becomes the tangible expression of spreading the good news, a sacramental act that both symbolizes and imparts grace. As believers lower the new disciples into the waters, they are enacting the death and resurrection of Christ, a vivid portrayal of the inner transformation that faith has wrought.

Just as Jesus emerged from the waters to the affirmation of His Father, so too do new believers rise to a new life, affirmed by the body of Christ surrounding them. Baptism, therefore, is not merely a tradition or a religious obligation; it is a command, an integral component of discipleship that connects us to the ministry of Jesus and to one another in the most profound way.

This divine mandate to baptize is not just the apostles of old but is a perpetual inheritance for all who claim the mantel of discipleship. Through it, the love and salvation of Christ are perpetually offered, a cascade of grace that flows from the heart of God, through the hands of His followers, into the lives of those they touch. It's a chain of redemption, each link forged by the waters of baptism, as strong and as enduring as the command that initiated it.

========

Submerged in Truth

Once upon a time, in a quaint village nestled among rolling hills and murmuring streams, there lived a young man named Eli. At the age of 30, he was a carpenter, known for the meticulous care he took in crafting furniture—not merely as pieces of wood cobbled together, but as stories of families that would use them. With a warm smile and hands roughened by his trade, he wore a simple leather bracelet, inscribed with the word "Veritas"—truth.

But beneath the composed exterior, Eli wrestled with a relentless dragon—a yearning for something more profound, a truth that seemed just beyond his grasp, keeping him awake as the moon climbed the night sky. He sought solace in tradition and the legacy left by his forebears, yet the dragon of unrest breathed its fire still.

One day, as the sun began its descent, painting the sky with hues of amber and gold, Eli encountered an old man by the river, a man known for his wisdom and serene countenance. The old man was gently immersing people in the river, one by one, speaking of new life, of rebirth in water and Spirit. Eli watched, intrigued as each face emerged from the river alight with an ineffable joy.

In that moment, Eli's heartbeat quickened, a silent explosion of clarity that shattered the stillness of his long-held doubts. As the old man extended an invitation to the water, Eli realized the solution lay not in battling for truth, but in surrendering to it, allowing the waters to cleanse and renew.

Stepping into the river, Eli felt the cool embrace of the water as the old man whispered, "In the name of the Father, and of the Son, and of the Holy Spirit." As he was submerged, it was as if the river itself was washing away the scales from his eyes. Rising from the water, Eli felt the heavy armor of his uncertainties fall away, replaced by a lightness of being he had never known. The dragon, that once fearsome best of doubt, had been vanquished not by a sword, but by the gentle power of the flowing river.

This act of baptism, as simple as it was profound, changed Eli. He became a testament to the village, his life a canvas upon which the value of faith was vividly painted. He still crafted furniture, but now he imbued each piece with the story of his transformation, inviting others to find their truth in the river's timeless flow.

And so, the villagers came to understand that while Eli was still their beloved carpenter, he had become something more—a living testimony to the grace found in the waters of baptism, a symbol of a truth that could be theirs as well.

—————

The Baptismal Vow

Step into the sun-drenched room where echoes of ancient truths still resonate, where a single decision marks the collision of past and promise. This is the moment of the baptismal vow, a profound public affirmation where the whispers of the heart are given voice, and the soul's silent transformation is announced to the world.

Imagine, if you will, a young woman named Patricia, standing with trembling hands before her congregation. Her voice, a gentle murmur at first, grows firm as she recites her covenant. It is here, in the waters of baptism, she will symbolically bury her old life, just as Romans 6:4 says, "We are therefore buried with Him through baptism into death in order that, just as Christ was raised from the dead through the glory of the Father, we too may live a new life."

Patricia's vow is more than a rite; it's the embroidery of conviction on the fabric of her existence. Acts 2:38 echoes through her pledge, "Repent and be baptized, every one of you, in the name of Jesus Christ for the forgiveness of your sins. And you will receive the gift of the Holy Spirit." This scripture is not just etched in her mind but woven into her very being, a promise that stirs within her a sense of redemption and renewal.

With each word of her vow, Patricia stands as a testament to 2 Corinthians 5:17, "Therefore, if anyone is in Christ, the new creation has come: the old has gone, the new is here!" her declaration is a narrative of metamorphosis, an acknowledgment that in the act of baptism, the stories of fallen humanity and divine grace are intimately entwined.

The congregation watches, a sea of supportive faces, as Patricia's declaration culminates in the baptismal waters, a theater of transformation. For in those still, reflective depths, every believer sees the reflection of their own journey. And as Patricia emerges, dripping and radiant with joy, the truth of Galatians 3:27 unites them all, "For all of you who were baptized into Christ have clothed yourselves with Christ."

In this sacred act, the baptismal vow is both an end and a beginning, a solemn farewell to a life lived in shadow, and a joyous greeting to a path illuminated by faith. It's a narrative as old as the church itself, a story that continues to be written in the lives of believers like Patricia, across the globe, wherever and whenever the waters of baptism stir to the rhythm of repentant hearts.

The Act of Baptism

As dawn's first light stretches across a serene body of water, a congregation gathers, their voices subdued in reverence for the sacred ritual about to unfold. This is the stage where faith moves from the private chambers of the heart into the open embrace of community witnesses. It's the act of baptism, a simple yet profound immersion that paints a vivid picture of a spiritual journey—a descent and a rising, an ending and a new beginning.

Consider a man named Joseph, whose journey to this moment has been long and fraught with trials. His steps into the water are tentative, echoing the inner turmoil of a soul seeking rebirth. As he stands waist-deep, the coolness of the water is a stark contrast to the warmth of the rising sun, symbolizing the awakening of his spirit.

"Baptism is an outward testimony of an inward transformation," the minister begins, his voice carrying over the water. Joseph nods, his heart pounding with the weight of this truth. It's a portrayal of Romans 6:3–4, which states, "Or don't you know that all of us who were baptized into Christ Jesus were baptized into his death? We therefore were buried with him through baptism into death in order that, just as Christ was raised from the dead through the glory of the Father, we too may live a new life."

The congregation watches, a testament to the shared faith that binds them, as Joseph is gently laid back into the water. This immersion is more than a physical act; it is the embodiment of his old self being laid to rest, buried with Christ. The water closes over him, a brief shroud of the life he leaves behind, and for a moment, there is a hush, a sacred pause where time seems to stand still.

Then, as he is raised from the watery grave, the air breaks with applause and cheers. Joseph's face emerges, cleansed and beaming with joy, a vivid illustration of Colossians 2:12, "Having been buried with Him in baptism, in which you were also raised with Him through your faith in the working of God, who raised Him from the dead."

The act of baptism is a testament to belief, a public pronouncement that echoes through the ages: "I am with Christ, in death and in resurrection." It is a declaration made not in words, but in the powerful symbol of water—of washing away, of dying and rising, of old made new. It is both a personal milestone and a communal celebration, for in every droplet that cascades from Joseph's renewed form, there is a reflection of a story much greater than his own—a story of redemption, hope, and the everlasting promise of eternal life.

Is Water Baptism Required for Salvation?

The question of whether water baptism is essential for salvation has stirred waters of theological debate for centuries, and the ripples of this discussion touch the very core of Christian belief and practices. Let's plunge into the depths of Scripture to seek clarity in the currents of Peter's teachings.

Acts 2:38 stands as a towering beacon in this exploration. Here, Peter declares, "Repent and be baptized, every one of you, in the name of Jesus Christ for the forgiveness of your sins. And you will receive the gift of the Holy Spirit." On the surface, this seems to forge a strong link between the act of baptism and the reception of salvation.

Yet, the journey does not end here. As we navigate further into the book of Acts, the waters become both clearer and more complex. Acts 3:19 beckons us to "repent, then, and turn to God, so that your sins may be wiped out, that times of refreshing may come from the Lord." Here, Peter's emphasis is on repentance and turning to God, with no explicit mention of water baptism.

Fast-forward to Acts 5:29–32, where Peter and the apostles, after facing imprisonment, confront the religious leaders of the day. "We must obey God rather than human beings!" Peter proclaims. He continues to recount Christ's death and resurrection, His exaltation, and His role as Savior—sent to enable Israel to repent and be forgiven. Yet again, the focus is riveted on repentance without an express command for baptism.

The waters of Scripture flow swiftly to Acts 10, where we witness Cornelius and his household. Peter preaches to these Gentiles, and as they believe, the Holy Spirit descends upon them even before they are baptized with water. This sequence of events reveals that the Holy Spirit is not confined to the act of water baptism. Indeed, the Gentiles' hearts were sprinkled clean by faith, a point underscored in Acts 15:9, where Peter reflects on how God "made no distinction between us and them, for he purified their hearts by faith."

This episode crystallizes the essence of the gospel message that Peter consistently heralds: Repentance and belief in Christ lead to the forgiveness of sins. Water baptism, while a significant and commanded act of obedience, is portrayed not as the mechanism of salvation but as the outward testimony of an inward grace already received.

In the end, the harmonious melody of Peter's sermons and actions throughout Acts forms a symphony that resounds with the primacy of faith. Acts 11:18 captures this beautifully as Peter recounts the events at Cornelius' house: "When they heard these things they fell silent. And they glorified God, saying, 'Then to the gentiles also God has granted repentance that leads to life.'"

So, we arrive at a shore of understanding: water baptism is a vital expression of faith and obedience, a declaration of allegiance to Christ in the presence of many witnesses. It is a sacred act that mirrors the death, burial, and resurrection of Jesus—a profound statement of identification with Him. Yet, according to the harmonized testimony of Peter, salvation—this glorious grace—is gifted through repentance and faith, a treasure held in the earthen vessels of our hearts, sealed by the Spirit, and celebrated through the waters of baptism.

———

Ripples of Faith: The Knight's Testimony

In the quaint village of Evergrace, nestled between verdant hills and a crystal-clear river, lived a knight named Eliam. A man of 30-years, with eyes as deep as the waters he stood beside, Eliam was known not for the battles he fought but for the inner dragons he sought to conquer. The sword at his side was a family heirloom, gleaming and unblemished, a silent witness to the turmoil within.

Eliam's dragon was doubt, a smokey wraith that crept into his thoughts at the cusp of night, whispering questions about worth, faith, and salvation. The villagers saw his shining armor and his confident stride, but they did not see the creases of worry that lined his forehead when he was alone, pondering the path to true peace.

The moment that would change Eliam's life came unexpectedly. It was during the annual celebration of remembrance when the village gathered to honor the history of their faith. That year, a traveler, a humble man of God named Silas, came speaking of salvation not as a burdensome quest but as a gift—free, unearned, yet requiring a response.

Silas spoke of the waters of baptism, not as the sword that defeats the dragon but as the declaration of a battle already won. "Repentance," he said, touching his heart, "is where the dragon is slain, and belief is your shield. Baptism? It is the banner you raise to show the world which King you serve."

In the hush of the gathered crowd, Eliam's armor felt heavy. It was a weight he no longer needed to carry. As Silas poured water from the river, speaking ancient words that echoed through the hills, Eliam stepped forward. His hand did not go to his sword; instead, he removed his gauntlet and let it fall to the ground.

The water was cool, and as it enveloped him, Eliam realized the moment had come. The dragon's smoke cleared, and he emerged from the river with a joyous gasp, a knight reborn not by the sword but by the water's grace and his heart's true confession. It was not the act itself but the faith it represented that transformed Eliam.

The villagers saw Eliam's soaked hair and his radiant smile, and they understood. This was not the same knight who had walked stoically through their streets. Here was a man who had found the answer to the questions that once haunted him, and in doing so, he gave them a glimpse of their own potential journey to peace.

The sword remained by the river that day, a symbol of the old battles. Eliam's new strength lay in the testimony of his faith, a story that would ripple through the village, changing lives as it had changed his.

Peace—this was the elusive treasure that Eliam had been seeking, the antidote to his nightly unrest. Silas's words were simple, but they addressed the knight's deepest fears. In the acceptance of grace, through the waters of baptism, Eliam found the peace that armor and sword could never give.

It was not the plunge into the river that shifted the world for Eliam, but the instant his gauntlet hit the ground—a resolute thud that silenced the whispers of his dragon, signifying a release from the burdens of doubt and the embrace of a faith renewed.

The gauntlet, once a necessary protection, now lay abandoned, while the river, once just a part of the landscape, became sacred in the eyes of the beholder. The villagers would always remember the sight of the knight, the weight of his armor discarded, standing drenched and triumphant, a true warrior of faith.

The Immediate Aftermath

In the wake of the sacred waters of baptism, a myriad of emotions cascades through the soul like the sun's rays piercing through the morning mist. Believers, emerging from the depths, often speak of a euphoria, a sense of purity that envelops their being, as if the old garment of their past has been shed, and they stand cloaked in a raiment of light.

This transformative experience mirrors the words of 2 Corinthians 5:17, "Therefore, if anyone is in Christ, the new creation has come: the old has gone, the new is here!" The tangible feeling of being born anew is not merely a symbolic interpretation but a spiritual reality that marks a definitive line in the sand between who they were and who they have become.

The dripping water from the brow of the newly baptized might as well be the anointing oil of the Holy Spirit, for many recount a palpable sense of empowerment, a courage that whispers of unseen mountains moved and giants toppled. It's as though the words in Acts 1:8 become a personal testament, "But you will receive power when the Holy Spirit comes on you; and you will be my witnesses . . ." They step out of the water not just washed, but also endowed with a purpose, called to witness with the vibrancy of their refreshed spirits.

A sense of cleansing is almost universally described, akin to the Psalmist's exaltation in Psalm 51:7, "Cleanse me with hyssop, and I will be clean; wash me, and I will be whiter than snow." The water, simple in its essence, becomes a conduit for divine purification, a hallowed element that seems to wash away the dust of past errors and transgressions.

But perhaps the most profound of all experiences is the soul's quiet, steadfast recognition of a promise fulfilled. In the act of baptism, the words of Romans 6:4 resonate deeply, "We were therefore buried with him through baptism into death in order that, just as Christ was raised from the dead through the glory of the Father, we too may live a new life." It is a spiritual symbiosis; as the believer rises from the water, so too, they are reminded of Christ's resurrection, and with it, their own.

The immediate aftermath of baptism is a collage of divine touchpoints. Each droplet of water carries with it a note of grace, every shiver a testament to a spiritual flame ignited, and every breath a chorus of ancient words that declare the enduring truth of transformation through Christ. It is not an end, but a breathtaking beginning.

―――――

Submerged in Hope: The Knight's Transformation

Once upon a time, in the heart of a bustling modern metropolis, there was a young man named Elijah. He wasn't your typical hero adorned in armor, but rather a 28-year-old social worker, armed with compassion and a relentless drive to better the world around him. Yet, despite his noble profession, Elijah faced a formidable dragon—the overwhelming sense of unworthiness and spiritual stagnation that showed his every step.

The sword in our tale isn't forged of steel but comprised of sacred waters—the ancient ritual of baptism. It wasn't the waters themselves that held power, but rather what they represented in Elijah's journey.

Each night, Elijah wrestled with the thought that his life lacked a significant purpose. His internal battle was not against flesh and blood but against the doubts and fears that haunted him—his dragon. No success at work could slay this persistent foe; no accolade was enough to silence the inner turmoil. What he sought was a transformation not just of mind, but of spirit.

The moment of change came unexpectedly. At a small community church he'd passed countless times, a banner caught his eye: "New Beginnings: A Baptism Service." Something within him stirred—a whisper of hope, a ripple in still water. On impulse, he attended the service.

As Elijah listened to the pastor speak of renewal, citing 2 Corinthians 5:17, a profound truth resonated within him. When he witnessed others rise from the baptismal waters, reborn and invigorated, the silence that followed was more than an absence of sound—it was the presence of possibility. In their stories of redemption, Elijah saw his own.

The decision to be baptized came like a dawn breaking upon a night that had lasted too long. Dressed in plain garments, symbolizing the shedding of his old self, Elijah stepped into the water. It wasn't just a pool but a crucible of change. As he was submerged, the waters whispered of ancient paths and promised futures.

Rising from the water, the weight of his internal strife seemed to dissolve into the liquid grace that now cascaded off him. He felt a kinship with the words of Romans 6:4, understanding that just as Christ was resurrected, he, too, was rising to walk in a newness of life.

Elijah's life was transformed. Baptism, the symbolic sword, had not slain his dragon—Elijah had. The waters were merely the tool that facilitated his victory. The true power lay within his heart and spirit, awakened and affirmed by the act of obedience and faith.

To those bearing witness, Elijah's story was a testament to the enduring power of spiritual rebirth. It was a specific detail in the larger narrative of human struggle and divine grace. As they watched Elijah embrace his new path, they found themselves whispering, "He gets it—and because he does, so can I."

The Ongoing Journey

In the lingering embrace of his baptismal waters, Elijah found the first steps of his ongoing journey illuminated before him. Baptism was not the culmination of his spiritual quest, but the commencement of a grander adventure—one that would stretch the fabric of his soul and weave him into the tapestry of a broader faith community.

Just as the Israelites entered the Promised Land with steps of faith, Elijah began to seek a place where he could plant his roots and grow. He found himself drawn to the vibrant community that had become the setting of his rebirth. The church doors, once mere architectural features, now stood as gateways to fellowship. He joined this family of believers, each with their own stories of grace and transformation.

Hebrews 10:24–25 became the rhythm of his new life: "and let us consider how we may spur one another on toward love and good deeds, not giving up meeting together . . . but encouraging one another." In the warm smiles and earnest prayer of his new brothers and sisters, Elijah found encouragement and the very essence of discipleship. They were his Aaron and Hur, holding up his hands when the battle grew weary, just as Moses had needed in his time of trial.

Elijah's steps in discipleship were as deliberate as the words of Matthew 28:19–20 that had been echoed in his baptism. He now understood the Great Commission as a personal call to engage in the world—not just as a social worker, but as a disciple of Christ, teaching and learning the profound depths of God's Word. The Scripture was no longer abstract text; it was alive, a compass that navigated him through the trials and joys of life.

This ongoing journey was a pilgrimage marked by continual growth. Like the mustard seed mentioned in Matthew 13:31–32, Elijah's faith started small but was destined to grow into something grand, providing shelter and hope to those around him. His actions and words began to reflect the love of Christ, a love he aimed to exemplify every day.

Discipleship was more than a series of lessons; it was life lived in the echo of Christ's footsteps. It was loving the unlovable, forgiving the unforgivable, and touching the untouchable. It was, as James 2:17 put it, a faith that was alive and vibrant, evidenced by works and not just carried by belief.

The sacrament of baptism had initiated Elijah into this lifelong journey—a journey not marked by a single event but by an ever-unfolding story of faith, hope, and love. And as he continued to walk this path, every step was a testament to the transformative power of those sacred waters that had once enveloped him, marking the beginning of an eternal walk with God.

CHAPTER THREE

Breath of the Divine: Embracing the Holy Spirit

"And if the Spirit of Him who raised Jesus from the dead is living in you, He who raised Christ from the dead will also give life to your mortal bodies because of His Spirit who lives in you."

—ROMANS 8:11 NIV

Welcome, dear reader, to this chapter, a journey through the ethereal and profound presence of the most enigmatic member of the Holy Trinity. As we step into the sacred dance of understanding and relationship with the Holy Spirit, we embark on a path that winds back to the very dawn of time and stretches into the boundless eternity promised to us.

In this chapter, we will whisper alongside the winds of Genesis, where the Spirit of God first hovered over the depths, a divine artist poised above the canvas of creation. We will walk through the annals of ancient Israel, witnessing the Holy Spirit shaping nations and anointing leaders. Prophetic voices will echo through the corridors of time, their words heavy with the breath of the Spirit.

We shall draw near to the dusty roads of Galilee, where Jesus of Nazareth, the anointed Messiah, lived and moved in inseparable unity with the Spirit. Together, we will linger in the upper room in Jerusalem, where tongues of fire descended, and the church took its first gasping breaths in the power of the Spirit.

As we traverse through the ages, the gifts of the Spirit will unfold before us in vibrant display, each one a testament to the Spirit's living presence in the Body of Christ. We will delve into the orchard of spiritual fruit, where love, joy, peace, and kindness grow, nourished by the spirit's indwelling.

Our guide, the Holy Spirit, is both counselor and comforter, the still small voice and the roaring wind, present in our deepest sorrows and highest joys. In the quiet chambers of our hearts, in the moments of fervent prayer, the Spirit intercedes, translating groans into the language of heaven.

And finally, with reverent awe, we will gaze into the future, where the promise of the Spirit seals us for a day beyond days. Here, in the eternal embrace of God, ,we find our truest identify and destiny.

So, take a deep breath, for every breath is a taste of the divine, an invitation to embrace the Holy Spirit, the Breath of God. Let us begin.

Whispers of Genesis

In the hushed anticipation of the void, before the stars flung into their appointed places and the mountains heaved their way to the skies, there was a whisper. Not just any murmur, but the very breath of God moving upon the face of the deep. The Holy Spirit, often perceived as the enigmatic force of the Trinity, took center stage in the universe's grand overture.

Imagine the scene as depicted in Genesis 1:2, "And the Spirit of God was hovering over the face of the waters." Here, in the vast expanse of nothingness, the Holy Spirit was present, vibrating with potential and promise, ready to orchestrate the symphony of Creation at God's command. This wasn't a passive breeze but the dynamic, life-giving wind of divine action.

As the Creator said, "Let there be light," and there was light, we witness the first act of divine collaboration (Genesis 1:3). The Spirit and the word, together, brought forth the genesis of all that is known and unknown. Each "Let there be . . ." resonated through the cosmos, a testament to the Spirit's power to execute the Father's will with perfect fidelity.

In the poetic language of Psalm 33:6, we read, "By the word of the Lord were the heavens made; their starry host by the breath of his mouth." The Hebrew word for "breath" here is akin to the Spirit—it is the Holy Spirit that breathes life into the Word, catalyzing the emergence of galaxies, landscapes, and creatures great and small.

And it doesn't stop there. The Spirit doesn't merely set the world spinning and step back. No, this Divine Whisper breathes into the nostrils of humanity, bestowing life to Adam, molding him from the earth itself as a potter with clay (Genesis 2:7). In this intimate act, we see the Spirit's role not just as Creator, but as the Giver of Life, intimately involved in shaping mankind's very essence.

As we ponder the magnitude of the Holy Spirit's involvement in Creation, we are reminded of the continual presence and activity of this same Spirit in our lives. The apostle Paul later reflects in Romans 8:11,

"But if the Spirit of Him who raised Jesus from the dead dwells in you, He who raised Christ from the dead will also give life to your mortal bodies through His Spirit who dwells in you." The same power that hovered over the formless earth, that called into existence the myriad of life, is at work in us.

Whispers of Genesis, then, are not mere echoes of a distant past but the ongoing voice of the Spirit, calling us to remember our sacred origin and our part in the unfolding story of Creation—a story that continues with each breath, each moment, each life touched by the Breath of the Divine.

Crafting a Melody of Creation

In the dim glow of his workshop, Gregg, a middle-aged craftsman of fine instruments, hunched over his latest creation—a violin that refused to sing. The problem wasn't with his skill or the quality of the wood. The issue was deeper, more profound—it was the absence of soul in the music it produced. Despite being a master of his craft, Gregg faced the dragon of self-doubt, a silent question that kept him awake at night: "Can I ever create an instrument that touches the divine?"

Gregg was no knight, and his instruments were no swords, but the parallel was there. His violins could slay the silence of a hall, evoke tears and laughter, yet something was amiss. This particular violin, with its curves as graceful as any he'd made, held back a secret he couldn't grasp.

One night, as the moon cast long shadows across his workbench, a breeze fluttered through the open window, carrying with it the distant echo of a church choir. It was the moment when the world stood still, the air charged with a silent understanding. The wood he worked on came from an old tree that grew by the church where he once found refuge in dark times. The realization dawned on him—the wood wasn't lacking; it was waiting for the breath to awaken its spirit.

With renewed purpose, Gregg set to work, carving delicately, shaping the wood not just with his hands but with his heart, infusing his faith into every stroke. He whispered prayers with each shaving that fell away, every note he imagined the violin could play, an invocation to the Holy Spirit that had stirred the waters of Creation itself.

Weeks later, in the hush of the local parish, the completed violin was poised to prove its worth. Gregg, with trembling hands, drew the bow across the strings, and a sound filled the space—a sound both new and ancient, as if the whispers of Genesis had found a home in the grain of the wood, the curves of the violin.

The congregation held its breath, not just because of the beauty of the melody but because they recognized the feeling it evoked. It was the sound of creation, of life, of the Divine Breath itself. Gregg's problem had never been about making a violin that could play. It was about crafting an instrument that could pray, that could carry the legacy of the Spirit that hovered over the waters at the dawn of time.

Gregg's violin didn't just change the course of his life; it transformed the lives of those who heard its sacred melody. The story of his violin whispered a promise—that the Spirit moves in all acts of true creation, be it the universe of a simple instrument, awaiting the moment to sing through our labor of love. And in the melody, people found a shared truth: The Holy Spirit was not a distant force but a present, breathing influence, making all things new, including them.

The Spirit in the Covenant

As the Israelites traversed the rocky deserts and lush valleys of their tumultuous history, there was an unseen force guiding, nurturing, and empowering them. This force was the Holy Spirit, an integral aspect of God's dealings with His chosen people.

In the twilight of human history, when the stars of man's destiny had barely begun to shine, a covenant was struck between the Divine and Abram—a covenant of profound implications. "I will establish my covenant as an everlasting covenant between Me and you and your descendants after you for the generations to come, to be your God and the God of your descendants after you" (Genesis 17:7). This promise wasn't merely a contract; it was imbued with the breath of the Holy Spirit, sealing a sacred bond.

The Spirit wasn't a silent spectator but an active participant in the drama of Israel. When the Israelites were cornered by Pharoah's chariots, it was the Holy Spirit that blew with power, parting the Red Sea and leading them to a deliverance so mighty that it echoed through their songs and stories for generations (Exodus 14:21).

Moses, with his staff and stammer, might have seemed an unlikely leader. Yet, "the Spirit of the Lord" rested upon him (Numbers 11:25), transforming his weaknesses into strengths, enabling him to speak to Pharaoh, and to be mediator of a new covenant at Sinai. The tablets of the law were not just stone but inscribed by the finger of God, perhaps the divine metaphor for the Holy Spirit's engraving of truth upon human hearts (Exodus 31:18).

And what of the judges? Individuals like Deborah, Gideon, and Samson? They were not superheroes in their own right; their might and wisdom were not self-sourced. "The Spirit of the Lord came upon him [Gideon] so that he became Israel's judge and went to war" (Judges 6:34). It was the Holy Spirit that endowed them with supernatural strength and wisdom, turning the tides of battles and leading Israel through their darkest hours.

The covenant promise and the presence of the Spirit were not just for the bygone days of the desert but for the entire narrative of Israel. It was the Holy Spirit that inspired kings and empowered prophets to call God's people back to the heart of the covenant. David, a man after God's own heart, knew this intimately when he pleaded, "Do not take your Holy Spirit from me" (Psalms 51:11), recognizing the Spirit as the source of his life's melody.

As we reflect upon the Spirit in the Covenant, we see a tapestry of divine fidelity woven through the ages. The Holy Spirit was, and is, a beacon of God's unwavering commitment to His people—a pledge of His presence, a guarantee of His power, and a whisper of His eternal love. The story of Israel is incomplete without the golden thread of the Spirit, entwining every moment of promise, every act of deliverance, and every stone of the Law with the heartbeat of the covenant God.

The Breath of Commitment

Forget the sword, what's the battle within? In the heart of ancient Israel, there walked a man burdened not by the weight of his armor but by the promise of his lineage. Meet Eliav: a 40-year-old scribe whose life's work was to transcribe the scrolls of his forefathers, with ink-stained fingers and a furrowed brow marking his daily toil. His battle was not against flesh and blood but against the creeping doubt that plagued his people—the loss of hope in the promises of old.

Eliav, whose name echoes "God is my Father," is known for his meticulous care for the Word and the unwavering belief in the Spirit's presence. He's clad not in armor but in the humble garb of a scribe, a quill tucked behind one ear and the weight of history on his shoulders. He's the keeper of promises, a silent guardian of the covenant made generations ago. It is the integrity of these scrolls that has changed the course of Eliav's life, and with, he hopes to change the lives of his people.

As night falls and the oil in his lamp begins to dwindle, so too does Eliav's resolve. The signs of his people echo through the stone walls—the temple's glory has faded, the nations encroach, and the whispers of the forefathers seem distant. What keeps him up at night is the question: Will the Spirit that guided Moses, emboldened judges, and whispered to prophets still breathe life into these dry bones?

It's in the silent hours of an ordinary Thursday, when a cool breeze slipping through the window, that Eliav unrolls a freshly completed scroll. The words of the prophet Ezekiel stare back at him: "I will put my Spirit in you and you will live" (Ezekiel 37:14). The room is still, but something stirs within him. It's the moment the words leap from the parchment into his heart, a flame reignites, and hope is no longer a distant memory but a present warmth. The Spirit that once hovered over the chaos of creation now moves upon the waters of his soul.

The smell of parchments and ink, the texture of the scroll rough under his fingertips, the soft creak of the wooden table—these are the details that place you there, in Eliav's chamber. The gentle whisper of the wind carries the distant sound of temple songs, and the flickering flame casts a dance of shadows upon the walls, as if the stories of old are coming to life. "They get me," whispers Eliav, and in that moment, he understands that he's not just a scribe of history; he's a vessel of the Spirit, part of the living, breathing covenant.

In Eliav's story, we see our own—the quest for a tangible sign of an ancient promise. The Holy Spirit is not the sword that cleaves the darkness but the hand that guides it, the breath that fuels it, and the voice that calms the storm within. Through Eliav's eyes, we learn that the true value lies not in the clanging of armor but in the quiet, steadfast heart that carries the promise forward.

Prophetic Utterances

In the tapestry of faith, the prophets stand as the vibrant threads, weaving a narrative of divine communication that cuts through the epochs. Their voices rang out, not as their own, but as conduits of a Higher Power, the Holy Spirit, who filled them with words that would echo into eternity.

In the days of old, the Holy Spirit did not thunder indiscriminately from the heavens but often spoke in a hush, a whisper that only the attuned heart of a prophet could discern. Consider Elijah, standing upon the mountain, not in the wind, the earthquake, or the fire, but in the still, small voice—the gentle whisper—came the Spirit's utterance (1 Kings 19:12).

The Holy Spirit was not only a gentle murmur but also a fervent fire within the prophets, urging them to speak, even when their messages were not of comfort but of conviction. Jeremiah proclaimed, "His Word is in my heart like a fire, a fire shut up in my bones. I am weary of holding it in; indeed, I cannot" (Jeremiah 20:9). The Spirit compelled them, consumed them with a zeal that could not be quenched by human means.

The prophets, visionaries of their time, saw beyond the veil of the temporal, into the heart of the divine will. The Spirit granted them glimpses of what was to come, dreams and visions that held within them the seeds of hope and the call to repentance. As Joel prophesied, "I will pour out my Spirit on all people. Your sons and daughters will prophesy, your old men will dream dreams, your young men will see visions" (Joel 2:28).

In moments of peril, the Spirit was the steadfastness in the prophet's resolve. When Daniel faced the lions' den, it was not solely his courage that sealed the mouths of the beasts but the Spirit of the Living God that sustained him (Daniel 6:22).

The Holy Spirit, through the prophets, was not a voice of doom but a call to return to the covenantal embrace. Through Hosea, the Spirit expressed God's enduring love and yearning for His people, "I will heal their waywardness and love them freely, for my anger has turned away from them" (Hosea 14:4).

The Spirit imbued the prophets with a burning passion for justice, to be the voice for the voiceless, to defend the cause of the widow and the orphan, to rebuke the oppressor, as commanded in Isaiah: "Learn to do right; seek justice. Defend the oppressed. Take up the cause of the fatherless; plead the case of the widow" (Isaiah 1:17).

In their divinely inspired foresight, the prophets heralded the coming of the Messiah, a savior who would embody the Spirit in its fullness. Isaiah proclaimed, "The Spirit of the Lord will rest on Him— the Spirit of wisdom and of understanding, the Spirit of counsel and of might, the Spirit of the knowledge and fear of the Lord" (Isaiah 11:2).

The prophets, through the Spirit, reinforced the everlasting bond between the Divine and humanity, a promise etched in eternity, an unbreakable covenant. "I will put My Spirit in you and move you to follow My decrees and be careful to keep My laws" (Ezekiel 36:27).

The Holy Spirit, through these chosen vessels, spoke of renewal and restoration, of rivers in the desert and a way in the wilderness, for nothing was too desolate for the Spirit's rejuvenating breath (Isaiah 43:19).

Ultimately, the prophets, guided by the Spirit, were the enduring witnesses to the faithfulness of God, to His unchanging nature, and His inexhaustible grace. "The grass withers and the flowers fall, but the word of our God endures forever" (Isaiah 40:8).

In the symphony of the Spirit and the prophets, we hear the ancient echoes that continue to resound in the hearts of the faithful, a melody of divine love, justice, and redemption that stirs the soul and shapes the course of history.

———

Divine Whisper: Eli's Revelation

In the dimly lit chamber of his heart, where silence had built its citadel, Ashton, a young scribe, wrestled with a dragon of doubt. The texts he copied by day spoke of wonder and prophecies, yet the nights brought questions that echoed through the halls of his soul, relentless and unforgiving.

Ashton was no armored knight; his battle was not against flesh and bone but against the creeping shadows of despair that threatened to extinguish the flame of his faith. His armor was a threadbare robe, his sword a quill, yet the dragon he faced was as real as any of legend.

At the age of twenty-five, Ashton's eyes had seen much—the suffering of the people, the corruption of the powerful. His heart, once buoyant with the zeal of youth, now felt heavy with the authenticity of his emotions. Where was the Spirit that the prophets spoke of? How could he cling to promises that felt so distant?

One night, as a storm raged outside, Ashton sat transcribing the words of Isaiah, his quill trembling in the candlelight. The verses spoke of a Spirit that would come, not only upon a chosen few but to all flesh. The words were familiar, but in that moment, as thunder shook the foundation of his abode, something shifted within him.

The words on the page seemed to ignite, not with fire, but with life. It was as if the silence in the room, in his heart, was broken by a voice that was not a voice, a presence that was palpably absent before. The dragon's oppressive weight lifted, not by the might of a sword, but by the gentle, yet powerful realization that the Spirit was not confined to the ancient days of prophets but was here, now, within and around him.

Ashton had found the solution, not through his own understanding but through an encounter that transcended words on a page. The product—the scripture—was but a vessel, and he, a humble scribe, had touched the divine that breathed life into those sacred texts.

As dawn broke, Ashton emerged from his chamber changed. Those who saw him noticed a subtle but unmistakable difference. His eyes held a new light, his words carried a weight that was not his own. He began to speak of the scriptures with a fervor that resonated with the young and old alike. He spoke not of a distant deity but of a present help, a Spirit that moved as much in the corridors of the human heart as it had through the annals of history.

Ashton's story rippled through the community, a testament that the same Spirit that whispered to the prophets could still transform an ordinary life into a wellspring of hope. And in this, they found a truth that echoed through their own experiences, a voice saying, "I understand, I am here, I am for you."

The Anointed Messiah

In the grand narrative of faith, few chapters are as compelling as the one concerning the anointed Messiah—Jesus of Nazareth, and the inseparable dance with the Holy Spirit from His earthly inception to His glorious resurrection.

Picture the quiet town of Nazareth, where a young woman named Mary receives the news that would alter the course of history: "The Holy Spirit will come on you, and the power of the Most High will overshadow you" (Luke 1:35). This divine breath whispers life into the virgin womb, crafting the Incarnation, not through the will of flesh or man, but by the Spirit.

Then visualize the banks of the Jordan River, where John baptizes Jesus. As He rises from the water, heaven opens, and the Spirit descends like a dove—a seal of approval, a confirmation of divinity— as a voice from heaven proclaims, "This is my Son, whom I love; with Him I am well pleased" (Matthew 3:17).

Jesus' ministry is a testament to the Spirit's power. Each miracle, parable, and step toward the oppressed is a rhythm moved by the Spirit. "The Spirit of the Lord is on me," Jesus announces, "because He has anointed me to proclaim good news to the poor" (Luke 4:18). His life becomes a canvas where the Spirit paints in bold strokes of grace, mercy, and truth.

The cross—a symbol of suffering and sacrifice—unveils the depth of Jesus' obedience. Yet, even death's shadow holds no sway without the Spirit's decrease. Romans 8:11 thunders with promise, "The Spirit of God, who raised Jesus from the dead, lives in you." The resurrection is the crescendo of the Spirit's work, a testament to the power that not only renews life but defeats death.

In every facet of Jesus' journey, we see the Spirit: from whispers of divine inception, through the torrents of Jordan's waters, across the dusty roads of Galilee, and beyond the tomb's dark despair. The Holy Spirit—an eternal companion to the Messiah—guides, empowers, comforts, and ultimately, triumphs.

For believers today, this partnership offers more than a historical glimpse—it's a mirror reflecting their own walk with the Spirit, a source of strength, guidance, and an assurance that the same power that raised Christ from the dead is at work within them, animating each step of their faith journey.

Spirit Empowered: Barry's Awakening

In the heart of a bustling city lived Barry, a 35-year-old community organizer known for his tireless advocacy and compassionate heart. His worn-out sneakers and the coffee stains on his shirt were testaments to the countless hours he spent walking the streets, listening to the voices of the marginalized. Barry's problem wasn't a lack of passion or purpose—it was the overwhelming feeling of fighting a losing battle against an unseen dragon of societal indifference.

The dragon's fiery breath was the burnout that haunted his dreams, the cynicism creeping into his once-hopeful vision. Each night, as he laid his head on a pillow damp with the day's sweat, Barry wrestled with the fear that perhaps he was just one man against an invincible force.

The moment of change arrived unannounced on a Sunday morning, with the sunlight piercing through the stained-glass windows of a small neighborhood church. As the preacher spoke of a man who, empowered by the Holy Spirit, turned the world upside down with love and miracles, something within Barry shifted. The story wasn't new to him, but in that moment, the Holy Spirit ceased to be an abstract concept. It became his revelation—the sword in his hand, not just a relic from a biblical time but a present and powerful force that could animate his weary bones.

It was the specificity of Jesus' life that resonated with Barry—the dusty roads, the touch of healing, the voice that spoke with authority not from titles but from an authentic place of service and sacrifice. The narrative of the Anointed One, carrying the Spirit within, transformed the course of history with acts that defied human limitations.

Barry left the church with a different kind of stride, one that carried a newfound resonance. He understood now that his fight was not in vain and that the same Spirit that raised the dead, healed the sick, and empowered the outcast to speak was in him. His work wasn't just a career; it was a calling, a participation in a divine narrative that promised that the same Spirit that worked through the Anointed Messiah was at work in him—turning small acts of kindness into ripples that could break down walls and heal divisions.

The community noticed a change in Barry. There was a steadiness in his voice, a light in his eyes. They whispered among themselves, "What happened to him?" And in their hearts, a hope kindled—that perhaps the dragon wasn't so invincible after all.

Pentecostal Fire

In the bustling streets of Jerusalem, something extraordinary was about to unfold—a divine event that would be etched into the annals of history as the fiery dawn of the Church.

Imagine the scene: The apostles, a mosaic of once ordinary men, huddled together in a humble room, united by the promises of a Messiah who had ascended, leaving them with the anticipation of a Helper to come. Their hearts beat in unified suspense, their eyes laden with the weight of waiting.

Suddenly, the air itself seemed to charge with power, and from the heavens, as if a mighty wind was rushing to fulfill an ancient vow, came the Holy Spirit in a display that defied the limitations of earthly elements. "And suddenly there came from heaven a sound like a mighty rushing wind, and it filled the entire house where they were sitting" (Acts 2:2). Tongues of fire settled upon each of them, a vivid and pulsating testament to the fulfillment of God's Word, "I will pour out my Spirit on all flesh" (Joel 2:28).

The apostles, once simply fishermen, tax collectors, and common folk, found themselves ablaze with divine eloquence, a speaking in languages not their own, yet understood by every ear in the cosmopolitan throng outside their door. The crowd was bewildered, for each one heard them speaking in his own language about the mighty works of God (Acts 2:11).

This was no ordinary fire; it was the fire of transformation. As Peter stood up, his voice rang out, emboldened beyond human capacity, cutting to the heart of every listener. He recounted prophecies and spoke of Jesus, the Nazarene, a man attested by God with mighty works and wonders. Conviction pierced the crowd like a sword, and they cried out, "Brothers, what shall we do?" (Acts 2:37).

And so, in that moment, the church was birthed from the embers of the Spirit's descent, as thousands were baptized, their lives transformed by the power of the Spirit that had been promised long ago. The disciples, once cowering in the shadows of uncertainty, became the torchbearers of a new covenant, igniting the path for countless souls seeking redemption.

Pentecost was not merely an event but the inauguration of an age—the age of the Spirit, where every believer would carry the flame of God's presence, a beacon of hope for a world entangled in darkness. Through the Spirit, we are all witnesses, and the same fire that descended upon the apostles beckons us to continue the legacy, to be the light that guides the lost to the harbor of salvation.

In this extraordinary convergence of divine promise and human history, we find our own invitation to embrace the Spirit, to let the fire of Pentecost refine us, and to walk in the boldness of those who first carried God's word to the ends of the earth.

―――――

Spirit's Embrace: Zach's Awakening at Pentecost

In the heart of Jerusalem's winding streets, Zach, a leatherworker by trade, labors under the weight of Roman occupation. At 42, his hands are as rough as the hides he works with, a testament to years of toil. His deep-set eyes, usually full of a quiet resilience, now flicker with an unresolved quest for something more than the clatter of his workshop and the familiar scent of tanned leather.

The problem? It isn't the Romans, nor is it the struggle to make ends meet; it's a profound spiritual hunger, a dragon of discontent breathing restlessness into his every night. Zach's spirit aches for deliverance, not from the chains of his trade, but from the bondage of an unfulfilled promise—a promise of a Messiah, a hope that seems as distant as the stars.

One day, as Pentecost approaches, the city buzzes with strange news. People speak of a new movement, of men who were with the Nazarene, Jesus. Zach's curiosity piques, but his skepticism holds firm. What could these men offer but more empty words?

The moment that changes everything arrives unexpectedly. On his way to the market, Zach stumbles upon a gathering. A fisherman named Peter speaks with an authority that commands the air itself. As Zach listens, his heart begins to race—the words cut through him, sharper than any leatherworker's knife. "Repent and be baptized every one of you in the name of Jesus Christ for the forgiveness of your sins, and you will receive the gift of the Holy Spirit" (Acts 2:38).

This moment, raw and piercing, is Zach's explosion. The solution isn't a revolution against Rome or a new technique in his craft—it's the Holy Spirit, the very breath of God that promises to fill the emptiness that had been gnawing at his soul.

In a flood of authentic emotion, Zach steps forward, his decision made—he prays a prayer of salvation. The dragon of despair is slain, not by Zach, but by the Holy Spirit—Peter's words merely the sword that delivered the decisive blow. It's not the words themselves, but what they carry, a divine power that transforms.

Zach's baptism is more than a ritual; it's a rebirth. His life, once bound by the cyclical rhythm of his workbench, is now a canvas for the Spirit's work. He becomes a beacon in his community, his shop a place of discourse and hope. The Holy Spirit, the Helper that Jesus promised, is now his guide, counselor, and ever-present companion.

Zach's story is our story, echoing through time. His struggles mirror our own, his questions are ours. When the Spirit descends upon Zach, we see our own potential for transformation, the true value of Pentecost. It tells us that the Holy Spirit is not just a chapter in ancient history but a vibrant, present force ready to fill our sails and guide us to shores beyond our vision. Through Zach's eyes, we understand that the true work of the Spirit is not confined to the walls of a church but is alive in the hearts of the faithful, in the everyday walk of life, just as it was on that fateful day in Jerusalem.

Gifts of the Spirit

In the tapestry of faith, the Holy Spirit weaves strands of extraordinary capability, bestowing upon believers gifts that surpass human skill and wisdom. These gifts, as vibrant and varied as the hues of a sunset, are not for personal glory but for the strengthening of the Church, the Body of Christ. Each believer is a thread in this divine fabric, endowed with a special gift meant to complement and complete the beautiful design intended by the Creator.

1 Corinthians 12:4–6 resonates with this truth: "There are different kinds of gifts, but the same Spirit distributes them. There are different kinds of service, but the same Lord. There are different kinds of working, but in all of them and in everyone it is the same God at work." This passage unveils the profound diversity yet unity in the spiritual

gifts, underscoring that the Spirit's intent is harmonious cooperation, not discordant competition.

As we explore the nine gifts mentioned by the apostle Paul, consider the miraculous nature of each:

1. **The Word of Wisdom**: An utterance of profound insight, often revealing solutions to complex problems. It's like a beacon of divine light slicing through the fog of human uncertainty.

2. **The Word of Knowledge**. This is a supernatural awareness, knowledge that could only be revealed by the Holy Spirit, a sacred whisper that unveils truths hidden in the shadows.

3. **Faith**. Not the everyday faith that tilts at windmills, but a mountain-moving certainty that stands unflinching in the face of the impossible, an anchor in the stormy seas of life.

4. **Gifts of Healing**. These are hands that become conduits of divine restoration, where illnesses and infirmities bow to the will of the Healer.

5. **Working of Miracles**. Here lies the power to intervene in the natural course of events, a divine disruption of the ordinary, making way for the extraordinary.

6. **Prophecy**. This is the voice that speaks forth the heart and mind of God, often bringing edification, exhortation, and comfort to the hearers, a holy echo of divine intention.

7. **Discerning of Spirits**. An ability to see not with physical eyes but with spiritual insight, distinguishing truth from deception, purity from defilement.

8. **Diverse Kinds of Tongues**. A spiritual language that transcends human understanding, often a mystery to the speaker, yet a vessel of profound intercession and praise.

9. **Interpretation of Tongues**. The key that unlocks the messages enfolded in tongues, transforming enigmatic utterances into messages of clarity.

1 Peter 4:10 encapsulates the call to steward these gifts: "Each of you should use whatever gift you have received to serve others, as faithful stewards of God's grace in its various forms." Here lies the heartbeat of the gifts: service—not self-service, but service to others, service that glorifies the Giver rather than the gift-bearer.

In understanding these gifts, we discover not a hierarchy but a mosaic, not a competition but a symphony. They invite us to look beyond our limitations and lean into the Spirit's empowering presence, to embrace a life where our natural talents are supernaturally enhanced for the common good. It is in this divine collaboration that we find the Church edified, the broken restored, and the name of Christ lifted high.

The Woven Threads of Purpose

Forget this spiritual gifts, what's the problem? The problem is the individual feeling of insignificance in the grand tapestry of life. Meet Cynthia, a 32-year-old community center director from a bustling city neighborhood. Despite her dedication, she often lies awake at night, wrestling with a gnawing question: "Am I making a real difference?" Her life is a portrait of service, yet her heart whispers doubts about her purpose and impact.

Cynthia's daily armor isn't shining, and it's not made of steel—it's her well-worn sneakers and the lanyard of keys jangling at her hip, symbols of her service and commitment. Her vibrant scarf is as much a part of her as her compassionate spirit, an emblem of her creativity and desire to bring color to the lives of others. The spiritual gifts are her untapped potential, the sword that lies unclaimed.

It's that sinking feeling of invisibility that keeps Cynthia up at night—the fear that her actions are but drops in an overwhelming ocean of need. The youth she mentors, the families she supports, they all weigh upon her, each face a reminder of her inner turmoil: "Is my presence in their lives truly beneficial?"

The shift occurs one unassuming Tuesday evening during a community prayer meeting. As Cynthia listens to a message about the diversity of spiritual gifts, a silent explosion occurs within her. She feels a resonance, a call to seek deeper within herself. The speaker quotes 1 Corinthians 12:7: "Now to each one the manifestation of the Spirit is given for the common good." It is her epiphany, the moment she understands that her natural talents are but seeds that, when watered by the Spirit, can grow into gifts far beyond her own capabilities.

The scene is her small, cluttered office, filled with children's artwork and stacks of paperwork. The glow of the sunset through the blinds bathes the room in golden light, mirroring the warmth spreading through her chest. It's the familiar smell of aged paper and the cacophony of the city that grounds her. She looks at the community board, plastered with flyers and thank-you notes, and sees not just her own work, but the potential for so much more.

The real value Cynthia discovers is not just in understanding her spiritual gifts, but in the profound realization that she is part of a greater whole. As she embraces her gift of administration, suddenly, the daunting problems of her community begin to seem surmountable. Each organized event, every planned program, becomes a conduit of grace, impacting lives in ways she never imagined.

Cynthia's story is our story. It's the recognition that within each of us lies a latent power, waiting to be ignited by the Holy Spirit. Our natural abilities, when fused with divine purpose, can slay the dragons of doubt and insignificance, awakening us to our part in the eternal narrative. The spiritual gifts are not just tools; they are extensions of our being, a means to transform not only our lives but the world around us. They whisper a profound truth: we are seen, we are known, and we are empowered to make a difference.

The Fruitful Life

In the bustling orchard of humanity, where the branches are heavy with varied actions and the air is thick with the scent of striving, there blooms a quiet revolution known as "The Fruitful Life." It's the life that any believer is invited to lead, marked not just by what one does, but by who one becomes. This transformation is beautifully detailed in Paul's letter to the Galatians, where he lists the fruits of the Spirit as love, joy, peace, forbearance, kindness, goodness, faithfulness, gentleness, and self-control (Galatians 5:22–23).

Imagine a life where love is not just a fleeting emotion but a constant presence, as enduring as the sun that rises faithfully each morning. Where joy is not dependent on circumstances but is a stream that flows steadily beneath the surface of every moment. This joy radiates, even when shadows fall, because it is rooted in something— or Someone—far greater than transient events.

Picture a peace that does not falter in the face of chaos, a peace that stands firm like a lighthouse amid tempestuous seas. This peace is a reflection of the Prince of Peace Himself, a testament to a life surrendered to the whisper of the Holy Spirit. "Peace I leave with you;

my peace I give you. I do not give to you as the world gives. Do not let your hearts be troubled and do not be afraid" (John 14:27).

Envision forbearance that manifests as a patience that does not wane, even when trials stretch long and weariness clings like morning mist. This is a patience that "bears all things, believes all things, hopes all things, endures all things" (1 Corinthians 13:7), standing as a fortress of faithfulness in a world of instant gratification.

Imagine kindness and goodness that are not acts put on for show but the very fabric of one's being, a reflection of the One who "is kind to the ungrateful and wicked" (Luke 6:35). These are not just traits but testaments, evidence of a Divine touch in the human heart.

Contemplate faithfulness that does not waver, a constancy in the face of a fickle world, a mirror of the faithfulness of God, who remains true even when we are faithless. "If we are faithless, He remains faithful, for He cannot disown Himself" (2 Timothy 2:13).

Reflect on gentleness, a strength under control, a might that does not crush but cherishes, an echo of the gentle whisper that Elijah heard on the mountain (1 King 19:12).

Consider self-control, not as a binding of the self but as freedom from enslavement to impulses and passions. It's a liberating force, as Paul writes, "I will not be mastered by anything" (1 Corinthians 6:12).

"The Fruitful Life" is not a call to a passive existence but an active cultivation of these divine qualities that grow from a life intertwined with the Holy Spirit. It is a journey of becoming, a transformation so deep that it changes not just behaviors but the very desires that drive them. This life is an open invitation, a path lined with the evidence of divine companionship and empowerment, leading ever onward to life that is abundantly fruitful.

The Gardener's Awakening

In the bustling heart of the city, where the clamor of daily existence often drowns out the whispers of the soul, lived a man named Nico. Nico, a 45-year-old community center director, was known for his stoic demeanor and his seemingly unflappable nature. He wore his responsibility like a badge, but beneath his steady gaze was a turmoil that kept him awake at night. The city was his dragon, a beast that never slept, with problems as numerous as its stars.

Nico's suit and tie were less about fashion and more a suit of armor, defending him against a world that demanded constant strength. Yet in the solitude of his apartment, the armor fell away, revealing the weight of loneliness and the longing for a life of more profound meaning and connection.

One night, a silent plea escaped his lips, a whisper for something real amidst the facade. In that moment, Nico felt a shift, like the soft but certain turning of a page. The next day, on his way to work, his usual route was blocked, and he took a detour through a local park. There, he stumbled upon a community garden, a splash of green serenity in the gray landscape. The contrast was jarring, the silence almost tangible. It was as if the garden was waiting for him.

Drawn to the tranquility, Nico began to volunteer at the garden. His hands, once accustomed to the sterility of paperwork, now delved into the richness of soil. Each seed he planted, each plant he nurtured, began a mirror a transformation within him. The garden became his quiet place of refection, a space where he could cultivate the fruits of a life enriched not by accolades, but by attributes of the Spirit.

The authenticity of growth, the patience required for cultivation, the joy in blooming flowers, and the peace amidst the greenery began to resonate with Nico. The garden was not just a place; it was a living metaphor for a spiritual journey he hadn't realized he'd embarked upon.

Galatians 5:22–23 became a mantra for him, as he saw love, joy, peace, forbearance, kindness, goodness, faithfulness, gentleness, and self-control not just as virtues to aspire to, but as the natural outcome of a life rooted in something beyond himself. "But the fruit of the Spirit is love, joy, peace, forbearance, kindness, goodness, faithfulness, gentleness, and self-control . . ."

Months turned into seasons, and the community center began to reflect the change in Nico. Programs became more compassionate, interactions more genuine. People noticed. They would often say, "There's something different about him," without quite being able to pinpoint what had changed.

Nico would just smile, a knowing twinkle in his eye, because he had discovered the true dragon was not the city or its problems, but the disconnection within his own heart. And the sword that slew the dragon was not his position or his intellect, but the fruits of a life transformed by the tender work of the Spirit. His garden thrived, as did his soul, and thus, the city felt a little less daunting, the night a little less dark. And the garden? It became known as "The Oasis," a testament to one man's journey to a Fruitful Life.

———

The Counselor Within

In the midst of life's tumultuous sea, where waves of confusion and the gales of decision-making often threaten to capsize our fragile boats, there sails a vessel guided by an unseen force. This section dives into the profound role of the Holy Spirit, known to many as the Counselor within, whose gentle yet compelling guidance can turn the sails of our souls towards safe harbors.

Imagine Sarah, a middle-aged teacher in a small town, known for her wisdom and her uncanny ability to solve problems that left others bewildered. She wasn't just solving algebraic equations on the blackboard; she was known to untangle the more complex variables of life's challenges. Yet, even a teacher has moments when the answers seem as distant as stars in a cloudy night sky.

In one such moment, with a heart heavy with uncertainty, Sarah sat quietly in her room, pondering the course her life was taking. "When the Spirit of truth comes, He will guide you into all the truth," (John 16:13) she recalled, a verse that had always intrigued her, as it promised a guide beyond the map of her own understanding.

It was in the quiet hours of the dawn, while the world was still in slumber, that Sarah experienced the whisper of the Counselor within. The Holy Spirit, much like a compass in the hands of a mariner, began to orient her towards a direction that resonated with peace and clarity. It wasn't an audible voice, nor a dramatic revelation, but a subtle knowing that coursed through her being, much like the silent unfolding of dawn dispels darkness without a sound.

As days passed, Sarah found herself enveloped in a sense of confidence that was not her own. Her choices reflected a wisdom that wasn't born of books or scholarly article but of the gentle promptings of the Spirit within her. "But the Counselor, the Holy Spirit, whom the Father will send in My name, will teach you all things and will remind you of everything I have said to you," (John 14:26) echoed in her actions, as she navigated through life's decisions with an otherworldly precision.

Her students and colleagues began to notice the serene assurance with which she approached her work. It was as if she had an internal guide, a counselor, who whispered truths in the quiet corners of her heart, prompting her to lead, to comfort, and to shine light in places where shadows fell.

The Holy Spirit as the Counselor within is not merely a theological concept for those like Sarah, but a lived experience. It is the warm glow of certainty when the world presents questions; it is the soft nudge towards love when anger seems easier; it is the infusion of strength when the flesh is weak.

For the believers, the Holy Spirit is the Counselor who teaches and reminds, guides and comforts. Through Him, the words of Christ become alive, not just inscribed on the pages of a sacred book but written upon the heart. In the intricacies of life's journey, the Holy Spirit is the guide, the Counselor within, who turns our midnight musings into dawn's glorious certainty.

Intercession and Power

Amidst the vibrant tapestry of faith, there is a thread that weaves through the very fabric of a believer's prayer life, glowing with a divine luminescence—this is the role of the Holy Spirit in prayer, a celestial advocate that speaks with sighs too deep for words.

In the quiet sanctuary of her garden, where roses bloom and time seems to stand still, we find Hannah, a woman of steadfast faith. Yet even the faithful can find themselves grappling with the groans of an unspeakable yearning, reaching for the heavens with prayers that seem to falter on trembling lips.

Hannah knows well the verses that speak of the Holy Spirit's power in prayer, how "the Spirit helps us in our weakness" (Romans 8:26). As she kneels among the roses, the fragility of her own efforts to pray becomes palpable. Her soul yearns for a depth of communion with the Divine, as intercession that transcends her own limitations.

As she quiets her thoughts and opens her heart, she feels the gentle stirrings of the Holy Spirit, a sacred wind that begins to fill the sails of her spirit. Her words may stumble, her requests may be muddled, but the Spirit within her rises with a celestial voice, interceding on her behalf "with groanings too deep for words" (Romans 8:26).

In this hallowed moment, Hannah understands that she is not alone in her prayers; she is accompanied by a power far greater than her own. The Holy Spirit pleads for her, aligning her deepest needs with the will of God, transforming her silent whispers into a symphony of divine communication.

The intercession of the Spirit is not an abstract doctrine for Hannah—it is as real as the roses that witness her communion. She takes comfort in knowing that the Spirit intercedes for the saints "according to the will of God" (Romans 8:27), making her simple garden a gateway to the heavens.

Through the Spirit's intercession, Hannah finds a power that does not merely echo on the walls of cathedrals or resound in the hymns of the faithful; it pulses within the very core of her being. Her prayers are now enfolded in the assurance that the Spirit is at work, taking the sighs of her heart and lifting them to the throne of grace with divine eloquence.

In the life of a believer, the Holy Spirit is not a silent observer but an active participant in the communion of prayer. For those who, like Hannah, kneel in gardens or sit in pews, or even those who whisper their prayers in the stillness of their minds, the Holy Spirit is the intercessor, the celestial advocate, ensuring that even the most fragile prayer is heard and held in the hands of God.

The Eternal Promise

In the narrative of faith, there is a culminating crescendo, a moment that secures the believer's story with an indelible mark of divine promise—the sealing of the Holy Spirit. This is not merely a theological concept, but a celestial stamp, the guarantee of an inheritance that surpasses all earthly treasures.

We find ourselves walking alongside Eliana, a woman whose journey of faith has been a mosaic of trials and triumphs. She carries within her a promise, one that is as steadfast as the dawn and as eternal as the stars. The concept of the Holy Spirit as a seal over her life is a profound assurance that whispers of a future beyond the horizon of her earthly existence.

Eliana holds close to her heart the words of Ephesians 1:13–14, where it is written, "Having believed, you were marked in Him with a seal, the promised Holy Spirit, who is a deposit guaranteeing our inheritance until the redemption of those who are God's possession—to the praise of His glory."

As she reflects on this, the worries of life seem to fall away like leaves from an autumn tree. The Holy Spirit has been given to her as a seal, a confirmation of her faith, and a prelude to the promises that await. This seal is not a mere symbol; it is the living presence of God within her, the down payment of a celestial heritage that is kept in the vaults of heaven for her.

The tangible reality of this promise fills Eliana with an unspeakable joy. She envisions the seal not as a static mark but as a vibrant, living presence that guides her, comforts her, and reminds her that she is not just passing through this world; she is journeying towards an eternal home.

The presence of the Holy Spirit in her life is her eternal promise, a testament to the fact that she is indeed God's possession, precious in His sight and held in His hands. The seal is her constant reminder that, though she faces the ephemeral shadows of this world, she is destined for an unshakable kingdom—an inheritance that is incorruptible, undefiled, and unfading, kept in heaven for her (1 Peter 1:4).

For Eliana, and for every believer who carries this seal, the Holy Spirit is the whisper of eternity in the midst of temporal chaos, the warmth of divine assurance in the coldness of life's uncertainties. It is the promise that whatever trials come, they are but the turning pages in a much grander story—a story that ends not with a period, but with an ellipsis leading into the infinite realms of God's glory and everlasting love.

CHAPTER FOUR

Daily Bread
The Habit of Bible Reading

"Man shall not live by bread alone, but by every word that comes from the mouth of God."

—MATTHEW 4:4 ESV

Welcome to the journey of a lifetime—one that you are about to undertake with nothing more than a book in your hands. But this is no ordinary book; it is a living, breathing tapestry of truths, woven with the threads of divine wisdom. This is your invitation to the table where the feast never ends and every morsel is a taste of eternity. This chapter isn't just a chapter in your life; it is the opening of a continuous dialogue between the Divine and you.

In a world that clamors for your attention with relentless urgency, carving out moments for quiet reflection and nourishment for your soul can seem as an insurmountable task. Yet, here you stand at the precipice of decision. Will you step into a routine that transforms the mundane into the sacred, the ordinary into the extraordinary?

As we embark on this chronologically ordered sojourn through scripture, you will not simply move from page to page, but from glory to glory. From the first whispers of truth that beckon you to taste and see, to the deep wells of wisdom that call you to come and drink, each topic is a stepping stone across the river of revelation.

Together, we will set the table, understanding why each word in the Bible is a portion to be savored. We'll take our first bite, initiating a rhythm that will dance to the heartbeat of revelation. With a play in hand, our daily manna, we will traverse the landscapes of history, poetry, prophecy, and epistle.

Meditation will become our resting place, a pause in the rush of life where the Word is chewed slowly, allowing its flavors to release and its nutrients to absorb into the very fabric of our beings. Interpretation will be our guide, helping us to digest the bread of ancient text in a modern world.

And then, we'll encounter Jesus—the bread of Life in all of scripture—discovering the scarlet thread that runs through every book, every story, every prophecy. As our faith feeds on the Word, it grows strong, reshaping our beliefs and sharpening our vision.

Hand in hand with the text comes the whisper of prayer, the conversations that arise naturally from the communion of reading. And with the wisdom gained, we turn towards our lives, seeking to apply the truths that rise like dawn upon our days.

Finally, we don't hoard this bread; we share it, breaking it with others so that they too may know the sustenance and satisfaction that comes from God's Word.

Prepare yourself for transformation, for as you turn each page, you will be turning the soil of your soul, planting seeds that will bear fruit in every season of life. Let's begin this feast together, savoring each word, for man does not live on bread alone, but on every word that comes from the mouth of God.

Welcome to your "Daily Bread."

Setting the Table: Understanding the Importance of Daily Bible Reading

Imagine a table set before you, not with an array of fleeting delicacies, but with a feast meant to sustain you eternally. This isn't just any table; it's one that is laid out daily with a spread that is both ancient and fresh, ready to feed the deepest hunger within you—the hunger for spiritual truth and guidance.

In the physical realm, we never question the need for daily meals. Our bodies have a built-in alert system that rumbles and reminds us when we need to eat. Similarly, our spirits require nourishment, and there is no richer diet than the Word of God. Just as Moses told the Israelites in Deuteronomy 8:3, ". . . man does not live on bread alone but on every word that comes from the mouth of the Lord," we too must understand the sustenance that comes from daily communion with scripture.

The spiritual bread is not just food for thought; it is the very sustenance of our souls. As we break the bread of scripture, we are not simply reading words; we are partaking in a meal prepared by God Himself. Through the Holy Scriptures, He speaks directly to us, providing guidance, comfort, and the strength to face our daily battles.

The psalmist declares, "Your word is a lamp for my feet, a light on my path" (Psalm 119:105). In a world that can often be dark and confusing, the Bible illuminates our way, guiding our steps with the brilliance of divine wisdom. Each verse, each story, each commandment is a morsel of light, helping us to see and walk the path laid out for us.

But this meal requires an active engagement. It's not enough to simple read; one must digest, savor, and allow the nutrients of heavenly wisdom to permeate every aspect of life. As James 1:22 exhorts, "Do not merely listen to the word, and so deceive yourselves. Do what it says." The true value of this meal is realized when it translates into lived experience, when the words jump off the page and become part of who we are.

So, as you approach this divine table set before you, do so with a heart ready to receive and a life ready to be transformed. Make it a daily habit to sit and dine, to read and reflect, to listen and to live out the rich truths found in the Holy Scriptures. In doing so, you will find that every other table you approach in this life is secondary to the one that offers the bread of life—Jesus Christ, the Word made flesh (John 1:14).

This spiritual discipline is not just for the scholars and saints; it's for the weary, the seeking, the broken, and the hopeful. It's for those yearning for something more, something deeper, something eternal. In a world chasing after quick fixes and fast food, choose the better part—choose the sustenance that will never perish, the food that endures to eternal life, which the Son of Man will give you (John 6:27).

Setting the table for daily Bible reading is not an antiquated ritual; it's the laying out of God's promises, presence, and power in your life. Every verse a vitamin, every chapter a course, every book a banquet—this is the meal that truly satisfies.

The Quiet Awakening

Rebecca is a 34-year-old nurse. Every day she wraps her stethoscope, a symbol of her healing vocation, around her neck. Her brown hair is usually tied back in a no-nonsense bun, and laugh lines crease the corners of her eyes, evidence of her warmth despite the stress of her profession.

Lately, Rebecca's laughter has been less frequent. The weight of long, taxing hours in the hospital and the emotional toll of caring for the sick have begun to shadow her once bright spirit. At night, instead of rest, her mind races with a litany of patient names, medication dosages, and the relentless buzz of the emergency room.

One particularly trying evening, after losing a young patient, Rebecca found herself alone in the hospital chapel, the quiet stark contrast to the chaos of her day. Her hands found a neglected Bible in the rack in front of her—its leather cover worn, pages thumbed through by countless seeking hands before hers. As she flipped through it, a passage seemed to leap out at her: "Come to me, all who labor and are heavy laden, and I will give you rest" (Matthew 11:28). In that moment, the weight she had been carrying began to lift. It wasn't a miraculous cure for her fatigue, but a quiet awakening to a source of strength she had long forgotten.

The very next day, Rebecca started a new morning ritual. Before the sun rose, before the alarms buzzed, she sat with her Bible at her small kitchen table, the one with the mismatched chairs and the coffee mug ring stains. As her eyes traveled over the verses, she found not just words, but a conversation, a source of renewal, a daily bread that began to nourish her in ways she hadn't anticipated.

This practice became her armor, not visible like the stethoscope she wore, but stronger in many ways. It equipped her for the daily battles she faced, not with steel, but with hope, resilience, and a peace that transcended understanding. The dragon of burnout still reared its head, but now she had a sword, forged in the quiet moments of dawn with scriptures that whispered of a love louder than any chaos.

Through this daily habit of Bible reading, Rebecca rediscovered her laugh, her purpose, and a well of strength that carried her through the double shifts and heartbreaking moments. And for those who witnessed her transformation, who saw the way she seemed to stand a little taller, to shine a little brighter amidst the sterile halls of the hospital, it was clear that this was a nourishment they yearned for too. In Rebecca's revival, they found an invitation to seek their own.

The First Bite: Beginning Your Journey in Scripture

Embarking on the journey of daily scripture reading can be as daunting as standing at the base of a towering mountain, especially when you're not sure where the path begins. Yet, just like any journey, the secret to beginning is to take the very first step.

1. **Choosing Your Time and Place**. "Your word is a lamp for my feet, a light on my path" (Psalm 119:105). As the Psalmist poetically notes, scripture illuminates the steps ahead. But to let this light shine, you must carve out a moment in your day. Dawn, with its quiet and promise, might beckon to some, while others find the stillness of night more comforting. Pinpoint a time when your heart can be most receptive, when the static of life dims enough to hear the soft whisper of divine wisdom.

2. **Establishing Your Routine**. "And let us not grow weary of doing good, for in due season we will reap, if we do not give up" (Galatians 6:9). Starting a new habit isn't without its

challenges. There will be mornings when the bed's embrace is too warm, nights when fatigue blankets your resolve. Yet, the apostle Paul encourages persistence. Create a ritual around your reading. Maybe it's a particular chair that cradles you, a candle whose sent lifts your spirits, or a journal where reflections can be penned. Embrace these routines as sacred companions on your journey.

3. **Overcoming the Initial Hurdle**. "So then faith comes by hearing, and hearing by the Word of God" (Romans 10:17). The first steps of any endeavor are often the hardest, laden with resistance. Remember, faith isn't built on fleeting feelings but on the steady, often challenging, steps of commitment. The initial hurdle is surmounted not by a giant leap but by the simple act of opening the Book, letting your eyes rest on the words, and allowing them to speak to you.

4. **Feeding on the Word**. "Man shall not live by bread alone, but by every word that comes from the mouth of God" (Matthew 4:4). Your soul hungers for more than what this world offers; it yearns for the spiritual sustenance found within the scriptures. As Jesus reminded Satan, our lives gain true fullness not from earthly bread but from the divine word. With each passage you read, you're taking a bite of the Bread of Life, allowing it to fill you, sustain you, and prepare you for the day's journey.

5. **The Shared Feast**. "Iron sharpens iron, and one man sharpens another" (Proverbs 27:17). Perhaps consider inviting others into your journey. Share the verses that move you, the lessons you glean. As you do, you'll find your understanding deepening,

your commitment solidifying, and your journey enriched by the shared wisdom of fellow travelers.

So, take the first bite. Let the richness of the Word settle on your palate, taste its complexity, and feel its power. With each day, with each verse, you'll find yourself walking a path illuminated by the very Light of the Word.

———

Awakening to a New Routine

In the quiet cobblestone lanes of a small village, nestled between the undulating hills and whispering woods, there lived a young scribe named Felicity. With chestnut hair cascading like a waterfall and eyes as clear as the summer sky, she was a picture of youth and vigor, adorned always with a locket containing a mustard seed—a reminder to keep faith even when it seemed as small and inconspicuous as the trinket around her neck.

Night after night, Felicity sat by the flicker of candlelight, quill in hand, her heart heavy with an inexplicable yearning. The manuscripts and scrolls she transcribed spoke of history, of wars and kings, but her spirit hungered for something more profound, more satiating. Her nights were restless, her days a sequence of shadows, for the dragon she faced was a silent one—a life lacking in spiritual depth and understanding.

The locket's weight against her chest was a constant reminder of the faith she wished to deepen. What kept her up as the moon climbed high was not the fear of what lay in the dark, but what seemed absent in the light—purpose, direction, and a connection with the Divine.

Then came the morning when the mist hung low, and Felicity stumbled upon an old, leather-bound book in the market square. Its pages were worn, its script faded, but as she turned the pages, a hush fell over her world. The words "In the beginning was the Word, and the Word was with God, and the Word was God" seemed to dance before her eyes, igniting something long dormant within her.

Felicity began to rise with the dawn, her routine born in that moment of discovery. Each morning, as the first light crept over the horizon, she would sit at her oak desk, the locket lying beside her, and read from the ancient scriptures. This was no longer just a habit; it was a sacred communion. The village began to notice a change in her—a lightness in her step, a clarity in her voice, an assurance in her gaze.

It wasn't the book alone that changed Felicity; it was her willingness to let the words permeate her being, to digest them slowly, savoring each morsel of wisdom, each syllable of truth. As she made scripture her daily bread, she found the sustenance her soul had been craving.

Through the shared verses with friends, the discussions that flowed like rivers, and the quiet moments of revelation, the mustard seed in her locket seemed to grow. Felicity was no longer just a scribe; she was a beacon of the Word, a testament to the transformative power of embracing a discipline that fed not just the mind, but the heart and soul as well.

As Felicity's story spread, it carried a simple yet profound message: the dawn awaits all who seek it. The solution to her restlessness was not in conquering a dragon of grandeur, but in facing the dragon within, armed with the sword of the Spirit—the Word of God. Her journey had just begun, a path lit with the promise of growing light.

Daily Manna: Choosing a Bible Reading Plan

Navigating the vast sea of Scripture can seem as daunting as plotting a course through uncharted waters. For the earnest but overwhelmed believer, finding a way to consume the Word of God is a manner that is both structured and spiritually nourishing is paramount. Jacklyn, our diligent scribe, once adrift in a sea of parchments, discovered the very thing that would guide her vessel: a Bible reading plan.

Just as a tree is known by its fruit, a believer is nourished by the Word, and there is a veritable banquet of plans laid out for the hungry soul. One can embark on a journey from Genesis to Revelation with a chronological plan—the Cornucopia plan—witnessing the unfolding of God's grand narrative in a linear dance of divine sovereignty. "For everything that was written in the past was written to teach us, so that through the endurance taught in the Scriptures and the encouragement they provide we might have hope" (Romans 15:4).

Alternatively, a thematic plan weaves through the Bible like a golden thread, gathering pearls of wisdom on specific subjects, connecting disparate strands of thought into a cohesive tapestry of understanding. "All Scripture is God-breathed and is useful for teaching, rebuking, correction and training in righteousness" (2 Timothy 3:16).

For those who delight in structure and order, the canonical plan presents the Bible in the sequence that the books appear, an approach that honors the historical and ecclesiastical journey of the Bible as we have it today.

Jacklyn found her rhythm in the ebb and flow of the thematic plan, savoring the interconnectedness of scriptures that spanned from the poetic musings of David to the prophetic visions of Isaiah, from the wisdom of Solomon to the parables of Jesus. This method allowed her to delve into the heart of God's love, justice, and redemption as seen throughout the whole counsel of Scripture.

With each plan offering its own unique vista, Jacklyn charted her spiritual growth, marking each passage with the joy of a traveler discovering new lands. She experienced the fullness of God's story, saw the beauty of redemption threading through each testament, and the mirror it held up to her own life's journey.

This section of our tale is not just about feeding on the "daily manna," recognizing that man does not live on bread alone, but on every word that comes from the mouth of God (Deuteronomy 8:3). Jacklyn's story is an invitation to every believer to find their plan, their structure, their daily bread, and in doing so, discover the feast that awaits in the Word of God—a feast that sustains, enriches, and empowers the soul for the voyage of life.

Savoring the Flavor: Learning to Meditate on Scripture

In the quiet chambers of the heart, where the hustle of the world fades into a whisper, there lies a banquet hall for the soul. It is in this hallowed space that the art of meditation transforms the act of reading Scripture into a feast of divine flavors. Let us draw up a chair beside Mariah, a seeker whose hunger for spiritual depth led her to the ancient practice of Lectio Divina.

Mariah discovered in Lectio Divina a four-course meal for her soul. Each step a deeper dive into the heart of God's Word.

1. **Lectio (Read)**. She begins with a slow, deliberate reading of the Scripture, savoring each word as one would savor the first bite of a cherished dish. As she reads, a phrase shimmers before her, inviting her to linger. "Your word is a lamp for my feet, a light on my path" (Psalm 119:105).

2. **Meditatio (Meditate)**. Mariah ponders the text, rolling it over in her mind, extracting the nuances of its flavor, allowing the Holy Spirit to marinate her thoughts with the truth she has tasted. "Blessed is the one . . . whose delight is in the law of the

Lord, and who meditates on his law day and night" (Psalm 1:1–2).

3. **Oratio (Pray)**. With the words of Scripture softening her heart like warm bread softens with butter, Mariah's meditation naturally seasons her prayers. She converses with God, her words a fragrant offering of reflection and response. "Do not be anxious about anything, but in every situation, by prayer and petition, with thanksgiving, present your requests to God" (Philippians 4:6).

4. **Contemplatio (Contemplate)**. Finally, she rests in contemplation, sitting in silence before the Lord, the truths of Scripture infusing her being, nourishing her spirit, the presence of God encompassing her like the sweet aroma of a well-prepared meal. "Be still, and know that I am God . . ." (Psalm 46:10).

Mariah also explored other meditative strategies. She practiced "scriptio continua," reading Scripture continuously and repetitively, which allowed the Word to wash over her repeatedly, each wave depositing fresh insight. She engaged in "praying the Scriptures," where she turned the words of the Bible into personal prayers, making the ancient text alive and relevant to her life.

As Mariah grows in her practice of meditation, the verses she reads are no longer just words on a page but life-giving morsels to be chewed, digested, and treasured. Her daily readings become more than a discipline; they are an encounter with the Divine, leaving a lingering sweetness that sustains her throughout the day.

This section is an invitation to you, dear reader, to partake in this sacred practice. To let the words of Scripture settle in your heart as you meditate on them, allowing them to shape your thoughts, guide your prayers, and bring you into the peaceful presence of contemplation. For in the quiet tasting of God's Word, we find the sustenance for our souls, the wisdom for our lives, and the joy of intimate fellowship with the Creator.

Digesting the Word: Understanding and Interpretation

Embarking on a journey through the vibrant tapestry of Scripture, we must become students of context and cultivators of understanding. It's like stepping into a grand library filled with ancient manuscripts, each one rich with history and alive with meaning. Here we meet Carson, a modern-day disciple with a passion for unlocking the treasures within the Bible's pages.

Carson approaches Scripture with reverence and an inquisitive heart, knowing that to digest the Word fully, one must first understand its ingredients—the culture, the language, the people, and the spirit of the times. He delves into hermeneutics, the art of interpreting biblical texts, with the eagerness of a scholar and the humility of a seeker. "All Scripture is God-breathed and is useful for teaching, rebuking, correcting and training in righteousness" (2 Timothy 3:16).

He begins by examining the historical context, placing himself in the dusty sandals of those who walked the earth during biblical times. Carson understands that the events, customs, and social dynamics of the ancient world shed light on the depth of Scripture's meaning. "For everything that was written in the past was written to teach us, so that through the endurance taught in the Scriptures and the encouragement they provide we might have hope" (Romans 15:4).

Guided by hermeneutical principles, Carson discerns literal meanings from metaphors and parables, and he weighs the different genres of Scripture—from poetry to prophecy, from narrative to law.

Each genre requires a unique approach, much like the varied cooking methods needed to bring out the distinct flavors in a gourmet meal. "Your commands are always with me and make me wiser than my enemies" (Psalm 119:98).

Understanding is not just for the mind; it's for life application. Carson seeks to translate the ancient wisdom into contemporary living, finding ways to apply the eternal truths to his daily walk. "Do not merely listen to the word, and so deceive yourselves. Do what it says" (James 1:22).

The Bible becomes for Carson a living conversation across millennia, a dialogue that informs his values, decisions, and perspectives. Through careful interpretation, he uncovers principles that transcend time, cultures that reveal humanity's collective story, and divine wisdom that guides his path.

Now, consider yourself invited to this feast of understanding. May you, like Carson, be equipped with the tools of hermeneutics to unearth the rich layers of biblical text. May historical context illuminate your reading, and may the principles of interpretation be the compass by which you navigate the living Word. For in the thoughtful digestion of Scripture lies the nourishment of the soul, the transformation of the mind, and the shaping of a life that reflects the wisdom of the ages.

The Bread of Life:
Encountering Jesus in All of Scripture

Within the tapestry of scripture, from the first promise in Genesis to the final Amen in Revelation, a single thread is woven throughout: the redemptive story of Jesus Christ, the Bread of Life. To partake of this Bread is to see the grand narrative of redemption come alive with every turn of the page.

Meet Nancy, a woman of vibrant faith, who opens her Bible each morning with anticipation, searching for the footprints of Jesus in every book, every law, every prophecy, and every psalm. Her soul yearns for the deep, sustaining nourishment that only an encounter with Christ can provide. "Then he opened their minds so they could understand the Scriptures," Jesus proclaimed, as He unveiled His presence in all of the Scriptures (Luke 24:45).

Nancy marvels at how the story of salvation is skillfully penned in the shadows of the Old Testament, waiting to be revealed in the light of the New. The foreshadowing of the sacrificial system, the parallels in the Passover lamb, the symbolism found in the feasts—all point to the One who would come to fulfill them all. "You search the Scriptures because you think that in them you have eternal life; and it is they that bear witness about Me," Jesus said, beckoning all to find Him in the sacred texts (John 5:39).

With each narrative, prophecy, and law she encounters, Nancy finds the unexpected glimpses of the Savior. In Joseph's forgiveness, she sees Jesus' grace; in David's kingship, His sovereign rule; and in Isaiah's prophecies, His suffering and glory. The Bible becomes a mosaic where every piece, no matter how seemingly small or obscure, reflects a facet of Jesus' character and mission. "For Christ is the end of the law for righteousness to everyone who believes," Paul writes, affirming the culmination of the law's purpose in Jesus (Romans 10:4).

For Nancy, encountering Jesus in Scripture is not merely an academic exercise; it is a personal, transformative experience. As she reads, she does not just learn about Jesus—she meets Him, she dines with Him. He is the Living Word that speaks into her life, the Bread of Life that satisfies her deepest hunger. "I am the Bread of Life; whoever comes to Me shall not hunger, and whoever believes in Me shall never thirst," Jesus promises, inviting all to this eternal sustenance (John 6:35).

Let us join Nancy in this sacred search. May we open the Scriptures and see the face of Jesus looking back at us, inviting us to understand the Bible not just as a collection of books, but as a coherent story that finds its meaning in Him. Through prophets and poets, lawgivers and storytellers, let us trace the scarlet cord of redemption.

May our journey through the Word be a continuous encounter with Jesus, the Bread of Life, until we come to see Him face to face in the fulfillment of His Kingdom. For in Him, we find not just the story of the Bible, but the very source of life itself.

Feeding Faith:
Allowing Scripture to Shape Beliefs

As believers draw daily from the well of Scripture, they allow the very words of God to sculpt their innermost beliefs and perspectives. Like a gardener tending to a plant, the consistent reading and reflection upon the Bible nurtures the seed of faith, allowing it to grow deep roots and produce a sturdy, life-giving tree.

Meet James, a man whose faith was once like a flickering candle, vulnerable to the winds of change and circumstances. His believes wavered with every passing doctrine and his worldview was as mutable as the shifting sands. But then, he discovered the steadfastness that comes from anchoring oneself in the Word of God. "So then faith comes by hearing, and hearing by the Word of God," declares Romans 10:17. As James delved into the daily practice of Bible reading, he found his faith not only hearing but thriving.

The Scripture began to work in James like yeast through dough—silently, powerfully, thoroughly. The narratives of faith in the face of adversity, the wisdom found in Proverbs, the teachings of Christ in the gospels, all started to redefine his understanding of truth, justice, love, and redemption. "All Scripture is breathed out by God and profitable for teaching, for reproof, for correction, and for training in righteousness," Writes Paul in 2 Timothy 3:16. It was this divine breath that revived James's dormant faith.

With every verse and chapter, James's worldview shifted. The cultural lenses through which he once viewed the world were replaced with a biblical framework. He learned to see beyond the temporal, to discern matters of eternal significance. The Bible became his compass, guiding his decisions, his actions, and his outlook on life. "Your word is a lamp to my feet and a light to my path," sings the Psalmist in Psalm 119:105. James now walked a path illuminated by the enduring light of Scripture.

The faith that grew in James's heart was not passive; it demanded action. The biblical principles of love, service, and sacrifice found their expression in how he lived. His relationships, his work ethic, his contributions to society were all reflections of the beliefs shaped by the Word. "But be doers of the word, and not hearers only, deceiving yourselves," James the apostle advises in James 1:22. Similarly, our James became a living testimony to the transformative power of engaging with Scripture.

Let us walk alongside James and take up the daily bread of God's Word. May we allow the Holy Scripture to challenge us, change us, and ultimately, to strengthen the very fabric of our faith.

The Living Water:
Integrating Prayer with Bible Reading

Picture a garden where streams of fresh water meander through, nurturing every plant and flower. Such is the union of prayer with Bible reading—a divine conversation where the water of the Word refreshes the soul and prayer allows the garden of our hearts to flourish.

Meet Tracey, a seeker of wisdom, whose journey with the Bible was like walking through a magnificent garden. She treasured every leaf of scripture, every blossom of prophecy, and every fruit of wisdom. But it was when she began to sprinkle her walk with the living water of prayer that the words leaped off the pages and took root in her heart. "This book of the law shall not depart out of your mouth; but you shalt meditate therein day and night," Joshua 1:8 tells us, suggesting a perpetual engagement with the Word, a call Tracey took to heart.

As Tracey read, she paused to whisper words of awe, of thanks, or of petition. The scriptures became a dialogue, with each verse a voice of God to which her prayers were the eager reply. "Let my prayer be set before you as incense; the lifting up of my hands as the evening sacrifice," echoes the Psalmist in Psalm 141:2. Tracey's prayers, inspired by scripture, became a fragrant offering, pleasing and personal to the Lord.

Each narrative, law, and proverb became a stepping stone for Tracey's prayers. She would read about the faith of Abraham, and her prayer would become one of trust; David's psalms turned her prayers into songs of praise; Jesus' words moved her to seek the Kingdom first in her supplications. "Pray without ceasing," urges 1 Thessalonians 5:17, a command made richer against the backdrop of God's Word. Tracey's prayers were unceasing because they were in constant conversation with scripture.

The Holy Scriptures guided Tracey's prayers, preventing them from becoming mere echoes of her own desires. Instead, they aligned her petitions with the heart of God, His promises, and His will. "If you abide in Me, and My words abide in you, you shall ask what you will, and it shall be done unto you," Jesus promises in John 15:7. Tracey abided in Christ as His words abided in her, shaping the prayers that flowed from her lips.

As Tracey integrated prayer with her reading, she found herself growing in grace and knowledge, her faith deepening and her spirit flourishing. The scripture was her soil, prayer was her water, and together they cultivated a vibrant spiritual life.

Let us take inspiration from Tracey's story. May we, too, learn to immerse our reading in prayer, allowing the living waters of our response to mingle with the rich soil of God's Word. In doing so, we can expect a harvest of wisdom, peace, and closeness with the Creator that can only come from such a sacred communion.

Fruitful Harvest:
Applying Biblical Truth to Everyday Life

In the lush landscape of our lives, scripture is not merely to be admired, but to be absorbed and applied, yielding a harvest of good fruit in our everyday existence.

Meet Marcus, a man with a planner always at hand, a life full of decisions, responsibilities, and the all-too-familiar challenge of aligning daily life with deeper values. Marcus found his compass in the pages of the Bible, his decisions and actions guided by the timeless truths nestled within. "But be you doers of the word, and not hearers only, deceiving your own selves," James 1:22 compels us. Marcus took this exhortation to heart, letting scripture leap from the page into his daily walk and talk.

Each morning, Marcus's day began with a passage of scripture, which he would ponder, seeking to unearth the practical wisdom it held. To love one's neighbor (Mark 12:31), for instance, transformed into tangible acts of kindness—a helping hand to a colleague, a warm meal for a neighbor, a listening ear to a friend. "Whatever you do, work heartily, as for the Lord and not for men," Colossians 3:23 told him, and so his work became an offering, done with the excellence and integrity that befits service to the divine.

Faced with choices, Marcus turned to biblical principles as his guide. The wisdom of Proverbs shaped his financial decisions, the patience of John helped him navigate trials, and the courage of Esther emboldened him to stand for what's right. Your word is a lamp for my feet, a light on my path," Psalm 119:105 reminded him, and thus, his path was illuminated by the precepts and commands of God, steering him clear of the pitfalls of shortsightedness and the snares of impulsivity.

In moments of adversity, instead of being swayed by the tumultuous waves of circumstance, Marcus found his anchor in scriptures such as Philippians 4:13, "I can do all things through Christ who strengthens me." This assurance empowered him to meet challenges with a resilience and strength that had its roots in divine promise.

Knowing that life is lived among others, Marcus shared the insights he gleaned from the Bible with friends, family, and his community. By doing so, he not only applied the lessons to his own life but also sowed seeds of wisdom in the lives of others, multiplying the impact of the truths he cherished. "Iron sharpens iron, and one man sharpens another," Proverbs 27:17 tells us. Marcus lived this, engaging in conversations that refined his understanding and application of scripture, while also challenging and encouraging his peers to do likewise.

Let us walk in Marcus's footsteps, treating the Bible not as an exhibit to be viewed from afar, but as a field to be worked, that we might enjoy the fruits of a life lived in accordance with its precepts. For it is through such lived application that the Word of God truly transforms us and our world.

Passing the Bread:
Sharing Scripture with Others

In the warm glow of fellowship, the sharing of bread has always been a symbol of community, sustenance, and shared life. So it is with the Word of God—meant to be savored personally, but also shared generously with those around us, enriching the fabric of our shared existence.

Meet Lydia, whose heart overflows with the richness of the scriptures. Her journey with the Word is not a solitary trek but a communal pilgrimage, where the truths she discovers become beacons of light for others. "Therefore encourage one another and build each other up, just as in fact you are doing," 1 Thessalonians 5:11 echoes through Lydia's life. She sees every verse as not only a personal treasure but a communal gift to be given away.

Lydia begins at home, weaving the threads of scripture into the tapestry of daily family life. Bible stories become the bedrock of bedtime for her children, planting seeds of truth and wisdom in their young hearts. "Train up a child in the way he should go; even when he is old he will not depart from it," Proverbs 22:6 shapes her parental guide. Every parable told, every verse shared, is a stepping stone for her children to encounter God and His world.

With friends and peers, Lydia shares verses that lift the spirit and challenge the soul. She encourages through the scriptures in times of joy and comforts in times of sorrow, making God's Word a shared language of the heart. "A word fitly spoken is like apples of gold in settings of silver," Proverbs 25:11, Lydia's conversations are thus framed, always seeking the right verse for the right moment, a precious offering to the listener.

Out in the wider community, Lydia's scriptural sharing takes on the mantle of service. She volunteers, she teaches, she participates—always ready with a story or a verse that brings hope and perspective. "Let your light so shine before men, that they may see your good works, and glorify your Father which is in heaven," Matthew 5:16 is Lydia's mission statement, her scriptural sharing intertwined with acts of kindness and community building.

Lydia knows that sharing scripture is an art—it requires listening deeply, understanding the needs of others, and speaking with both clarity and love. "Let your speech always be gracious, seasoned with salt, so that you may know how you ought to answer each person," Colossians 4:6 guides her dialogue. She shares not to preach, but to uplift; not to argue, but to enlighten.

She makes use of stories and parables, much like Jesus did, to connect with ancient words to contemporary life. She asks questions that stimulate reflection and she listens, truly listens, to the responses, making the exchange of scripture a true dialogue.

In sharing the Word, Lydia doesn't just pass on information; she extends an invitation to a feast—a banquet of wisdom, love, and transformation. In doing so, she fulfills the call of the great commission, "Go you therefore, and teach all nations," Matthew 28:19, through the simple, profound act of passing the bread of life to those around her.

Thus, as Lydia's life illustrates, the sharing of God's Word is a natural overflow of its work in our hearts, a sacred tradition that nourishes and binds us, a testament to the fact that the most divine truths are made more powerful still when given away.

Home in His Word:

Finding Your Place in a

Bible-believing Community

"And let us consider how we may spur one another on toward love and good deeds, not giving up meeting together, as some are in the habit of doing, but encouraging one another—and all the more as you see the Day approaching."

—HEBREWS 10:24–25 NIV

In the tapestry of faith, each thread is a story, a life interwoven with the Divine, and while our personal journeys with God are immensely precious, they are not meant to be walked in isolation.

Welcome to chapter five, where we embark on a heartfelt exploration of the vital role that community plays in the life of a believer.

From the bustling streets of ancient Jerusalem to the modern digital highways that connect us across continents, the call to fellowship remains a constant echo from the heart of God. This chapter is an invitation to discover the warmth of fellowship, the strength found in collective worship, and the unparalleled joy of learning and growing together in a community that cherishes the Bible as the true north of its existence.

We'll begin by laying down the foundational stones of biblical fellowship, tracing its roots back to the early church, where believers broke bread with glad and sincere hearts. As we delve deeper, we'll uncover the hallmarks of a Bible-believing community, and why, like a beacon, it attracts those yearning for spiritual kinship and growth.

We'll guide you on how to find your spot within this mosaic of believers—how to become not just an attendee, but an active, vibrant member of a local church. We'll navigate the intimate settings of small groups and Bible studies, where the Word of God often leaps from the pages into the very fabric of our daily lives.

Together, we will roll up our sleeves and explore the joys of service, the profound journey of discipleship, and the grace of mentorship. Yes, there may be challenges—doctrinal differences will arise, opinions will diverge—but within these pages, we'll learn how to embrace diversity with love and grace, finding unity in the sacred scriptures.

As we look beyond the four walls of a church building, we'll discover how the spirit of community transcends physical boundaries, flourishing in online spaces and beyond, nurturing souls across the globe. And finally, we'll address the importance of commitment—not as an obligation, but as a joyful response to God's steadfast love for us.

So, take a seat, open your heart, and let's journey together through the beauty of God's family—diverse, robust, and united by the living Word. Welcome home.

The Foundation of Fellowship

The concept of fellowship isn't just a mere aspect of the Christian life; it is the very bedrock upon which the church is built. From the intimate gatherings in the humble homes of the early believers to the modern-day congregations in soaring cathedrals and cozy chapels, the heart of fellowship has pulsed with a steadfast rhythm of shared faith.

In Acts 2:42, we read a powerful depiction of the early church: "They devoted themselves to the apostles' teaching and to fellowship, to the breaking of bread and to prayer." This scripture is not just a historical account; it is a template for our gatherings. Here, in the simplicity of their devotion, is a profound truth—the gathering of believers is a spiritual mortar that holds the bricks of the church together.

The foundation of fellowship is rooted in more than just communal tradition; it is woven into the very fabric of our spiritual DNA. 1 John 1:7 affirms this by saying, "But if we walk in the light, as he is in the light, we have fellowship with one another, and the blood of Jesus, His Son, purifies us from all sin." Walking in the light is walking in community—united, purified, and purposeful.

In a world that increasingly values individualism and self-sufficiency, the biblical call to community stands countercultural. It is a call to lay down the idol of independence to embrace interdependence—a sacred tapestry of lives intertwined by faith and love.

But what does this look like practically? It's more than just attending services or signing up for a church event. It's about engaging deeply, sharing lives, bearing burdens (Galatians 6:2), and exhorting one another (Hebrew 3:13). It's about laughter shared over a meal, tears shed in a time of prayer, and hands joined in service. It is, as Romans 12:5 declares, "so in Christ we, though many, form one body, and each member belongs to all the others."

The foundation of fellowship is thus both a divine gift and a holy responsibility. In community, we find strength, we are equipped, we are honed, and most importantly, we see the fullness of Christ's body in action. Here, within the fellowship of believers, we find a home, a place to grow, and a foretaste of the eternal community we are promised in Christ.

This foundation is not just historical; it is living, active, and essential. It is our heritage, our present joy, and our future hope. Let us then hold fast to this sacred gathering, for in it we find the very heartbeat of the church.

Digital Solitude to Fellowship

In the bustling city of solitude, where skyscrapers stretched like Babel's ambition and the cacophony of ambition drowned out the whispers of community, lived Kyle, a 30-year-old software developer. Her life was a series of code and coffee, keystrokes echoing in the silent voice of her apartment. Kyle's armor was her sharp mind; her sword, the laptop she wielded with deft precision. But the dragon she faced was not one of fire and scale, but of isolation and disconnection.

Kyle's friends were thumbnails in a chat window; her family, voices over a phone line. At night, the city's glow did little to warm the creeping chill of loneliness that settled over her. The thoughts that kept her up were not fears of failure at work, but of the quiet dread that perhaps life was more than projects and promotions, something deeply relational that she was missing out on.

Then came the moment of silence. It wasn't dramatic—no crescendo of music or flash of light—but the quiet of a Saturday morning when her internet blinked out. No emails, no messages, no artificial chatter. In that silence, Kyle found a flyer from a local community group that had been slipped under her door. Out of habit, she had set it aside, but now, in the digital quiet, she read it. It spoke of a gathering, a fellowship of individuals who sought to connect, to share, to belong.

On a whim, Kyle went. Walking into the room, the atmosphere shifted palpably. There was laughter, genuine and warm; there were handshakes, hugs, and introductions. She was welcomed not for her skillset but for her very self. The group was diverse—a mosaic of tales and backgrounds—but the common thread was a shared faith and a mutual commitment to support, encourage, and uplift one another.

The fellowship she encountered changed Kyle's trajectory. The void of loneliness began to fill with invitations to volunteer, to study, to eat and celebrate together. The specific detail of her favorite scarf, which she wore to every meeting, became a symbol of her new identity within this community. It was in this fellowship that Kyle realized the problem was never her career or capabilities; it was the absence of deep, human connection, the kind that could only be found in shared life.

Kyle's story resonates with many who feel adrift in the digital age, where interactions are as fleeting as a swipe on a screen. Her journey from isolation to community mirrors the longing in many hearts for a place to call home, a group to call family. It's a reminder that while technology and talent can build careers, only shared life can build a life worth living.

Identifying a Bible-believing Community

When seeking a spiritual home, the quest often begins with a fundamental question: What does a Bible-believing community look like? This isn't merely about a congregation that reads the Bible, but one that embodies its truths, making the Word alive through their actions and interactions.

In a world of shifting sands, a Bible-believing community stands as a beacon of steadfastness, its foundations deeply rooted in the enduring Word of God. Such communities are not just identified by the Bibles in their pews but by the scripture engraved on their hearts.

Marks of authenticity:

1. **Adherence to Scripture**. "All Scripture is God-breathed and is useful for teaching, rebuking correcting, and training in righteousness" (2 Timothy 3:16). A Bible-believing community holds Scripture as the ultimate authority, applying its wisdom as the litmus test for all teachings and traditions.

2. **Christ-Centered Living**. At the heart of their doctrine and practice is the pursuit of a Christ-like life, echoing the apostle Paul's words: "Follow my example, as I follow the example of Christ" (1 Corinthians 11:1).

3. **Love in Action**. Love is the undeniable signature of a believer, as Jesus stated, "By this everyone will know that you are my disciples if you love one another" (John 13:35). True communities actively live out this love, reaching out not only to each other but also to the marginalized and the lost.

4. **Communal Worship and Prayer**. They gather regularly, heeding the call of Hebrews 10:25, not giving up meeting together but encouraging one another.

5. **Discipleship and Growth**. A thriving community is marked by growth, not just in numbers but in the depth of spiritual understanding, as they "grow in the grace and knowledge of our Lord and Savior Jesus Christ" (2 Peter 3:18).

6. **Service and Mission**. Their faith is not idle, for they are the hands and feet of Jesus, engaging in service and missions, as mandated in Matthew 28:19–20, to go and make disciples of all nations.

The journey to find such a community may be daunting, but it is by seeking that one shall find; by knocking, the door will be opened (Matthew 7:7–8). It's about finding a collective of believers where the Bible isn't just a book that's read but is the very fabric that binds every aspect of communal life.

Upon finding such a community, engagement is key. Dive into the study groups, contribute to the outreach programs, and be part of the tapestry of fellowship. For as you knit yourself into the community, you allow the richness of God's Word to weave through your life, enriching not only your faith but also those around you.

In essence, identifying and joining a Bible-believing community is about more than finding a place to worship—it's about finding a family, a body of Christ, where together, believers can grow, serve, and live out the transformative power of the living Word.

The Quest for Communal Ground

Once upon a time, in the vibrant cityscape, there was a young man named Morgan. At 29, he was an earnest graphic designer, known for his sharp eye and the splash of red that was always present in his attire—a nod to his zest for life. But beneath the bright colors and easy smiles, Morgan wrestled with a gnawing emptiness. It was as if he was a knight, armor polished and sword at the ready, yet without a cause to fight for, no dragon to slay.

His dragon was not one of scales and fire but an invisible beast that fed on isolation and spiritual hunger. Nights were the toughest; the city's hum would fade, and the silence in his small apartment became a loud reminder of the community he longed for, the family of believers he had yet to find.

One dusky evening, as the orange hues bled into the city skyline, Morgan found himself walking past an old stone church, its stained glass windows a mosaic of stories. A gentle melody, a hymn of old, seeped through the walls, and for reasons he couldn't explain, he pushed the door open.

The moment he stepped in, he felt it—a shift in the atmosphere, a warmth that went beyond the physical. The congregation's voices rose in harmony, and the stained glass seemed to come alive with their song. He was an outsider, yet he felt an unspoken invitation to belong.

As the weeks went by, Morgan became a regular face in the pews. The community welcomed him, not just into their building, but into their lives. He discovered the product, so to speak, wasn't the majestic church or the well-versed pastor; it was the genuine love and fellowship that they offered. They were a community deeply rooted in scripture, living out the love commanded in John 13:35. Their actions were the hands and feet of Jesus, bringing the Bible to life beyond words on a page.

The impact was profound. Morgan found himself involved in their mission projects, adding his creative flair to their outreach programs. The void that once kept him up at night began to fill with shared prayers, shared meals, and shared lives.

But the true moment of change, the explosion in his tale, was during a small group meeting. As he shared his testimony, eyes wet with gratitude, he realized he had found his cause. The dragon of loneliness was defeated, not by the sword of eloquent words or grand gestures but by the simple, consistent acts of Christ-like love.

Now, when Morgan lays his head down at night, the silence is no longer an enemy. It's a canvas for reflection, a soft space to rest in the assurance of a newfound family. His story—marked by authentic emotion, a pivotal moment, and the vivid specifics of his red-themed wardrobe and the stained glass light—resonates with those searching for their own place in a Bible-believing community.

In the end, Morgan's life was changed, not by a product but by a people who lived their faith out loud. And just maybe, his story whispers to the heart of another knight-in-waiting, "Keep searching, keep knocking. Your fellowship of believers is out there, waiting to welcome you home."

The Role of Community in Spiritual Growth

In the tapestry of faith, community is not merely a fringe benefit; it is the thread that intertwines through the fabric of individual belief, strengthening and enriching the pattern of our spiritual lives. "For where two or three gather in my name, there am I with them," Jesus tells us in Matthew 18:20. This divine promise highlights the fundamental role of fellowship in the Christian walk.

Imagine, if you will, a lone ember plucked from a fire. Separated from its source, it glows with waning resilience, its heat diminishing until it is little more than a cold, grey ash. Such is the plight of the solitary believer, striving for spiritual growth in isolation. But place that ember back into the heart of the fire—amidst the company of its fellows—and watch as it bursts back into flame. This is the picture of spiritual growth within the community.

In Acts 2:42–47, the early church presents us with a blueprint of communal life, one where believers "devoted themselves to the apostles' teaching and to fellowship, to the breaking of bread and to prayer." Their lives were an intricate dance of learning, sharing, worshiping, and supporting one another—a dynamic environment where spiritual growth was as natural as the rising of the sun.

The writer of Hebrews exhorts us to "consider how we may spur one another on toward love and good deeds, not giving up meeting together . . . but encouraging one another" (Hebrews 10:24–25). Herein lies the secret ingredient of community: encouragement. It's the spiritual greenhouse where the fruits of faith can flourish, where prayers are lifted, burdens are shed, and joy is multiplied.

In a Bible-believing community, we find mirrors reflecting the grace of God in myriad ways. There, the Word of God is not just read, but lived out in relationships that mold and shape us. Proverbs 27:17 asserts, "As iron sharpens iron, so one person sharpens another." It's in the context of others that our character his honed, our patience tested, our compassion kindled, and our love deepened.

Community is where our personal narratives intersect with the grand, redemptive story God is telling. It's where we learn to live out the love commanded in 1 John 4:12, "No one has ever seen God; but if we love one another, God lives in us and his love is made complete in us." Here, love is not an abstract concept, but a concrete reality experienced through the hands and feet of those walking beside us on this journey of faith.

So let us embrace community, not as a mere accessory to our faith, but as the very crucible in which our spiritual growth is forged. For it is within the vibrant tapestry of fellowship that we truly find ourselves knit together in the body of Christ, growing up into the fullness of Him who is the head over every power and authority (Colossians 2:19).

Embers Rekindled

In the heart of a bustling city lived Terry, a 30-year-old digital artist known for his sharp wit and trademark red sneakers. He spent his days crafting visuals that spoke without words, yet when the screens went dark, a palpable silence filled his world. Beneath the layers of his cool demeanor was a battle with solitude that left him restless at night. The dragon he faced was not of scales and fire, but an invisible monster named Isolation that clawed at his spirit, leaving him feeling disconnected, not only from others but from the deeper meaning he yearned for in life.

Terry's church attendance had dwindled to an occasional Easter and Christmas visit. The Bible, a gift from his grandmother, gathered dust on his shelf. It wasn't that he lacked faith; rather, it was the lack of connections to that faith in his daily life that troubled him. What kept him up at night was the whisper of purpose that seemed just out of reach, a purpose he knew was tied to something greater than himself.

The moment everything changed was a regular Wednesday evening. Walking home from work, Terry's path took him past a small community church. Through the open windows, he heard voices mingling in a harmony so pure it seemed to reach straight into his chest and reawaken a long-forgotten song of his own. On a whim, he entered. The group was small, a circle of chairs filled with people of all ages and walks of life, their faces turned towards each other, their eyes alight with something Terry recognized as hope.

It was here, in this unassuming church hall, that Terry rediscovered the ember of his faith. He wasn't greeted with judgement or expectation, but with genuine smiles and open Bibles. They delved into scriptures, not as a scholarly study, but as a living conversation, each verse a thread weaving them closer. Terry found solace in the words of

Proverbs 27:17, "As iron sharpens iron, so one person sharpens another." In this community, he wasn't just another face; he was a valued voice.

Each detail of that room—the worn carpet, the flickering candlelight, the shared laughter over steaming cups of coffee—built a scene that felt like home. The Bible wasn't just a book here; it was the living water that quenched his parched roots, allowing him to grow. The stories of love, redemption, and strength he heard didn't just fill the room; they filled the emptiness he had carried.

The community became Terry's crucible for transformation. Not only did he rediscover his faith, but he also found his purpose woven into the lives of others. In helping serve food at the shelter, joining the prayer group, or simply listening to a friend's troubles after the meeting, Terry found that the grand story of the Bible was a story he was meant to live out loud. It was not the church that changed his life; it was the fellowship within it, the shared journey, the communal flame that turned his faith from a flickering possibility into a roaring blaze.

The value Terry discovered in this fellowship was immeasurable. It was not in simply going to church, not in the act of reading the Bible, but in being part of a community that lived out its message. As the apostle Paul wrote in 1 Corinthians 12:26, "If one part suffers, every part suffers with it; if one part is honored, every part rejoices with it." This wasn't just a verse; it was the reality of his new life.

This is the story for anyone who has felt the cold touch of isolation, for those who seek a place where faith is not a solitary act but a shared journey. It is a testament to the transformative power of a Bible-believing community, a story that resonates with the truth that we are truly stronger together.

———

Engaging with the Local Church

Engaging with a local church can be like finding a new family in your own backyard. It's a place where you can put down roots and watch them grow deeper, nurtured by the shared love and wisdom that flows from being in fellowship with others.

Hebrews 10:24–25 offers the perfect encouragement for this journey, "And let us consider how we may spur one another on toward love and good deeds, not giving up meeting together, as some are in the habit of doing, but encouraging one another—and all the more as you see the Day approaching."

But how do you go from being a Sunday spectator to a thriving branch of this living, spiritual tree? Here are some verdant verses and fruitful tips to help you plant yourself firmly within the local church:

1. **Bloom Where You are Planted**. Just like the mustard seed in Matthew 13:31–32 which grows into a tree where birds can perch, start small. Volunteer for a duty that fits your schedule, even if it's just once a month. Every act of service helps the church grow.

2. **Cultivate Relationships**. The early church in Acts was all about community. Acts 2:46–47 tells us, "Every day they continued to meet together in the temple courts. They broke bread in their homes and ate together with glad and sincere hearts, praising God and enjoying the favor of all the people." Join or start a small group to study the Bible, pray, and share life together.

3. **Harvest Your Talents**. In 1 Peter 4:10, it says, "Each of you should use whatever gift you have received to serve others, as faithful stewards of God's grace in its various forms," Are you

a musician, a cook, a carpenter? The church is a place where your skills can be a blessing to others.

4. **Seed New Ministries**. Is there something you're passionate about that the church isn't doing yet? Romans 12:6 encourages us, "We have different gifts, according to the grace given to each of us. "Perhaps your vision could lead to a new outreach or support group.""

5. **Water with the Word**. Don't just read the Bible; let it read you. Involve yourself in Bible studies and apply what you learn. Psalm 119:105 says, "Your word is a lamp for my feet, a light on my path." When you walk in His Word, you illuminate the way for others too.

6. **Prune Through Participation**. Just like pruning helps plants to flourish, your active participation helps both you and the church to grow. Get involved in the decision-making process, attend congregational meetings, and provide feedback.

7. **Propagate Prayer**. Prayer is the power source of the church. James 5:16 reminds us, "The prayer of a righteous person is powerful and effective." Commit to being part of the prayer life of the church, whether in corporate prayer meetings or in a prayer chain.

By engaging with your local church, you're not just filling a seat; you're fulfilling a role in the body of Christ. As 1 Corinthians 12:27 states, "Now you are the body of Christ, and each one of you is a part of it." Your presence, your prayers, and your participation are the threads in a beautiful tapestry that showcases the vibrant life of your church community. So, step in, reach out, and become an integral part of the tapestry that is your local church.

Rooted and Built Up

Meet Chris, a 38-year-old art director with a gentle demeanor, known for his quirky bow ties and a burgeoning collection of rare books. His passion for design is only matched by his love for contemplative, early-morning walks. But beneath his calm exterior, Chris wrestles with a dragon—a profound sense of isolation. Despite his successful career and online followers, he finds himself yearning for genuine connection and a place where he can share his faith and creativity.

The pews of the local church are familiar to Chris, yet they symbolize his silent battle. He attends service every Sunday, sits in the back row, and slips out as soon as the benediction is pronounced. He's surrounded by a community, yet feels invisible within it. The question that haunts him every night is simple yet profound: "How do I find my place among these people?"

The turning point arrives during a community picnic. Chris, initially standing on the periphery, is approached by Mia, the church's vibrant outreach coordinator, known for her infectious laugh and an uncanny ability to remember every member's birthday. She invites him to contribute a design for an upcoming charity event. In that moment, something shifts. Chris sees an opportunity, a bridge between his solitary existence and the community he longs to be part of.

Empowered by Mia's genuine interest and armed with his unique skill set, Chris steps forward. His design for the event isn't just noticed; it's celebrated. He feels a ripple of change as he's introduced to the congregation, not as a spectator, but as a contributing member whose talents bring beauty and connection to the church family.

As Chris becomes more involved, volunteering his skills and joining a small group, the details of his life weave into the fabric of the community. The once overwhelming dragon of isolation shrinks back as he forms meaningful relationships. Church members begin to wear the bow ties he designs, and his love for rare books leads to the start of a church library.

The church, once a product in Chris's life—static and unchanging—becomes the setting where his story unfolds. He discovers that it's not the rows of seats that define his church experience, but the shared laughter, the collaborative projects, the prayers, and the support he both gives and receives. The church becomes his home, the congregation his family, and his talents a tool to slay the dragon of loneliness.

In his transformation, Chris embodies the truth that church is more than a place to go; it's a place to belong. For others like him, the message is clear: there is a spot within the church where every talent, personality, and heart can find a home, transforming not only their own lives but the community around them.

Small Groups and Bible Studies

Picture this: a cozy living room filled with a mix of earnest faces—some fresh and eager, others etched with the wisdom of life's many seasons. It's Tuesday evening at the Quaid's, and the small group is gathering, as they do each week, a microcosm of the church at large, nestled on the corner of Maple and Fifth. It's here, in this intimate setting, that the beauty of Acts 2:46 unfolds: "they broke bread in their homes and ate together with glad and sincere hearts."

In these small groups and Bible studies, believers find a unique and nourishing environment that the Sunday service alone cannot cultivate. It's where James 5:16 comes to life, as members "confess your sins to each other and pray for each other so that you may be healed." These are sacred spaces where the mask of "I'm fine" can be laid down, where prayers ascend, and burdens are shared—where the unity commanded in Psalm 133:1, "How good and pleasant it is when God's people live together in unity!" is experienced in its fullest sense.

These small gatherings are the fertile soil where seeds of scripture are planted deep into the heart, watered by discussion, and warmed by friendship. As the group dives into the Word, they don't just skim the surface but delve into the depths of scripture, "rightly handling the word of truth" (2 Timothy 2:15), and like the Bereans, they examine the Scriptures daily to see if what they learn is true (Acts 17:11).

Here, in the safety of trusted company, difficult passages are wrestled with, doubts are voiced, and the Holy Spirit illuminates the Word, making it a lamp unto their feet and a light unto their path (Psalm 119:105). These gatherings fulfill the "one another" commands of scripture—encourage one another (1 Thessalonians 5:11), teach and admonish one another (Colossians 3:16), love one another (John 13:34) —in the most practical and life-giving ways.

The importance of these smaller gatherings cannot be overstated. They are the places where spiritual muscles are flexed and faith is stretched. They are sanctuaries of learning, where the milk of 1 Peter 2:2 is consumed by new believers and the meat of Hebrews 5:14 is chewed on by the mature. They are the settings of laughter and tears, where the joy of the Lord becomes their strength (Nehemiah 8:10) and where burdens are halved because they are shared.

For those who have yet to step into such fellowship, the invitation is as warm as the living room on Maple and Fifth. It's an open call to join a family within the family of God, to move from isolated reading to a collective journey through the pages of Scripture, and to discover, in the faces of fellow seekers, the transformative power of living the Bible out loud, together.

A Tale of Transformation

Meet Milania, a 33-year-old visual communicator, with a keen eye for beauty but a heart wrestling with the chaos of life. Her friends admire her creative spirit, but beneath her colorful handbags and cheerful demeanor, Milania grapples with a sense of isolation. Despite her active social media presence, her real-life connection to a faith community feels superficial, like a puzzle missing its centerpiece.

Lying awake at night, Milania's mind races with questions about purpose, belonging, and faith. The silence of her apartment amplifies the longing for a connection that goes beyond Sunday morning pleasantries. The vibrant faith she once pictured seems as dim as the flickering streetlight outside her window.

The shift happens one autumn evening when Milania hesitantly steps into a small group Bible study, invited by a colleague who sensed her searching heart. The warm glow from the living room window beckons, a contrast to the chill in the air. Crossing that threshold, she finds herself wrapped in the welcoming aroma of freshly baked bread and coffee.

As the group delves into a passage from Romans, the words leap from the page, sparking conversation that weaves the sacred into the ordinary. Laugher echoes, prayers ascend, and scripture is explored with a vulnerability that Milania never experienced before. Here, in this circle of newfound friends, the text becomes more than ink on a page—it becomes a dialogue, a shared journey, an anchor.

Milania discovers the product is not just the Bible study guide in her hands; it's the collective journey through scripture, the interwoven stories, the mutual encouragement, and the hands held in prayer. This community becomes her lifeline, turning her nightly wrestling into morning songs of hope. Her creativity flourishes with new inspiration, her work infused with deeper meaning.

Now, when Milania throws her colorful bag over her shoulder and steps out into the world, she carries with her the strength of a community. She has found the missing piece, not just the puzzle of her faith but for the grander design of her life. And as Milania's story unfolds, it whispers the promise of transformation to all who have yet to find their place in the living room of fellowship.

Service and Ministry

When we think of service and ministry, our minds often paint grandiose pictures of far-flung missions or large-scale community projects. But nestled within the heart of service is the essence of Jesus' teachings, where the act of giving become a mirror reflecting the Word of God in action.

Consider the early church, where believers were described as having "all things in common" and "selling their possessions and goods, they gave to anyone as he had need" (Acts 2:44–45 NIV). This wasn't merely a lofty ideal; it was the pulsating life of a community in love with God and His Word. Service was their heartbeat, their hands and feet moved by the compassion of Christ, who "came not to be served, but to serve" (Mark 10:45).

Engaging in service within a community transcends the simple act of healing others. It is a form of worship, a silent sermon preached through the labor of love. As we roll up our sleeves in the soup kitchens, organize books in a church library, or simply listen to a soul in need, we are walking in the footsteps of the greatest Servant.

Take the story of Dorcas in Acts 9:36–42, a woman "always doing good and helping the poor." Her service was her testimony, so powerful that her life became interwoven with the fabric of her community. When we serve, we are living epistles, known and read by all, manifesting the fruits of the Spirit "against such things there is no law" (Galatians 5:22–23).

Moreover, service is a profound teacher. James 1:22 exhorts us to "be doers of the word, and not hearers only," reminding us that the true understanding of Scripture is not merely cognitive but is demonstrated through action. When we serve, the verses of the Bible leap off the page and take on flesh and blood in the context of human needs and the simple, sacred acts of kindness.

In the tapestry of a Christ-centered community, each act of service is a thread interlaced with the golden strand of biblical truth. Whether it's the youth group painting a fence for the elderly or the choir visiting a nursing home, service knits the community closer, weaving together a living testament to the transformative power of the Word.

So let us embrace service as both a privilege and a discipline, for it is in giving that we receive, in ministering to others that we are ministered to, and in living out the scriptures that we truly come to understand the heart of God. As we serve, let's remember that "whatever you did for one of the least of these brother and sisters of mine, you did for me" (Matthew 25:40), and in this way, our ministry becomes a dynamic encounter with the Divine, a life-affirming dance with the Word made manifest.

Emma's Awakening

Dana, a 38-year-old accountant, stands in the stillness of her meticulously organized home office, her gaze lost in the spreadsheets that no longer seem to fill the growing void within her. A picture of efficiency, Dana's life is a well-oiled machine, but the gears of her heart have slowly ground to a halt. Each tick of the clock whispers of something missing, a deeper purpose that numbers and balance sheets can't calculate. The dragon that Dana faces isn't breathing fire; it's the silent echo of isolation in a crowded room, the disconnect between her routine life and the meaningful existence she yearns for.

Lying awake at night, the ceiling fan casts a repetitive shadow dance, mirroring the monotony of her solitary existence. Her mind replays the Sunday sermons she has heard, verses about love, community, and service. "Faith without works is dead," the preacher declared, a statement that haunts her in these quiet hours. It's not the fear of danger that keeps Dana up; it's the fear of never truly living.

Then comes the moment that changes everything. At a routine church coffee hour, Dana overhears a conversation about a local service project, a community garden that needs volunteers. Something stirs within her. It's a small flicker or curiosity, an ember of longing for connection that refuses to be snuffed out. Dana, who has never had dirt under her fingernails, who has calculated risk but never taken one, finds herself volunteering.

On that Saturday morning, as Dana steps into the garden, the scent of earth and growing things is a comfort to her restless spirit. Her hands, accustomed to the click of a mouse, now delve into the soil, pulling weeds, planting seeds—small acts, perhaps, but each one a declaration. In the garden, Dana meets Michael, a retiree with gentle eyes and a knowing smile, who quotes, "We are God's handiwork, created in Christ Jesus to do good works" (Ephesians 2:10). She learns about the families the garden will feed and feels a connection to the community she never knew was possible.

As the weeks pass, the garden grows, and so does Dana. The joy of service, the warmth of fellowship, the simple pleasure of a shared meal after a day's work becomes the new rhythm of her life. She starts a Bible study, not in a church hall, but right there among the tomato plants and sunflowers, where parables of sowing and reaping suddenly resonate with vibrant truth.

One day, standing before the lush greenery, a transformation clear on her face, Dana's story unfolds to a new volunteer. She speaks of her journey, the emptiness that once seemed insurmountable, and the community that became her lifeline. Her voice, vibrant with authentic emotion, doesn't just tell her story; it extends an invitation.

And in this story, every listener finds a piece of themselves. They recognize the ache, the silent longing for meaning beyond the material. They see in Dana not just an accountant or a gardener, but a fellow traveler on life's journey. Her courage becomes a beacon, guiding them to a truth we all seek: that the real value in our lives is not what we accumulate, but what we give away, and in our giving, we find ourselves.

As Dana ties back her hair with a bandana that has become her trademark, her laughter melding with the chorus of kindred spirits around her, she embodies the heart of service. And they think to themselves, "They get me." Dana's awakening is not just her own, but an echo of the awakening they too long for.

━━━━━━

Discipleship and Mentorship

In the tapestry of faith, each thread is vital, and among them, discipleship and mentorship are the vibrant strands that give strength and color to the picture of communal belief. Imagine, if you will, a bustling community where lives intersect not just in service, but in the sacred dance of learning and guiding, questioning and understanding, stumbling and steadying.

Enter Stephanie, a young teacher whose vibrant energy and quick smile make her a favorite among her students. But beneath her sun-bright exterior lies a tumult of questions about her purpose and how her faith should shape her life. Stephanie is no stranger to Sunday sermons or Bible studies; she's grown up knowing the scriptures, can recite verses with ease. Yet, she thirsts for something more, a way to weave the ancient words into the fabric of her everyday life.

"Teach me your way, O Lord," she whispers from Psalm 27:11, a prayer that escapes her lips in the quiet corners of her classroom. It's the same plea that echoes in the hearts of many who walk beside her in faith but have yet to grasp its depth.

The answer comes, not with a thunderous voice from the heavens, but with the gentle presence of Mrs. Thompson, a silver-haired widow with a lifetime of wisdom etched in the lines of her face. She is a pillar in the community, known for her unwavering faith and the gentle way she opens her home and heart to those seeking direction. Stephanie is drawn to her, sensing the depth of understanding that comes only from a life deeply rooted in the love and knowledge of God.

They begin to meet, initially under the guise of going through a devotional, but quickly their time blossoms into something richer—a discipleship that intertwines their lives. Mrs. Thompson doesn't come armed with all the answers; instead, she comes with an open Bible and an even more open heart. Together, they explore the Beatitudes, delve into the complexities of Paul's letters, and stand in awe at the poetic justice in the book of Esther, finding in each story a mirror for their own journey.

"As iron sharpens iron," Mrs. Thompson quotes Proverbs 27:17, "so one person sharpens another." And so it is with them. Stephanie learns to see her faith not as a static possession but as a living, breathing entity that grows and evolves with each passing day. It becomes clear that discipleship is not a mere transfer of knowledge; it is the sharing of life, with all its trials and triumphs.

The influence of their relationship ripples outward, inspiring others in the community to seek and foster these bonds of mentorship. Young men and women look to the seasoned, the brave, and the tenderhearted among them to guide them in the ways of faith and life. They find solace in James 5:16, "Therefore confess your sins to each other and pray for each other so that you may be healed." The call to openness and vulnerability becomes the building blocks of relationships that stand firm in the face of life's gales.

In discipleship and mentorship, the community finds not just growth, but transformation—a renaissance of spirit that draws them closer to the divine and to each other. And in this shared pilgrimage, they discover the essence of what it means to live a life not just marked by faith, but defined by it.

Navigating Doctrinal Differences

Navigating doctrinal differences within a faith community is akin to sailing through a sea dotted with islands of distinct landscapes—each one a representation of the diverse interpretations and beliefs that individuals hold dear. The journey isn't about avoiding these islands but learning the art of exploration and dialogue, understanding that the waters around us are held together by the same faith, even as the expressions of their faith vary from shore to shore.

Consider Levi, a devout man of faith with a keen intellect and a compassionate heart. He finds himself often in the midst of spirited discussions, whether he's at the local coffee shop or within the stained-glass embrace of his church. The apostle Paul's counsel in Ephesians 4:2–3 is a beacon for him: "Be completely humble and gentle; be patient, bearing with one another in love. Make every effort to keep the unity of the Spirit through the bond of peace."

Levi has sat through many Sunday school classes where the interpretation of a particular scripture became the day's hot debate. He knows the sting in the air when opinions clash like cymbals, when

Romans 14:1 "accept the one whose faith is weak, without quarreling over disputable matters" seems like a distant whisper.

Yet, Levi also knows the beauty of diversity within the body of Christ. He has witnessed how, when handled with grace, these differences can lead to deeper understanding and respect. He approaches each conversation with a James 1:19 mindset: "Everyone should be quick to listen, slow to speak and slow to become angry." This scripture is not just a verse to him; it's the very air he breathes when engaging in dialogue.

Levi also reminds his peers of the call in 1 Peter 3:15–16, to "give an answer to everyone who asks you to give the reason for the hope that you have. But do this with gentleness and respect, keeping a clear conscience." It's a call to know what you believe and why, but so share those beliefs without losing the love that is meant to define them.

In the microcosm of his community, Levi becomes a facilitator of sorts, helping others to navigate the sometimes treacherous waters of doctrinal differences. He encourages open forums where questions are not just allowed but welcomed, where scripture is dissected and discussed not to win arguments, but to seek truth collectively. He helps his community remember that "God is not a God of disorder but of peace" as in 1 Corinthians 14:33.

The result of such navigations is not uniformity—that would be too simple and frankly, unreflective of the rich tapestry of belief. Instead, the result is unity in diversity, a picture of a community that values each individual's quest for truth, while holding fast to the core of their faith—the life, death, and resurrection of Jesus Christ, the cornerstone.

For Levi and his community, navigating doctrinal differences becomes not a burden but an adventure, an opportunity to grow in love, understanding, and faith. They realize that while they may not always agree on every doctrinal point, they are united in the essentials and committed to journeying together in respect and brotherly love, as they seek to live out the truth in love (Ephesians 4:15).

Community Beyond Walls

In a world increasingly, connected by the invisible threads of digital communication and social media, the concept of a faith community has transcended the traditional boundaries of stained glass and wooden pews. Now, it encompasses the global village, where a prayer request can leap across continents in a heartbeat, and words of encouragement can be whispered through screens from a thousand miles away. This is the essence of Community Beyond Walls.

Let's take the journey of Bethany, a young fashion designer whose faith is as integral to her identity as her artistic flair. She lives in a bustling city, where skyscrapers seem to graze the heavens themselves. Bethany finds solace in Matthew 18:20, where Jesus said, "For where two or three gather in my name, there am I with them." For her, this gathering isn't limited to the physical realm. It happens every day through her laptop and smartphone, where she's part of an online Bible study group that meets weekly, sharing insights and supporting one another through pixels and prayer.

Beyond the digital space, Bethany also participates in her church's outreach program, which has partnered with a local shelter. She recalls the words in Hebrews 13:16, "Do not forget to do good and to share with others, for with such sacrifices God is pleased." Her community takes this message to heart, organizing food drives and offering services that go beyond the Sunday sermon, into the realm of the tangible, the immediate, the desperately needed.

Bethany's story is intertwined with that of Miguel, who lives half a world away. He has found his calling in mission work, often citing Mark

16:15, "Go into all the world and preach the gospel to all creation." His mission isn't confined to the spoken word but is lived through actions—building homes, providing medical aid, and teaching children. The impact is profound, the ripples of every kind deed felt in the very fabric of the communities he touches.

This modern tapestry of fellowship is rich with threads of connectivity. Whether it's through an encouraging email, a video chat prayer meeting, a Bible app devotional shared among friends, or a hashtag that rallies support for a cause, the essence of Christian community has found a new expression. It's John 13:34 in action—"A new command I give you: Love one another as I have loved you, so you must love one another"—but this time, the love transcends physical barriers and manifests in the digital realm.

Bethany and Miguel, though they have never met, are part of a global body of believers practicing Galatians 6:2, "Carry each other's burdens, and in this way, you will fulfill the law of Christ." They are modern-day disciples, using every tool at their disposal to extend the reach of their community, to touch lives, to offer hope, and to weave a network of faith that isn't confined by walls but is as boundless as the grace upon which it is built.

"Community Beyond Walls" isn't just a phrase; it's a reality—a call to all believers to embrace the potential of this era to share love and faith unceasingly. It is the understanding that while the church may have a postcode, the Church—capital C—is a global, borderless family, living out the love of Christ, every day, everywhere, in every way possible.

Commitment to Community

In a world rife with transience, where connections can be as fleeting as a swipe on a screen, the biblical call to plant deep roots in a community stands as a counter-cultural beacon. This is a call to steadfastness, to the kind of commitment that weathers seasons and storms, a theme resoundingly echoed in Psalm 92:13–14: "Planted in the house of the Lord, they will flourish in the courts of our God. They will still bear fruit in old age, they will stay fresh and green."

Picture Kevin, a middle-aged school teacher with a gentle demeanor, who believes that his life is a testament to Proverbs 27:17, "As iron sharpens iron, so one person sharpens another." Kevin has been a part of his local church for over two decades, and through the years, he has seen faces come and go, ministries blossom and fade, but through it all, his commitment has remained as steadfast as Daniel in the lions' den.

His story is not just about the pew he warms each Sunday but the lives he has touched and the countless ways he's grown. In his years with the community, Kevin has served in various capacities, from youth mentor to choir member, each role reinforcing Colossians 3:23: "Whenever you do, work at it with all your heart, as working for the Lord, not for human masters." His commitment is not just to an institution but to a family of faith, a commitment that has seen him through his own trials and triumphs.

The mutual benefits are clear, as the community has come to rely on Kevin's wisdom and gentle spirit. In return, Kevin has been supported through his own challenges, including the loss of a spouse, embodying Romans 12:15: "Rejoice with those who rejoice; mourn with those who mourn." His journey has shown that commitment is a two-way street, offering a sanctuary for him and allowing him to be a pillar for others.

And what of the younger generation, the millennials and Gen Z'ers who are often characterized by their quest for novel experiences? They, too, are finding that in the embrace of a committed community, there's a treasure trove of wisdom and a network of support that can't be downloaded or streamed. For them, Ecclesiastes 4:12 resonates with newfound relevance: "Though one may be overpowered, two can defend themselves. A cord of three strands is not quickly broken."

To commit is to decide that growth happens not in isolation, but in the fertile soil of fellowship. It is to be believed, as the early church did, in the power of Acts 2:42: "They devoted themselves to the apostles' teaching and to fellowship, to the breaking of bread and to prayer." It's a holistic investment—in each other's lives, in shared missions, and in the spiritual disciplines that form the bedrock of a thriving faith community.

Commitment to Community is more than a section title; it's a narrative that invites each believer to become a character in a story much larger than themselves—a story where every act of service, every shared meal, and every moment of vulnerability is a thread in a beautiful tapestry, displaying the richness of life done together, under the watchful eye of a faithful God.

PART TWO

Ambassador for God

CHAPTER SIX

Seeds of Generosity: The Joy of Tithing and Supporting Ministry

"Honor the Lord with your wealth, and with the firstfruits of all your produce; then your barns will be filled with plenty, and your vats will be bursting with wine."

—PROVERBS 3:9–10 ESV

Welcome to a journey of open hands and open hearts! In this invigorating chapter, we will wade into the verdant fields of giving, where each act of generosity plants a seed that promises a harvest far beyond our wildest dreams. This chapter isn't just a mere exploration of an age-old practice; it is a voyage into the very heart of what it means to live abundantly.

As we delve into the roots of tithing and the fruits it bears in our lives and the lives of others, we will discover that this is more than a duty; it's a privilege. The tithe is not simply a portion of our earnings returned to God, but a testament to our trust and faith in His provision. As we unravel the tapestry of biblical principles and heartwarming narratives, we will see that these seeds of generosity grow into strong, sheltering trees under whose shade many find refuge.

Together, we will examine how the simple act of giving transforms lives, empowers ministries, and reflects the generous nature of God Himself. We'll share stories that glow with the joy of those who give and those who receive, affirming that generosity is a cycle as endless as it is beautiful.

So, prepare to have your heart stirred and your spirit lifted. Whether you're a seasoned giver or taking your first step into the realm of sacrificial generosity, this chapter is an invitation to experience the deep joy and indescribable peace that comes from holding your treasures with an open palm. In the pages that follow, we shall learn that when we sow bountifully, we shall also reap bountifully. For in the kingdom of God, generosity is the seed, and joy is the harvest.

The Biblical Basis of Tithing

Imagine if you will, a treasure chest—not one buried on a distant island, but one residing within the very pages of Scripture. This treasure chest is brimming with golden truths about a practice as ancient as faith itself: tithing. The act of tithing isn't a mere transaction; it's a transformation, a divine investment strategy that predates even the oldest stock markets.

The Biblical Basis of Tithing takes us on an archaeological dig through the Scriptures, unearthing the rich soil of its foundations in both the Old and New Testaments. In the fragrant gardens of Genesis, we witness Abraham, the father of faith, giving a tenth to Melchizedek in a pure act of worship (Genesis 14:19–20). It's our first glimpse of tithing, set under a sky of promise, showing us that giving is not about law but love and recognition of God's sovereignty.

As we journey through the desert sands of Leviticus, we learn that tithing was instituted as a covenantal provision for the Levites and a perpetual statute (Leviticus 27:30–32). It wasn't a burdensome tax but a communal celebration, ensuring that no one, not even the stranger or the widow, was left in need (Deuteronomy 14:28–29).

Fast-forward to the cobblestone streets of the New Testament, and we find Jesus affirming the practice of tithing, not as a rigid rule, but as an expression of justice, mercy, and faithfulness (Matthew 23:23). The early church, ablaze with the Holy Spirit's power, gave generously, breaking bread with glad and sincere hearts, fully embodying the principle that "it is more blessed to give than to receive" (Acts 20:35).

This sacred practice of tithing is not a relic of the past, but a living principle that weaves generosity into the very fabric of our daily walk with God. As we unfold this section, we are not just flipping through ancient texts, but reviving a way of life that can transform our relationship with money, with others, and with God Himself.

So, let us approach this exploration with an eager spirit, ready to plant the seeds of generosity. For as we sow into the kingdom of heaven, we store up treasures not of this world but of a world to come, as enduring as the stars in the sky and as countless as the grains of sand on the seashore (Matthew 6:20).

John's Journey to Generous Living

In the heart of a bustling city, John, a 30-year-old accountant, sits in his well-ordered office, the gleaming skyline outside his window a testament to his professional success. He wears a silver cross handed down from his grandmother, a subtle yet constant reminder of his faith that seems at odds with his material success. John's sword, his financial acumen, has slain many a dragon in the corporate world, but there's one dragon he hasn't faced: the disconnect between his wealth and his spirituality.

At night, the glow of his smartphone replaces the skyline, and with it, the pangs of an authentic emotion: a gnawing sense of unfulfillment, a yearning for a purpose beyond ledgers and balance sheets. He reads articles about generosity, about living a life of giving, but the practical application seems as distant as the stars above his high-rise apartment.

Then, a moment. During a Sunday service, a verse projected on the wall strikes a chord within him: "For where your treasure is, there your heart will be also" (Matthew 6:21). The silence that follows is palpable, heavy with divine implications. It's an epiphany, a celestial explosion in his routine life. John realizes that his true value doesn't come from what he earns, but from what he gives.

Specific details of his ensuing journey are emblematic of a transformative path. He starts small, setting aside a portion of his income for the church. The first online transfer to his local ministry feels mechanical, but as weeks turn into months, each click is a step closer to his heart's true treasure.

The story of John is not an uncommon one. There are many like him, who don the armor of success yet face the dragon of emptiness. But as John discovers the joy of giving, his story echoes the deeper calling within us all: to invest not just in markets, but in souls, not just in business, but in eternity.

His newfound commitment to tithing reshapes his identity. Where once there were spreadsheets filled with numbers, now there are names and faces of those impacted by his generosity. He starts volunteering, mentoring young professionals in managing finances ethically, and using wealth for a greater good.

John's journey from affluence to altruism serves as a vivid narrative that resonates with many of us. It's not just a story about tithing—it's about discovering the real wealth in generosity, a value that changes not only John's life but also has the power to change our own. Through his eyes, we see a reflection of our potential, a call to action that reaches beyond the confines of personal gain into the expansive realm of divine purpose.

The Heart Behind the Gift

In the tapestry of faith, the threads of generosity weave a pattern far more complex and beautiful than the simple act of giving. It's not just about what is given, or how much is offered up, but the spirit that animates the giving hand. Let's delve into the heart behind the gift, where intention and love speak louder than the clink of coins or the rustle of banknotes.

The apostle Paul knew this well when he penned the immortal words in 2 Corinthians 9:7 (NIV): "Each of you should give what you have decided in your heart to give, not reluctantly or under compulsion, for God loves a cheerful giver." Herein lies a profound truth: the joy in giving is not merely for the receiver but for the giver as well. It is a holy exchange, where the currency is love and the dividends are eternal.

Consider the widow's mite, as narrated in Luke 21:1–4. Amidst the grand donations of the wealthy, her two small coins seemed to whisper in their fall. Yet, in Jesus' eyes, her offering thundered above the rest, for she gave out of her poverty, everything she had to live on. Her gift was measured not in value, but in sacrifice and trust. Here was a heart stripped of pretense, laid bare in devotion and reliance on God.

In the practice of giving, one might ask: "What does it mean to give wholeheartedly?" It's to echo the words of David in 1 Chronicles 29:14 (NIV), where he acknowledges that everything comes from God, and we give only what we have received from His hand. Giving, then, becomes an act of worship, a recognition of the Source of all blessings, and a testament of our stewardship of His grace.

But let's not forget, the gift without love is like a sun without warmth, a light without radiance. 1 Corinthians 13:3 (NIV) warns us, "If I give all I possess to the poor and give over my body to hardship that I may boast, but do not have love, I gain nothing." Thus, the true measure of any gift lies in the love that envelopes it, that earnest desire to bless and uplift another, reflecting the very heart of God.

To give with the right heart is to understand that our treasures are not for us to hoard but for us to steward with generosity. For as we open our hands, we become channels of God's love and provision to those around us, and in doing so, we discover the indescribable joy of true giving.

In giving, we are drawn into a deeper fellowship with the Giver of all good things. It's in this sacred space where our hearts align with His, that our gifts become more than mere transactions; they become transformative, both for the giver and the receiver. This is the beauty, the challenge, and the blessing of the heart behind the gift.

The Gift of Giving

In the bustling heart of a modern metropolis, where the neon glow outshines the stars, there lived a man named Ethan. He was an unassuming financial adviser, mid-thirties, with a penchant for vintage ties and a soft spot for stray cats. His life was a rhythm of numbers and spreadsheets, and like clockwork, he performed his role with the precision of a well-oiled machine. Yet, when the city fell asleep and the glow of his laptop faded, Ethan lay awake, wrestling with a nagging emptiness that no ledger could balance.

It wasn't a dragon of scale and fire that Ethan faced, but a dragon of the heart—a yearning for purpose that transcended the meticulous order of his daily life. The sword he needed wasn't one of steel, but one of spirit: the act of giving, not as a transaction, but as an expression of love and faith.

One chilly December evening, as the city was draped in festive lights and the air was tinged with the promise of snow, Ethan's moment of epiphany arrived. It was not marked by fanfare or revelation; it was as simple as a hand-stretched out in generosity. It happened at the community center, amidst the laughter of children and the smell of warm soup, where Ethan volunteered to help serve dinner to those with nowhere else to go.

In the tender eyes of a little girl clutching a tattered doll, Ethan saw something that changed everything—a reflection of his own search for meaning. As he handed her a bowl of soup, their hands briefly touched, and a current of understanding passed between them. In her gratitude, he found his answer. The act of giving filled a void no amount of wealth could.

Ethan's story began to take on new hues. He started organizing fundraisers, offering financial advice to the less fortunate, and mentoring young people in his field. With each act of service, the dragon's shadow waned, and Ethan's heart grew fuller.

This was not a story of monumental shifts or dramatic upheavals, but one that spoke volumes in the quiet truth it revealed: the act of giving, infused with genuine love and selflessness, holds the power to slay the deepest of internal dragons.

Those who heard Ethan's story recognized the echo of their own silent battles. They saw in his journey a mirror to their own and whispered to themselves, "They get me." For they too knew the restless dragon, and now they saw a sword—a way to transform their own trials into triumphs, not with grand gestures, but with the simple, profound power of the heart behind the gift.

The Impact of Tithing on the Giver

Tithing isn't merely an act of obedience; it's a testament to our trust and faith in God's provision. When we tithe, we're actively choosing to prioritize God's kingdom over our own needs and desires. But the beauty of this spiritual discipline goes beyond mere duty—it's about transformation.

In the act of giving, we find our hearts being reshaped. As we detach from the material grip of the world, we align closer with the heart of God, who gave the most generous gift of all—His Son. Paul reminds us in 2 Corinthians 9:7, "Each one must give as he has decided in his heart, not reluctantly or under compulsion, for God loves a cheerful giver." It's a reminder that the state of our hearts in giving matters immensely to God.

Tithing can also be a liberating experience. In a culture that constantly screams "more," choosing to tithe can help set our spirits free from the chains of consumerism. Jesus spoke of this freedom when he said, "It is more blessed to give than to receive" (Acts 20:35). Through giving, we experience the joy and blessing that comes not from holding on, but from letting go.

Moreover, the act of tithing isn't just a momentary transaction; it's a continuous journey of trust. As we give, we're reminded of God's faithfulness when he declares in Malachi 3:10, "Bring the full tithe into the storehouse, that there may be food in My house. And thereby put Me to the test, says the Lord of hosts, if I will not open the windows of heaven for you and pour down for you a blessing until there is no more need."

The spiritual discipline becomes a channel of blessings not only for the receiver but the giver as well. The joy, freedom, and peace that come from giving are spiritual blessings that enrich the giver in ways far beyond the monetary value of the tithe. It is in this sacrificial act of giving that we discover a deeper connection to God and His mission on earth. We realize that our tithes and offerings are more than just financial support for the church, they are an expression of our worship and a reflection of our hearts towards God.

The Alchemy of Giving

In the quiet town of Heartsville, there lived a man named Matthew. Not just any man, but a modern-day knight in the community's eyes, known for his gallant efforts in local charity and community service. Yet, beneath his routine of generosity, Matthew, a 42-year-old auditor, harbored a silent dragon: a lingering doubt about the impact of his actions and the genuineness of his own charity. Each night, as he counted blessings instead of sheep, he wrestled with the thoughts: "Is my tithing making a difference, or is it just a drop in the ocean?"

Matthew's giving wasn't just a mechanical transaction; it was a profound part of who he was. His tithes were not the sword but the expression of his faith—the faith that sometimes wavered in the dead of night. With every check he wrote, with every coin he dropped into the offering plate, he sought not praise nor acknowledgment, but a sign that his sacrifice was more than a financial gesture—that it was truly aligned with God's will.

Then came the moment, as distinct and pivotal as the turning of a page. During one Sunday service, as Matthew listened to the testimonies, a young woman spoke of how a scholarship, funded by the church's tithes, had allowed her to be the first in her family to attend college. In her voice, he heard echoes of his deepest prayers, and in her story, a reflection of his own values. It was as if the coins clinking into the offering plate were the sounds of chains breaking, the sound of that dragon—his doubt—releasing its grip on his heart.

Specific details of Matthew's life wove into the fabric of this moment. The watch he wore, a family heirloom, now ticked not just as a measure of time, but of impact. The well-worn Bible he carried, its margins filled with notes, was no longer a book of what could be, but what was—living proof of God's promises in action.

Heartsville had seen Matthew as a knight, and indeed he was. Not because he slew dragons with a glittering sword, but because he combated his inner doubts with steadfast faith and generosity. And as he realized the true value of his giving, the townspeople whispered not of his wealth, but of the wealth he had brought to others' lives, saying to themselves, "He gets us. He truly does."

In this tale of giving, the sword— Matthew's tithes—was not the hero. Matthew was, because he had slain the greatest dragon of all: the fear that his giving was in vain. And as the scripture says, "Do not neglect to do good and to share what you have, for such sacrifices are pleasing to God" (Hebrews 13:16). For Matthew, and for Heartsville, this was the moment when everything changed.

———

Tithing as Worship

When we think of worship, our minds might conjure images of raised hands, uplifted voices, and serene faces aglow with reverence in the sanctuary's hushed air. But there's a facet of worship often left in the shadows, unaccompanied by the organ's swell or the choir's harmony—tithing.

Tithing as worship turns the act of giving into a symphony of gratitude, a tangible chorus that reverberates with the sacred. It's not about the currency that slips through our fingers; it's about the declaration those resources make when we release them back to God. It's saying, "All that I have, and all that I am, is Yours, O Lord."

Consider the psalmist's cry: "I will not offer burnt offerings to the Lord my God that cost me nothing" (2 Samuel 24:24). Tithing becomes an intimate part of our worship when it costs us something, when it's a sacrifice made in joy, not in grudging compliance. It is here, in the hushed act of giving, that many find a deeper sense of nearness to the heart of God.

In the tapestry of worship, every thread counts, from the resounding "Amens" to the silent prayers, from the songs of praise to the gifts of tithing. Each is a color, a texture, an integral part of the whole. When we tithe, we weave our faith into this tapestry, not merely as observers but as contributors to the kingdom's unfolding story.

"Each one must give as he has decided in his heart, not reluctantly or under compulsion, for God loves a cheerful giver" (2 Corinthians 9:7). So, when we place our tithes in the offering plate, we're not just giving a portion of our earnings but participating in an ancient form of worship, echoing the faithfulness of generations before us.

Tithing, therefore, is a sacred echo of the heart's adoration, a worship that walks hand in hand with the songs we sing and the prayers we whisper. It's a beautiful surrender, a moment where our material blessings bow before the Giver of all good things. And in this act of worship, we remember that every gift, large or small, when given in a worshipful spirit, is a fragrant offering to the One who has given us everything.

Grace's Offering

In a quaint town where church steeples outnumbered stoplights, there lived a woman named Grace. At 52-years-old, with laugh lines etched around her eyes and silver strands weaving through her hair, she carried a quiet dignity. Grace owned a small flower shop, a place that smelled perpetually of spring, even in the bleakest winters. She wore a simple golden locket, a gift from her grandmother, which rested close to her heart—just like her faith.

The problem wasn't with the flowers or her business; it was deeper, a dragon that clawed at her heart. Grace lay awake at night, the silence of her room filled with the heavy weight of solitude and a gnawing sense that something was missing. Her hands, skilled in arranging bouquets, felt empty once clasped in prayer. Her faith was strong, yet it seemed like she was just going through the motions, lacking the joy and connection she once felt.

One Sunday, as sunlight streamed through the stained glass, casting kaleidoscopic patterns on the pews, Grace's pastor spoke of tithing not just as duty, but as an act of worship, an expression of faith. A moment—the explosion—came quietly when the offering plate reached her. For the first time, Grace saw not an obligation but an invitation to join in a deeper communion with God. The clink of her coin was more than a ritual; it was a surrender, a participation in something greater.

As she gave, her heart felt the shift. It wasn't about the amount; it was the willingness to place a piece of herself into the plate, trusting

God with not just her finances but her whole life. The flowers she arranged carried new significance, each petal a testament to the Provider of all.

Over time, the act of tithing wove into her routine, a thread in the fabric of her daily worship. Grace found that the more she gave, the less she felt the dragon's presence. In its place grew a garden of joy, peace, and connection with her community and her Creator. Her locket, once just a beautiful trinket, became a symbol of the legacy of faith and generosity she hoped to leave behind.

And so, Grace's story echoes the sentiment that when we give, it's not the sword we wield to slay our dragons, but the hand that holds it, guided by a heart of worship. For others peering into the stained glass windows of Grace's life, it was clear: her generous spirit was not just a testament to her character but to the transformative power of giving as an act of worship.

Stewardship and Accountability

In the tapestry of faith, each thread of action, each color of intention, and every pattern of habit weave together to form the picture of our walk with God. Stewardship and accountability represent not just singular strands but the very warp and weft of this divine image. They are the testimony of a life lived not in the pursuit of self, but in the humble acknowledgement that all we have is a trust from God, meant to be used for His glory and the good of others.

The principle of stewardship is poignantly captured in 1 Peter 4:10 (NIV), which urges believers, "Each of you should use whatever gift you have received to serve others, as faithful stewards of God's grace in its various forms." This verse doesn't merely suggest but implores us to see our resources, talents, and time as gifts not owned, but entrusted to us by a gracious Giver. As we delve into understanding stewardship, we're reminded that accountability is its inseparable partner. The call to wise management is also a call to transparent and responsible reporting. For as Jesus says in Luke 16:10 (NIV), "Whoever can be trusted with very little can also be trusted with much, and whoever is dishonest with very little will also be dishonest with much." It is this biblical principle that solidifies the truth that our integrity in the small things reflects our faithfulness in the larger narrative of God's kingdom.

What does this look like in a tangible sense? It's the careful budgeting of a church's funds, ensuring they're channeled into programs that feed the hungry, clothe the naked, and spread the gospel. It's the volunteer carefully logging hours, knowing that their service is an offering to God. It's the missionary reporting back to supporters, showcasing the impact of every penny given in faith. In these acts of stewardship and accountability, we echo the servant in Matthew 25 who, having been given talents by his master, diligently works and multiplies them, earning the master's commendation: "Well done, good and faithful servant!"

When we manage God's resources with wisdom and integrity, we are not just performing a duty; we are engaging in an act of worship. We are acknowledging His sovereignty, expressing our gratitude for His provision, and demonstrating our understanding that what we have is not ours to keep, but ours to share. As we embody these principles, we reflect the character of Christ, and through our stewardship and accountability, we provide a glimpse of the divine order in a world yearning for such clarity and purpose.

In conclusion, stewardship and accountability are not merely administrative duties; they are spiritual disciplines. They shape the character of the individual and the community, embedding the values of the Kingdom into every decision and action. As we steward our gifts with wisdom and submit ourselves to accountability, we honor God, advance His mission, and inspire those around us to do likewise.

―――――

A Tale of Trust and Triumph

Once upon a time in a bustling town nestled in the heart of a fruitful valley, there lived a man named Jared. At 42-years-old, Jared's hair was peppered with grey, a testament to years of toil under the sun as the town's most respected orchard keeper. He wore a wide-brimmed hat that had seen better days, which shadowed sharp, kind eyes that sparkled with a mix of wisdom and mirth.

Jared's problem wasn't unique, but it weighed heavily on him. He had been entrusted with a significant inheritance from a distant relative, an overwhelming sum that was meant not just for him but as a benefaction to the entire community. The weight of this responsibility was his dragon—how could he manage this gift to benefit not just his immediate circle but the generations to come?

Nights were long for Jared, with sleep playing a game of hide and seek as he wrestled with his task. The enormity of the stewardship kept him up, the pressure to not only preserve but multiply the inheritance was a constant companion.

Then came the moment that shifted everything. During one of the town's regular gatherings at the local church, a visiting pastor spoke of the parable of the talents, emphasizing not the quantity of the resources but the quality of the stewardship. The words struck Jared like a bell's chime at dawn, "Well done, good and faithful servant!"

In that instant, Jared realized the true value of his inheritance. It wasn't the currency or the land; it was trust. He decided then and there that he would invest in people, in the community, and in their future. He established a fund to educate the town's children, supported the local artisans to innovate, and invested in sustainable practices for the orchards.

The transformation was palpable. The once anxious man with furrowed brows became a beacon of calm confidence. His decision sparked a revival in the valley, with neighbors taking cues to invest their resources wisely for the collective good.

Specific details of Jared's story resonated with the town's folk; the wide-brimmed hat became a symbol of wise stewardship, his measured gait an assurance of thoughtful progress, and his late-night lantern glow a beacon of dedication and care. They whispered among themselves, nodding in collective agreement, "Jared gets it, and because he does, so do we."

Jared's tale is our reminder—stewardship is more than a duty; it's an honor, a form of worship, and a catalyst for change, both within and beyond the confines of our lives.

The Power of Collective Giving

As we step into the warmth and fellowship of our spiritual family, there's a palpable buzz that hums through the air—it's the sound of hearts united, of hands joined together for a purpose larger than themselves. It's the sound of collective giving.

In the scripture, we are reminded, "Each one must give as he has decided in his heart, not reluctantly or under compulsion, for God loves a cheerful giver" (2 Corinthians 9:7). This is the essence of giving within the church community, a cheerful, voluntary act that binds us together.

Imagine a patchwork quilt, each square lovingly sewn together, each thread an individual act of giving. Alone, each square is just a piece of fabric, each thread a mere filament. But together, they create warmth, comfort, and a story that's far richer and more complex than any single piece could tell.

The power of collective giving operates much like that quilt. When each member of the community brings their offerings, no matter how small, these acts of obedience and love weave together to form a strong and vibrant tapestry of support. It's the five loaves and two fish that, when blessed and shared, feed the multitude (John 6:9–11). It's the widow's mite, which in its humble way, surpasses the grandeur of wealthier donations (Mark 12:42–44).

Take for example, a church's mission to build a well in a community where clean water is a dream beyond reach. One person's tithe might fund the shovel that breaks the ground, another's the bricks that line the well, another's the pump that draws the water. Together, they bring forth a fountain of life, quenching physical thirst and nourishing souls with the living water of Christ's love.

Or consider the local food bank supported by the church's collective offerings. Each can of beans, each loaf of bread, each dollar donated, becomes a part of a greater movement of compassion and care. As Proverbs 22:9 tells us, "Whoever has a bountiful eye will be blessed, for he shares his bread with the poor." It's the shared vision, the bountiful eye of the congregation, that multiplies the blessings manifold.

This is the power of collective giving—it's more than just a sum of parts. It's the stirring of the Holy Spirit within a group of people who choose to live out the truth that "it is more blessed to give than to receive" (Acts 20:35). When we give together, we are not depleting our resources; we are investing them into God's kingdom, where the returns are measured in transformed lives and eternal impacts.

So, as we come together, let our tithes and offerings be like seeds sown in unity, growing into a garden of grace that extends far beyond the walls of our church, into the very heart of our community and out into the wider world. This is the power of collective giving—it's the embodiment of love in action, a testament to faith made visible, and a joyful echo of heaven's generosity.

Harvest of Generosity

In the heart of the city stood a towering, age-old church with stained glass that caught the sun's rays, casting kaleidoscopic patterns upon the faces of those who entered its hallowed halls. Among them was Jonathan, a middle-aged stockbroker known for his meticulous nature and the ever-present, slightly creased brow that spoke of constant, silent calculations running through his mind. Jonathan was a fixture in the community, his life a routine of numbers, ledgers, and a quietly harbored yearning for something more meaningful than the sum of his spreadsheets.

His emotion, a simmering blend of restlessness and a deep-seated desire to connect, to truly matter, often kept him up at night. His profession demanded precision, control, but his heart was searching for a place to invest that would yield a return no balance sheet could measure.

The moment that changed everything came quietly, subtly—like the soft turning of a page to a new chapter. During a regular Sunday service, as the pastor spoke passionately about a collective mission to build a community center for the underprivileged youth, Jonathan felt a stirring within him. It was a call to be a part of something greater, a shared vision that could only be realized through the unity and generosity of the congregation.

His hands, always so steady when they held a pen, trembled slightly as he wrote his commitment on the pledge card. It wasn't just a figure;

it was a symbol of his decision to become an active participant in a story bigger than his own.

In the weeks that followed, Jonathan watched and contributed as his fellow church members brought forth their unique offerings. There was JoAnn, the baker, whose pies seemed to taste of hope and whose laughter filled the fundraising events. Michael, the retired carpenter, whose skilled hands turned old wood into new treasures for the auction. Each contribution was a thread in the rich tapestry of their collective mission.

As the foundation of the community center was laid, something within Jonathan settled. It wasn't just the satisfaction of seeing a project take shape; it was the knowledge that his contribution had helped forge a sanctuary where young dreams could take flight.

Specific details of the change were etched in the laughter of children where silence once reigned, in the vibrant murals that now adorned walls that had been gray and lifeless, and in the community garden that flourished where waste once lay. The center became a beacon of the collective power of giving, and Jonathan's role in it a testament to the transformation that occurs when one invests in the currency of community and faith.

The community center stood as a testament to the change—a once abstract idea made concrete, its value measured not in currency, but in the smiles of children, the gratitude of parents, and the pride of a community that had come together to wield not swords, but shovels and paintbrushes, mixing bowls and auction gavels, to slay the dragon of despair and build a fortress of hope.

As Jonathan walked through the center, amidst the cacophony of joy and the harmonious murmur of life, he realized that the true power of his giving lay not in the financial figure he had contributed but in the collective spirit it had helped to nurture. This was his legacy—not a line in a ledger, but a line in a story that would be told for generations. The center was not just a building; it was a promise fulfilled, a dream realized, a community transformed.

Beyond the Tithe:
Offering Time and Talents

This section uncovers the oft-overlooked treasures we all possess—time and unique skills. This section is a heartfelt exploration of how the giving of ourselves in service echoes the scriptural call to live generously in all aspects of life.

In the fabric of the church, every thread counts—each volunteer hour and each skill offered weaves a tapestry of community and faith. 1 Peter 4:10 urges us, "As each has received a gift, use it to serve one another, as good stewards of God's varied grace." Here lies the essence of this section: to recognize that the gifts of time and talent are as critical to the vitality of the ministry as monetary offerings.

Envision the scene: a bustling church kitchen where laughter is the background music to clanging pots and the aroma of home-cooked meals. Martha, a retired teacher, stirs the soup, her years of nurturing children in the classroom now channeled into feeding the hungry in her local parish. Her time is a vessel of comfort, her teaching talents now serving to tutor young ones after school in the very same hall.

Just as the early church in Acts 2:44–45 shared everything they had, the modern ministry thrives when individuals like Martha live out this narrative. "All the believers were together and had everything in common. They sold property and possessions to give to anyone who had need." Today, the "selling" can be seen as the "giving up" of precious time, the "possessions" as the diverse talents each believer holds.

The story extends to the youth group, where Jeffrey, a local business owner, offers his acumen to guide teenagers in leadership and life skills. His input is not quantified by a paycheck but by the growth and confidence blossoming in the young people he mentors. "For we are his workmanship, created in Christ Jesus for good works, which God prepared beforehand, that we should walk in them," Paul writes in Ephesians 2:10. Jeffrey walks this path with purpose, his professional prowess now a cornerstone in the church's youth development program.

Beyond the Tithe doesn't just ask for more—it calls for a redefinition of "offering." It's a prompt to look within and find what we can share that, unlike money, doesn't diminish when given but multiplies. In the quiet moments of reflection, it beckons to remember Matthew 25:40, "And the King will answer and say to them, 'Truly I say to you, as you did it to one of the least of these my brothers, you did it to Me.'"

This section is not a directive but an invitation to journey down the often less-trodden path of giving, which starts with the self and extends into the boundless, where every hour volunteered and every skill shared becomes part of the ministry's heartbeat. The call is clear, echoing through the chambers of the church and the stillness of prayer: Beyond the Tithe is a call to action, a commitment to serve, and a living, breathing expression of faith.

The Silent Gift

Meet Amber, a 52-year-old web designer, known for her vibrant blazers that match her equally colorful personality. By day she crafts visual stories, but in the quiet of the night, a nagging thought tugs at her: "Is this all there is?" Amber longs for purpose beyond pixels and proofs.

The relentless pursuit of deadlines leaves her with a sense of emptiness. She craves connection, meaning, and a legacy that transcends her art. Her creativity yearns for a cause, something that would stir her heart as much as it challenges her skills.

It's during a Sunday service when the pastor speaks of serving with one's gifts that Amber's world tilts. The words "Let your light shine before others, that they may see your good deeds and glorify your Father in heaven" (Matthew 5:16) resonates deeply. There's a palpable silence around her as the idea takes root.

Amber begins volunteering her talents, designing flyers for charity events, and infusing life into the church's outreach programs with her visual flair. It starts small—a logo here, a banner there—but each stroke of her brush feels like a prayer, each completed project, a sermon.

The change in Amber's life is seismic. She's not just a designer; she's a storyteller for a cause. Her once lonely nights are now filled with community projects, her skills touching lives, her work a vivid tapestry of faith in action. The church's messages now reach further, the congregation grows, and Amber's once-whispered question finds its answer in every piece she creates.

Amber's story spreads, inspiring others to look within and offer their own gifts. Time and talents become the new currency of worship, with Amber as the unexpected evangelist. She's no longer chasing deadlines; she's fulfilling prophecies of goodwill and shared purpose.

In The Silent Gift, readers find a mirror to their own longing for significance. They see that the church is not built on tithes alone but on the backs of the faithful willing to serve. The value story of Amber becomes their story, one where every individual can slay their dragons of doubt with the sword of service, where every skill can be an anthem of worship, and every moment spent in giving becomes a lifetime of value realized.

CHAPTER SEVEN

The Giver's Path: Cultivating a Philanthropic Heart

"It is more blessed to give than to receive."

—ACTS 20:35 NIV

Welcome to The Giver's Path, a journey where the act of giving unfolds as a transformative experience, not just for the receiver but for the giver as well. In this chapter, we will embark on a chronological exploration of generosity, from this humble awakening in the human spirit to the fulfillment of living a life dedicated to giving.

As you turn these pages, you will discover that generosity is not a momentary act but a continuous path that evolves with every step you take. We begin by stirring the embers of generosity within, guiding you through the initial spark that ignites the desire to make a difference. It's about more than just opening your wallet; it's about opening your heart to the possibilities that generosity holds.

We will delve into understanding the depths of need that stretch across our neighborhoods and ripple out into the world, needs that call out for a compassionate response. You will learn to look within, to ask yourself what moves you, what calls you to act, and how you can turn your unique motivations into a powerful force for good.

As we progress, we'll lay out the tools you need to craft your philanthropic objectives. Whether you aspire to support local food banks, educate underprivileged children, or protect endangered species, your goals will shape the impact you leave on this world.

This chapter is not just about the theoretical aspects of giving; it's about practicality—how to channel your resources and intentions into strategies that amplify your impact. You'll learn how to give smartly, maximizing the reach of every cent and every second you dedicate to your cause.

Together, we'll confront the barriers that might discourage you and find ways to overcome them, for the path of giving, like all worthy journeys, is strewn with challenges. But it is through these challenges that your commitment grows stronger and your heart grows fuller.

And finally, we will celebrate the transformation that comes from a life rich with generosity. This is about who you become when you integrate giving into the very fabric of your being—when philanthropy is not just something you do, but a reflection of who you are.

Prepare to embark on a path that is as rewarding as it is enlightening, a path that shapes not just the lives around you but your own. Welcome to The Giver's Path.

Awakening to Generosity

Imagine standing at the edge of a tranquil lake at dawn. The world is quiet, the air is fresh, and the still waters are undisturbed. You're about to cast a pebble into that vast, serene expanse. You know, intuitively, that the ripples from this small act will travel far and wide, touching distant shores. This is the dawn of generosity in the heart of a believer, the very first ripple in the water. "Whoever is kind to the poor lends to the Lord, and he will reward them for what they have done" (Proverbs 19:17 NIV).

Generosity begins not with the act of giving itself, but with an awakening, a stirring in the soul that recognizes the profound interconnectedness of our lives. It's an understanding that what we possess—our resources, time, and talents—are not just for us to keep but to steward on behalf of others. This awakening often comes quietly, perhaps during a sermon that stirs the spirit or in a moment of silent reflection when the scriptures speak to us in new and profound ways. "Give, and it will be given to you. A good measure, pressed down, shaken together and running over, will be poured into your lap. For with the measure you use, it will be measured to you" (Luke 6:38 NIV).

When we first realize the power of giving, it's like seeing the world in a different light. We start to perceive need where we hadn't before, and with this perception comes an innate desire to respond. The early Christian church modeled this beautifully, sharing all they had, ensuring none among them was in need.

As we step out in faith to give, we align ourselves with the character of God, who gave His Son freely for us. Our giving is a reflection of His ultimate generosity. It's an act of worship, an acknowledgment that everything we have is a gift from above. "For God so loved the world that he gave His one and only Son, that whoever believes in Him shall not perish but have eternal life" (John 3:16 NIV).

The journey of a philanthropic heart often begins with a single, simple act—a moment of compassion, a decision to share. It's a step taken in faith, sometimes before the path ahead is clear. Yet, as the proverb assures us, it's a step that resonates with God's promise of provision and presence.

In this awakening to generosity, we find our hearts expanding. We give not out of duty, but from a place of joy. And as we do, we join in the eternal truth that it is more blessed to give than to receive, becoming ourselves a living testimony to the love we have received.

Let this awakening in your heart be the first ripple of many, cascading into a life rich with generosity, compassion, and love.

Ripples of the Heart:
The Journey of a Modern-Day Good Samaritan

Once upon a recent time, in the heart of a bustling city, lived Daniel, a 35-year-old software engineer. Known in his office for his keen eye for detail and his midnight-blue tie that never seemed to lose its knot, Daniel's world was one of codes and screens. He worked diligently, solving problems with a precision that made him a linchpin in his tech firm.

But when the screens dimmed and the city slept, Daniel wrestled with a recurring thought that kept him up at night—the haunting feeling of disconnection. For all his expertise in connecting systems, he felt a chasm between his well-ordered life and the chaotic world around him. The plight of those struggling in his own community seemed like a dragon he was powerless to slay.

One evening, walking home, Daniel's path was halted by the sight of a homeless man, shivering beneath a thin blanket. This wasn't the first time Daniel had passed by the needy, but in this moment, something shifted. The usual background hum of the city fell silent, and the man's gaze met his, a silent plea that struck a chord in Daniel's insulated heart.

Compelled by a surge of compassion he couldn't ignore, Daniel offered his midnight-blue tie to the man, along with his coat, and sat beside him. They talked, and for the first time, Daniel truly listened. The homeless man, Samuel, spoke not of need but of lost chances and a desire to reconnect with a world that had moved on without him.

This encounter sparked a transformation in Daniel. The tie, once a symbol of his professional success, became a token of a deeper calling. His talents, he realized, were tools, but it was he who must wield them to make a real difference. He began by creating a community app that connected volunteers with those in need, like Samuel.

The ripple effects were immediate and profound. People volunteered, resources were shared, and lives were changed—including Daniel's. The app was a success, but the true value lay in the community it built and the lives it touched.

As Daniel's story spread, others saw themselves in his journey. They too had ties, literal or figurative, that could be offered in service. They too could bridge the gap between wealth and want, between isolation and community. Daniel's sleepless nights gave way to a purpose-driven life, full of authentic connections and the joy that comes from serving others.

In sharing his story, a simple detail like the midnight-blue tie becomes a powerful symbol for the audience. They realize that the power to slay the dragons of disconnection and need isn't in the tools we possess, but in the heart that chooses to act, a heart like Daniel's, awakened to the true essence of generosity.

Understanding the Need

In the tapestry of our global village, every thread tells a story, and each is colored by different shades of need. As we step out of our doorways and into the world, our eyes open to a myriad of these needs—some as blatant as the hunger in a child's eyes, others as silent as the loneliness in an elderly widow's sigh.

Understanding the need is like learning a new language, the language of empathy and compassion that speaks across all barriers. The Bible whispers this language in passages like Proverbs 31:8–9, "Speak up for those who cannot speak for themselves, for the rights of all who are destitute. Speak up and judge fairly; defend the rights of the poor and needy."

This is not a call to simply observe, but to act—to be the hands and feet of a love that transcends. For if one part of our body suffers, does not every part suffer with it? If we have food to eat, clothes to wear, and a roof over our heads, we are called to recognize that there are those who do not, and in this recognition, find our shared humanity.

Consider the widow who must choose between medicine and her meal, the veteran who battles unseen scars, or the child whose potential is shadowed by the instability of a tumultuous home. The needs are as varied as the faces behind them, each yearning not just for help, but for understanding and dignity.

Jesus' parable of the Good Samaritan in Luke 10:33–34 reminds us, "But a Samaritan, as he journeyed, came to where the man was; and when he saw him, he had compassion. He went to him and bound up his wounds . . ." Here is a portrait of understanding the need—it starts with seeing, moves to compassion, and acts to heal.

Our communities are gardens that can flourish only when every flower is tended to. In understanding the need, we begin to water these flowers with acts of kindness, words of support, and the unspoken understanding that we are, indeed, our brother's and sister's keeper.

Let us then embrace the call of Galatians 6:2, "Bear one another's burdens, and so fulfill the law of Christ." For in the end, understanding the need is more than an act of charity; it's a fulfillment of the divine mandate to love our neighbors as ourselves.

Echoes in the Valley

In the shadowed valleys of the kingdom of Eldoria, where whispers of hope seemed to have faded long ago, there lived a knight whose armor had lost its gleam. Sir Caden, a warrior of 35 winters, had faced many a dragon in his lifetime. With a scar over his left eye, a remnant of battles past, he symbolized strength and bravery. Yet, in the silent hours of the night, it wasn't the fear of dragons that kept him awake. It was the sound of his people's despair, a constant reminder of the suffering he hadn't conquered.

Sir Caden's sword, named Verity, was known across the land, not for its ornate handle or its shimmering blade, but for the hope it embodied. The true dragon wasn't the beast that breathed fire, but the plague of poverty and sickness that ravaged his homeland.

One crystalline morning, the piercing cry of a peasant child sliced through the market's din, a sound that halted Sir Caden in his tracks. In the boy's eyes, he saw not just hunger, but a plea for a savior, someone to slay the true dragon they faced. It was the moment everything changed for Sir Caden.

He realized that Verity wasn't just a tool for battle; it was a symbol that could rally the wealthy lords and ladies of Eldoria to share their grain, their coin, and their medicine. This sword could cut through the heart of apathy that had held his kingdom in thrall.

Taking off his helmet, revealing his weathered but determined face, Sir Caden stood in the market square, lifting Verity high. He spoke not of dragons and glory, but of children and elders, of families and futures. He spoke of a new battle, one not against mythical beasts but against the dragon of need, of hunger, of despair.

As he shared his vision, a hush fell over the crowd. The lords and ladies, the merchants and farmers, they all saw in Sir Caden's plea a truth that resonated within them. It was as if they all, for the first time, heard the silent cries and saw the invisible tears of their brethren.

From that day on, Verity became more than a sword; it became a beacon of change. And as Sir Caden rode from village to village, the valleys began to echo with a new sound—the sound of rebuilding, of healing, of hope.

Every clink of coin into charity, every bundle of food shared, every potion brewed for the sick, began to forge a legacy far greater than any dragon slain. For in the end, it was not the sword but the knight's heart, the collective spirit of the people, that slayed the dragon of despair, breathing life back into the kingdom of Eldoria.

This tale of Sir Caden and his sword Verity serves as a parable for our own world. It tells us that the mightiest weapon against the trials we face is not forged of steel, but of collective will and compassion. And in its story, we see our reflection, a call to become knights in our own right, lifting our swords not just in battle, but in a pledge to defend and uplift those who need us most.

Self-Assessment and Motivation

Embarking on a journey of generosity is akin to planting a garden in your soul, where the seeds of giving can sprout into a bountiful harvest that nourishes not only those who receive but the giver as well. But before one sets out to till the ground, it's essential to pause and peer inward, to understand the soil of one's heart and the intention behind every seed sown.

The Scripture nudges us to such reflection in 2 Corinthians 9:7, "Each one must give as he has decided in his heart, not reluctantly or under compulsion, for God loves a cheerful giver." This verse isn't merely an instruction; it's an invitation to dialog with one's heart, to ask oneself, "Why do I give? What is the source of my generosity?"

In this meditative space, let's consider David, a man after God's own heart, who exclaimed in Psalm 51:17, "The sacrifices of God are a broken spirit; a broken and contrite heart, O God, you will not despise." David understood that the condition of his heart was paramount in his relationship with God and that his actions, including his giving, must stem from a place of humility and authenticity.

So, take a moment to contemplate your motives. Are you rooted in a desire for recognition, a sense of duty, or perhaps in the pure joy that comes from blessing others? Consider the parable of the widow's mite (Mark 12:41–44), where Jesus commends the widow for her sacrificial giving out of poverty, contrasting it with those who gave out of their wealth for show. It is the heart behind the gift that lends it immeasurable value.

As you ponder your personal reasons for giving, also think about what you hope to achieve through your philanthropy. The Proverbs tell us that "A generous person will prosper; whoever refreshes others will be refreshed" (Proverbs 11:25). This is not a call for transactional giving, but rather a reminder that generosity is a cycle where the giver, too, is nourished.

Reflect on the goals of your giving. Is it to provide shelter, to feed the hungry, to support the propagation of faith, or to lend a hand to the downtrodden? Let your motivations be as diverse and personal as the talents you've been given. For in understanding the "why" behind your gifts, you become more intentional in your giving, ensuring that each act of kindness is a fragrant offering to the Lord, pleasing and acceptable in His sight (Philippians 4:18).

In this self-assessment and the blossoming motivation that follows, you are invited to craft a narrative of generosity that resonates with your deepest values, inspired by the love and wisdom that flows from the Divine. Let your philanthropic journey be a testament to the transformative power of a heart aligned with purpose and graced by the spirit of giving.

The Heart Behind the Gift

Meet Margaret, a 42-year-old architect, known in her circles for her sharp mind and her even sharper pencil. She sketches grand buildings by day and by night, she's often found with her family around the dinner table, her hands clasped in prayer. Margaret wears a simple silver locket, a family heirloom, symbolizing the legacy of love and generosity passed down through generations.

Despite her success, Margaret wrestles with restlessness. Lying awake at night, she is haunted by a feeling of yearning, an ache to do more with the blessings she's received. Her heart is stirred by the needs she sees around her, and the desire to make a lasting impact weighs heavily on her spirit. She wonders, "Is my life's work meaningful beyond the structures I design?"

The turning point comes one crisp Sunday morning as she sits in the quiet solitude of her study, the early light casting blueprints in shadow. Her eyes fall upon the silver locket, its surface cool and comforting beneath her fingers. In this silence, she feels a profound connection to her grandmother, a woman of modest means but immeasurable generosity. Margaret recalls the stories of how her grandmother's open heart and hands blessed many, leaving an indelible mark on her community with simple, heartfelt acts of kindness. It is in this poignant moment that Margaret realizes that the legacy she yearns to build isn't made of stone and glass, but of love and giving.

A framed photo of her grandmother sits on Margaret's desk, a constant reminder of the strength found in gentle kindness. Her grandmother's favorite Bible verse, "Give, and it will be given to you. A good measure, pressed down, shaken together and running over, will be poured into your lap. For with the measure you use, it will be measured to you" (Luke 6:38), echoes through her mind. Margaret understands now that her true calling isn't to fill landscapes with her creations but to fill hearts with hope through her actions.

From that day forward, Margaret's blueprint for life includes the foundations of generosity. She volunteers her time at local shelters, designing spaces that are not just shelters but homes. She uses her talents to create community gardens, places where beauty and sustenance bloom. And in every beam she draws, every brick she lays, she pours the love and kindness of her grandmother's legacy.

Her nights are no longer restless but filled with peace, knowing that each act of giving constructs a legacy far greater than any edifice she could imagine. Margaret's story is not about the wealth she can accumulate but the wealth she can share—a testament to the transformative power of a heart motivated by pure generosity.

Setting Philanthropic Goals

In this section, we embark on a journey not unlike that of a master builder who, before laying a stone, envisions the cathedral in its full glory. The art of giving, too, requires such vision—a clear picture of the impact one wishes to make.

Consider the words of Proverbs 29:18, "Where there is no vision, the people perish." To give without aim is to walk without direction. Setting philanthropic goals is about aligning your heart's desires with heaven's purpose. It's about drawing the blueprints for change and prosperity, not only in your community but also in your own spirit.

This section of our chapter begins with a fundamental question: What moves you? Is it the gentle eyes of the orphan seeking companionship, or the humble hands of the widow in need of support? Perhaps it's the untapped potential of a community thirsty for knowledge and growth.

Once the cornerstone of passion is laid, we move to structure our aspirations with the wisdom of Matthew 6:21: "For where your treasure is, there your heart will be also." Defining your treasure—be it time, talent, or resources—determines where you will invest your heart's effort.

With your treasure identified, we then set forth the principle of measurability. As Luke 14:28 prompts us to consider, "For which of you, desiring to build a tower, does not first sit down and count the cost, to see if he has enough to complete it?" Your goals should be as tangible as the parable's tower, with milestones to mark progress and the cost counted to ensure their attainability.

In practical terms, this could look like setting a goal to fund the construction of a new community center, or to sponsor the education of children in a developing country. Perhaps it's a goal to dedicate a certain number of hours each month to volunteering, or to master a skill that could benefit others.

As you delineate these objectives, interweave them with the rhythm of Galatians 6:9: "And let us not grow weary of doing good, for in due season we will reap, if we do not give up." The path of a philanthropist is a marathon, not a sprint, and your goals are the markers that sustain and guide you towards the finish line.

By setting philanthropic goals, you transform the abstract into the concrete, shaping your vision of generosity into a living, breathing edifice of hope and help. It is a step of faith, one that begins with a vision and is fulfilled through steadfast purpose and action.

Blueprints of the Heart

In the heart of the bustling city stood Elmer, a 35-year-old project manager with a knack for problem-solving and a wardrobe that always included his well-worn, lucky red tie. By day, he orchestrated the chaos of construction sites, and by night, he lay awake, gripped by the echoing thoughts of "Is this all there is?" The problem wasn't his job; it was the dragon of purposelessness breathing its existential fire into his routine life.

Elmer's sword, the skills that he honed over a decade, felt unused in the battles that mattered. He sought more than just the steel of success; he craved the warmth of significance.

Then came the moment at his niece's school play, amidst the proud parents and beaming children, a silence settled in his heart—a stark, defining silence that unfurled a realization within him. As he watched the young actors on stage, illuminated by more than just the stage lights, Elmer recognized the power of a community united by a cause, the beauty of a shared goal.

Motivated by the desire to give back, Elmer began to leverage his expertise for philanthropic ends. He found himself on the board of a nonprofit dedicated to creating community spaces in underprivileged areas. Here, he was not just a manager; he was a craftsman of hope.

With every meeting, every plan laid out, every volunteer day coordinated, Elmer's specific talent for organization became his contribution to a larger narrative. Each project was a chapter in his value story, transforming empty lots into playgrounds, dilapidated buildings into community centers. The red tie became synonymous not with corporate boardrooms but with hands-on, heartfelt contributions to society.

In the shared joy of ribbon-cutting ceremonies and the gratitude in the eyes of community members, Elmer found the missing piece he had been searching for. The sleepless nights faded, replaced by a restful anticipation for the next day's opportunities to make a difference.

His story resonates with those who understand that significance comes not from what you have, but from what you give. In Elmer's journey, we see the embodiment of the sentiment that the sword alone doesn't slay the dragon; it is the will and heart of the knight that prevails.

Elmer's tale isn't just his own. It whispers to each of us who yearn to wield our abilities for a cause greater than ourselves, inviting us to write our own value stories, where the measure of our lives is not just in the success we achieve but the significance we create.

Strategies for Effective Giving

In the mosaic of life, every piece plays a part in the grand design. This section beckons us to approach our contributions with the wisdom of a master craftsman. It's about aligning the work of our hands with the intentions of our hearts, ensuring that each act of giving is not just a fleeting gesture but a cornerstone of change.

Proverbs 21:5 stands as a guiding beacon here, "The plans of the diligent lead surely to abundance, but everyone who is hasty comes only to poverty." This wisdom calls for a thoughtful approach to philanthropy, urging us to consider not just the act of giving, but the ripples it creates.

Imagine a farmer who sows his seeds with purpose, each one planted at the right depth, in the right soil, and at the right time. He knows that the wind or birds might carry some away, but he also knows that the ones planted with intention will take root and flourish. In the same way, strategic giving is about planting our resources where they will grow and multiply. It's about understanding the terrain—the needs of our community and the missions of organizations—and matching them with our personal convictions and capabilities.

2 Corinthians 9:7 echoes this sentiment, "Each one must give as he has decided in his heart, not reluctantly or under compulsion, for God loves a cheerful giver." The verse doesn't just call for generosity; it emphasizes the joy and sincerity behind it. This is the essence of strategic giving—it's thoughtful, it's heartfelt, and it's rooted in the genuine desire to make a difference.

As we navigate through the myriad opportunities to give, let us be diligent in our research, like the Bereans in Acts 17:11, who were of noble character and examined the Scriptures every day to see if what they heard was true. So too must we examine the causes we hear about, ensuring our contributions are well-placed.

In this strategic giving, we might find ourselves like the workers of Nehemiah in Nehemiah 4:6, who rebuilt the walls of Jerusalem with one hand working and the other holding a weapon. They were ready to protect their vision and their work, just as we must be ready to defend and sustain our philanthropic goals with wisdom and discernment.

Finally, let us embrace the words of Matthew 6:21, "For where your treasure is, there your heart will be also." In the context of effective giving, our treasure is not just our financial resources but also our time, attention, and action. Where we choose to place these treasures not only reflects the state of our hearts but also shapes the impact of our legacy.

So let's give like master builders, constructing a legacy that stands firm on the foundation of God's love and wisdom, ensuring our giving is not just effective, but eternally significant.

Turning Pages, Transforming Lives

In the quaint town of Cresthaven, Carrie, a warm-hearted 52-year-old records manager with an infectious smile and an affinity for colorful headbands, found herself grappling with a profound unease. The hushed whispers of her conscience kept her up at night, stirring within her a restless desire to do more for her community. The dragon she faced was not one of fire and scales, but of unmet needs and untapped potential within the worn walls of the town's aging community center.

One chilly October morning, the rustle of autumn leaves mirrored the turmoil in Carrie's heart as she watched children from low-income families walk by her library window, their dreams as brittle as the dried foliage underfoot. Her heart ached with the authenticity of someone who yearned to give, not from the excess, but from the essence of who she was. The problem was clear: the children needed a sanctuary, a place where dreams were nurtured, not neglected.

The moment of change arrive with the crisp subtlety of the fall air. It happened during the town's harvest festival, as Carrie sat at a rickety booth, selling used books to raise funds for the library. Amid the laughter and the clinking of coins, a simple conversation with a grateful parent illuminated the path ahead. The community center needed help, and Carrie realized she could be the architect of that transformation.

With a resolute spirit, she embarked on a mission to revive the center, not with sweeping donations, but with strategic giving. Carrie leveraged her position in the community, her network of ardent readers and kind-hearted volunteers, to begin a grassroots campaign. Each step she took was laden with the gravity of intention, from meticulously choosing local businesses to supply materials, to enlisting the aid of every willing hand to rejuvenate the derelict structure.

As the community center blossomed with new life—its walls painted with murals of Cresthaven's history, its shelves stocked with books, and its rooms echoing with the laughter of children—Carrie saw the embodiment of Matthew 6:21, "For where your treasure is, there your heart will be also." Her treasure lay not in the bricks and mortar but in the heartbeats and hopes of every child who crossed the threshold.

The transformation of the community center was a testament to Carrie's belief that strategic giving goes beyond the mere act of donation; it's an investment in human potential. Her journey was a mosaic of moments and emotions, each piece a story of community, perseverance, and love. And as the residents of Cresthaven would affirm, the true value of Carrie's giving was etched not in the ledgers of philanthropy but in the vibrant life a community reborn.

Overcoming Challenges

In the journey of giving, even the most generous hearts encounter roadblocks. Whether it's the scarcity of resources, the weight of emotional weariness, or the shadow of skepticism, these challenges can dim the light of altruism. Yet, it's through overcoming such trials that our resolve to contribute meaningfully to the world is refined and strengthened.

Consider the widow of Zarephath, who, with only a handful of flour and a little oil, extended hospitality to Elijah. In times of limited resources, we're called to trust and to give not from our abundance, but from our faith that He who calls us to be generous will also provide the means. "And my God will meet all your needs according to the riches of His glory in Christ Jesus" (Philippians 4:19).

To the givers wearied by empathy, remember the compassion of Christ, who, amidst His own sorrows, healed and comforted those in pain. Emotional fatigue is real, but it's also a reminder of our shared humanity and the comfort we can provide to each other. "Come to me, all who labor and are heavy laden, and I will give you rest" (Matthew 11:28).

Skepticism can cloud the path of a giver. Questions may arise: "Is my contribution making a difference?" Or "Are the recipients of my help truly in need?" In these moments, recall the parable of the sower. Some seeds fall on rocky ground, but some find good soil. Our role is to sow generously, discern wisely, and leave the growth to God. "Do not be overcome by evil, but overcome evil with good" (Romans 12:21).

As givers, we're reminded that every act of kindness is a step towards a grander vision—a world more reflective of the divine generosity that showers upon us daily. The path will have its challenges, but armed with faith and the assurance that we do not labor in vain, we can overcome and continue to plant seeds of hope and love in the hearts around us. "And let us not grow weary of doing good, for in due season we will reap, if we do not give up" (Galatians 6:9).

In this section, as we confront these challenges, we're not merely looking for quick fixes but seeking to cultivate a heart that perseveres in giving, fortified by faith and sustained by the knowledge that with every challenge we overcome, we mirror the steadfast love that has been so freely given to us.

The Weaver's Tale

In a quaint village perched at the edge of a dense forest, there lived a weaver named Jessica. At the age of 35, with her soft grey eyes often peering through the window as her hands danced over her loom, she was known for more than just the stunning tapestries she crafted. It was her spirit of generosity that wrapped the village in warmth, much like the blankets she wove.

Jessica's giving was not without challenges. Her "dragon" was not a beast of fire and scales, but the creeping doubt that came with each act of kindness. Were her contributions, made from the modest profits of her weavings, truly making a difference? The dragon's breath was the whisper of skepticism in her ear, questioning if her small deeds were but drops in an endless ocean.

Jessica was not a knight, and her loom was no sword. Yet, like the knight in shining armor, she faced her dragon day by day. She didn't wear armor; instead, she adorned a simple apron, always with a thread and needle in the pocket, ready to mend what was torn. Jessica's age and her gentle but determined character made her the beating heart of the village, her weavings a tangible symbol of her inner resolve.

What kept Jessica up at night was not the fear of the dragon but the pain of uncovered shoulders in the cold and the sight of bare walls in homes devoid of color. Her heart ached for warmth in every home and beauty in every corner. Her tapestries were more than art; they were her solace and her solution, her silent rebelling against the chill of neglect.

The moment that changed everything came unexpectedly. It was during the annual village gathering when the mayor unveiled a tapestry of Jessica's—a vibrant depiction of the village, interconnected by threads of various colors and textures. The silence that befell the crowd was a canvas of realization; her weavings were not just cloth. They were threads that bound the community, a weave of unity and support. Her doubts dissipated like mist as the villagers saw not just a tapestry but the story of their lives, intertwined and held together by Jessica's threads.

Jessica's loom, an aged oak heirloom, stood as a testament to the legacy of giving. Each shuttle pass through the warp threads was a commitment to her village, and the gentle clack of the beater bar was a rhythm familiar to every child's ear. The vibrant dyes she used were sourced from local plants, a detail that spoke of her dedication to community and sustainability.

Through Jessica's story, the villagers—and we, the audience— understand that the true value in her giving was not in the grandeur of the gestures but in the love woven into every fiber her tapestry became. Shielded against the dragon of doubt, a proof that even the smallest threads, when woven with intention and care, could create a tapestry strong enough to protect and warm an entire community.

Jessica's narrative whispers to us that in the fabric of our own lives, each act of kindness, each thread of generosity, strengthens the weave of our collective humanity. And just like Jessica, we realize that the true armor against our dragons is the goodness we weave into the lives of others.

Living a Life of Generosity

Living a life of generosity is not a singular grand gesture, but a series of small, consistent actions interwoven into the daily fabric of our lives. It's in the shared smiles with strangers, the extra time spent listening to a friend, and the silent prayers offered for those we may never meet. Such a life echoes the words of 1 Timothy 6:18, "They are to do good, to be rich in good works, to be generous and ready to share."

Generosity, must like the mustard seed in Matthew 13:31–32, starts small but grows beyond what one could imagine, providing shelter and comfort to many. It's about cultivating a heart that finds contentment not in accumulation, but in distribution. In the act of giving, we reflect the nature of God, who John 3:16 tells us, "so loved the world that He gave His one and only Son."

When we weave generosity into the routine of our daily existence, we find joy bubbling up in unexpected moments. Acts 20:35 reminds us of the words of Jesus: "It is more blessed to give than to receive." This blessing is not just in the act of giving itself but in the joy that springs from seeing the impact of our actions.

Sharing stories of generosity can ignite a similar passion in others. Just as the parables in the Bible impart wisdom and stir hearts, our own stories of giving can inspire friends, family, and even strangers to open their hearts. We are reminded in Hebrews 13:16 not to neglect doing good and sharing what we have, for such sacrifices are pleasing to God.

Living a life of generosity also means being stewards of the blessings we have been given, as outlined in 1 Peter 4:10: "As each has received a gift, use it to serve one another, as good stewards of God's varied grace." This stewardship extends beyond financial means; it encompasses time, talents, and our presence.

To integrate philanthropy into one's life, consider starting with these simple, actionable steps:

1. **Reflect on Values**. Start by considering what matters most to you. What are your core values? Understanding these will guide your philanthropic actions.

2. **Set Intentions**. Define clear intentions for your giving. Why do you want to give? What do you hope to achieve? Align these with your values.

3. **Educate Yourself**. Take the time to learn about the causes and organizations you care about. Understanding the landscape can lead to more impactful giving.

4. **Start Small**. Begin with manageable acts of kindness. Philanthropy doesn't have to be grandiose; even small contributions can make a big difference.

5. **Plan Your Philanthropic Journey**. Like any journey, philanthropy requires planning. Decide how much you can give, whether it's time, money, or skills, and how often.

6. **Involve Family and Friends**. Share your philanthropic goals with loved ones. Involving others can amplify your impact and create a community of giving.

7. **Volunteer Your Time**. Offering your time can be as valuable as financial contributions. Find opportunities to volunteer in areas that resonate with you.

8. **Measure Your Impact**. Keep track of the impact your giving has. This can be a powerful motivator and can help you understand where to focus your efforts.

9. **Adjust as Needed**. Be flexible and willing to change your approach as you learn what works best for you and the causes you support.

10. **Celebrate and Reflect**. Take time to celebrate the difference you've made. Reflect on your experiences and consider how you can continue to improve on your philanthropic path.

By breaking down the process into these steps, you can develop a comprehensive and sustainable approach to living a life of generosity, ensuring that your philanthropic efforts are both rewarding and effective.

Living a life of generosity is a transformative journey that aligns our earthly actions with heavenly principles. It's about allowing the love that has been poured into us to flow outward, and in doing so, finding that the wellspring of joy within us never runs dry.

The Generous Heart

Meet Harold, a 52-year-old community leader with kind eyes and a silver-flecked beard that speaks to his years of experience. He wears a simple wristband woven by his daughter, a constant reminder of the love he strives to share with the world. Harold has spent his life building bridges—literally and metaphorically—as a civil engineer and a volunteer. Yet, despite his accomplishments, an internal dragon casts a shadow over his heart: the question of his legacy and the depth of his impact.

Every evening, as the sun dips below the skyline of the city he helped shape, Harold wrestles with a gnawing feeling. It's the fear that, in the grand scheme, he hasn't done enough to combat the suffering he sees in the news, the poverty on the streets, the pain in the eyes of those he passes by. This restlessness haunts him, a relentless whisper questioning, "Is that all there is?"

Then comes the moment—the pivot that turns disquiet into action. It happens on a mundane Wednesday. Harold is at the park, sharing his lunch with the pigeons, when he overhears a conversation. A young woman is telling her friend about a group she's part of, one that gathers every week to pack meals for the homeless. Her voice is alight with passion, and her words are the flint that sparks Harold's transformative flame.

He notices the woman's threadbare coat, the earnestness in her eyes, the vibrant laughter that punctuates her sentences. She's not wealthy, not powerful in the traditional sense, yet her presence is rich with purpose. Harold realizes that generosity is not measured by the zeroes in one's bank account but by the willingness to act, to give, to be present. The wristband on his arm suddenly feels like a suit of armor, empowering him to join the battle against indifference.

Harold's life changes course that day. He approaches the woman, learns about the group, and becomes a regular volunteer. His professional skills prove invaluable, but it's his heart that truly builds bridges now. He rallies his colleagues, inspires his friends, and enkindles a spirit of giving that ripples outward. His legacy is no longer etched in stone and steel alone, but in the lives he touches, the smiles he crafts, and the warmth he spreads.

Through Harold's journey, we see our own potential reflected. The story whispers to us, "See, you have the power to slay dragons too." It's not about grand gestures or names carved in marble; it's about the daily choice to extend a hand, to share a meal, to listen—to love. In this story, we find our call to arms, to live a life of generosity, one unseen act of valor at a time.

———————

CHAPTER EIGHT

Intercessory Love: Praying for Those Yet to Believe

"I urge, then, first of all, that petitions, prayers, intercession and thanksgiving be made for all people—"

—1 TIMOTHY 2:1 NIV

Welcome to the heartfelt journey of intercession—a journey not measured in the miles we walk, but in the depths we dive into the sea of God's boundless love. This chapter invites you to embark on a scared question, one that goes beyond the reaches of our comfort and straight into the embrace of the Divine.

Imagine yourself standing at the edge of a vast field, the golden harvest swaying in the wind—a harvest of souls ripe with potential and longing for the touch of the Savior's love. Here, in the quiet stirrings of your heart, the spirit of intercession begins to take flight. It's a call that resonates with the whisper of the Spirit, beckoning you to stand in the gap for those who have yet to utter the name of Jesus with faith and conviction.

In this chapter, we'll start by laying the cornerstone—understanding intercessory prayer. What does it mean to intercede? Why does it matter? The Scriptures overflow the wisdom and commands that call us to this noble task, and together, we'll uncover the rich tapestry of biblical truths that support this form of spiritual advocacy.

As we progress, we'll delve into the very heart of intercession. It's a place where empathy meets earnest supplication, where our pleas for others mirror the intensity of a watchman on the city walls—vigilant, steadfast, and moved by a love that knows no bounds. We'll explore the emotions and attitudes that fuel our prayers, giving them wings to soar into the heavens.

But even the most seasoned travelers may encounter storms. And so, we'll navigate through the strategies to bolster our prayers against the gales of discouragement and the shadows of doubt. We'll learn to recognize the barriers that seek to silence our petitions and discover how to overcome them with grace and tenacity.

Community—a word that evokes the warmth of shared fires and the strength of intertwined arms. Our journey of intercession is one that thrives in the fellowship of believers. We'll witness how the symphony of collective prayer harmonizes individual voices into a chorus so powerful it shakes the very foundations of the unseen world.

And finally, we'll arrive at the crescendo—the fruits of our labor. This is where tears of intercession are turned into pearls of joy, where the whispered names of those we've prayed for are spoken aloud in the halls of redemption. We'll share in the stories of lives transformed and celebrate the victories won through the steadfast love poured out in prayer.

So, take my hand, dear traveler. Let us step forward with hope as our compass and love as our guide, ready to embrace the beauty and challenge of interceding for those yet to believe. This is not just a chapter in a book; it's an invitation to a chapter in your life that could change the eternity of another. Let's begin.

Understanding Intercessory Prayer

Intercessory prayer is the heartbeat of a compassionate life, a golden thread woven through the tapestry of scripture, where the whispers and cries of the faithful rise like incense for others. It's the Moses standing in the breach (Psalm 106:23), the Abraham pleading for Sodom (Genesis 18:23–33), and the Jesus on the cross whispering, "Father, forgive them" (Luke 23:34). In understanding intercessory prayer, we step into a realm where love knows no bounds, where the spirit touches the divine on behalf of those who are yet to see, to hear, to believe.

Imagine the world through the lens of 2 Corinthians 4:4, where the "god of this age has blinded the minds of unbelievers." In this place of spiritual battle, intercessory prayer becomes our profound response, a beacon that shines through the darkness. We are called, like warriors without armor but with the shield of faith, to pray persistently and earnestly for those yet to believe, embodying the essence of Ephesians 6:18, "And pray in the Spirit on all occasions with all kinds of prayers and requests."

This section will delve into the potent mix of divine intercession and human agency. It isn't about changing God's mind; it's about partnering with the heart of God, aligning our desires with His will, as mirrored in 1 John 5:14, "This is the confidence we have in approaching God: that if we ask anything according to His will, He hears us."

We learn that intercessory prayer is not a passive act; it's a dynamic engagement with the powers that veil the eyes of the heart. It is the love of Christ compelling us (2 Corinthians 5:14), driving us to our knees, not only for our friends and loved ones but for every lost soul wandering in the shadow of doubt. We stand in the gap as did Christ, the ultimate intercessor, whose life and death tore the veil, granting us access to the throne of grace (Hebrews 4:16).

So, as we embark on this journey to understand intercessory prayer, let us hold fast to the promise in James 5:16, "The prayer of a righteous person is powerful and effective." It's here we begin, with hearts wide open, ready to intercede for those yet to believe, trusting in the power of prayer to unlock the doors of faith.

━━━━━

The Armor of Grace

Once upon an ordinary life, there was Xavier, a seasoned carpenter known for his robust laughter and weathered hands that told tales of years shaping wood. At 58-years-old, his countenance carried the peace of a man well-acquainted with toil and the joy of simple blessings. A silver cross dangled from his neck, catching the sunlight as he worked, a testament not just to his craft but to his faith.

His community was the heart, his workshop a haven for those who sought not only furniture but counsel. But deep in the silence of night, his heart wrestled with a heavy burden—a daughter who had drifted, lost in the throes of doubt and disbelief. Her resistance to the faith he cherished was the dragon he faced, one that breathed fire into the core of his longing soul.

The product, you ask? It was prayer—intercessory prayer, not a physical sword, but one mightier in its reach, capable of touching a heart he could not. This was the tool that could change the course of his daughter's life, and subsequently, fortify his own faith.

The silence of his room was stark as he knelt down, his rugged hands clasped not in desperation but in hope, invoking the verses, "For we do not wrestle against flesh and blood, but against . . . spiritual hosts of wickedness" (Ephesians 6:12). The weight of what kept him awake was not a roof in disrepair but a soul he yearned to see bathed in light and truth.

Then came the moment—the turning point. Not when he fashioned his finest chair or restored the old church pews, but when his daughter, after years, stepped through the door of the very church he helped maintain. In that moment, as the wooden door creaked open and his eyes met hers, something had changed. It was a silent explosion of grace.

Details, like the way her eyes mirrored the stained glass window's story of redemption, the way her hesitant steps carried a rhythm of seeking, spoke to every parent's silent prayer for their child. And Xavier knew, he wasn't alone; countless others shared this silent vigil.

As Xavier's story unfolds, his quiet victory becomes a clarion call for others. In a world of noise and haste, the humble power of a prayerful life stands as a beacon, whispering a promise that echoes through time and space, "The fervent prayer of a righteous man avails much" (James 5:16).

In the tapestry of lives intertwined, Xavier's tale weaves a message clear and strong: sometimes the greatest battles are won on bended knees, and the most powerful armor is the unseen shield of intercessory prayer. Those who hear his story see not just a carpenter but a warrior, and in his reflection, they find their own.

———

The Heart of Intercession

In the tender journey of intercession, we wade through the depths of what it means to truly bear one another's burdens. The heart of intercession is not a task taken lightly—it's the very pulse of a soul stirred by love and compassion for others. It is the gentle yet profound realization that "if one member suffers, all the members suffer with it" (1 Corinthians 12:26).

Imagine Elizabeth, a nurse in her early forties, whose every day is a tapestry woven with the threads of care and concern for those who cross her path. Her tender touch and listening ear have become the healing balm for many a bruised soul. Yet, her heart is moved most deeply not by the physical wounds she tends but by the spiritual lostness she encounters.

Her compassion extends beyond the hospital wards, reaching into the quiet corners where her friends and loved ones wrestle with shadows of doubt and fear. It is in these places that Elizabeth kneels, her prayers a fragrant offering, rich with the empathy that follows from a heart touched by the suffering of others. She prays with the conviction that "the Lord is near to those who have a broken heart" (Psalm 34:18), believing that her intercessions are the threads that help mend the tattered spirits of those she loves.

As she lifts her voice in prayer, it's not just words that rise like incense but the genuine desire for her loved ones to know the fullness of joy and peace that comes from walking in the light of truth. Elizabeth understands that to intercede is to enter into a sacred space, where the heart's cry transcends the boundaries of heaven and earth. It is here, in the quiet sanctuary of her devotion, that the profound connection between the human and the divine unfolds.

The real crux of intercession lies in the transformation it beckons— not just for those being prayed for but for the intercessor as well. As Elizabeth prays, her own spirit is aligned with the heart of God, who "desires all men to be saved and to come to the knowledge of the truth" (1 Timothy 2:4). Her soul echoes the heavenly passion for redemption and restoration, and her life becomes a living testament to the power of a faith that acts through love.

The heart of intercession, then, is this beautiful tapestry of love in action—a divine synergy where the love Christ compels, the Spirit intercedes, and the Father listens. It's a sacred rhythm that beats to the words, "Bear one another's burdens, and so fulfill the law of Christ" (Galatians 6:2), reminding us that the deepest call to prayer is also the highest expression of love we can offer to this world.

———

A World in Need of Compassionate Prayer

Meet Lucy, a 38-year-old social worker with kind eyes that seem to absorb the pain of the world. Her hands, often clasped together, bear a simple silver ring engraved with the word "Hope." She is known in her community as a beacon of support, but her greatest struggle is the helplessness she feels for those she can't reach with her words or actions alone.

Every evening, as Lucy sits in her modest living room, the silence around her is heavy with stories of the day. There's the troubled teen who can't find his way home, the single mother drowning in despair, the old man who whispers to her of a life of regrets. Their pain is the dragon that haunts her nights, leaving her feeling powerless, her heart aching for a change she can't seem to make.

Then, one dusk-tinted evening, in the quiet solace of her porch, Lucy's hands unfold from their usual clasp, and she reaches for an old, worn Bible that had been her grandmother's. As she reads through the passages, a verse resonates with her, igniting a spark: "For where two or three gather in my name, there am I with them" (Matthew 18:20). In that hushed moment, Lucy realizes that her prayers can be the bridge for those lost in the darkness to the light they seek.

From that day forward, the silver ring isn't just a piece of jewelry; it becomes the symbol of her commitment to intercede for those she carries in her heart. Each day, Lucy dedicates a part of her morning to prayer, her hands wrapped around the ring, her soul wrapped around the lives of those she prays for.

The change is gradual but undeniable. The teen finds a program that guides him back; the mother discovers a community that lifts her up; the old man reconnects with a long-lost love. And Lucy, she finds a renewed sense of purpose. Her prayers become the sword with which she battles the dragon of despair, not just in her life but in the lives of those for whom she intercedes.

The value in Lucy's story is clear: the power of intercessory prayer isn't just in changing the lives of others, but in transforming the life of the intercessor. It's a testimony to the potential for authentic, heartfelt prayer to bring about real-world miracles, one life at a time. And in sharing her journey, she whispers to the world, "You are not alone; I'm here, praying with you and for you." And those who hear her story feel seen, understood, and a little less alone in their battles.

Strategies for Intercessory Prayer

In this section, we step into the shoes of those who have felt the stirring in their hearts to become warriors in prayer. This isn't about reciting empty words; it's about engaging in a spiritual exercise with intention, precision, and fervor.

Imagine you are at the potter's wheel. The clay is centered, and your hands are steady. The wheel begins to turn, and you are about to shape something magnificent. This is akin to the beginning of intercessory prayer: you are the potter, the prayer is your wheel, and the transformation you seek is in the clay. The Bible reminds us, "Yet you, Lord, are our Farther. We are the clay, you are the potter; we are all the work of your hand" (Isaiah 64:8).

Here, we delve into strategies that are less about changing the hearts of others and more about allowing God's spirit to direct and use our own. We start with commitment—a whispered promise in the quiet morning hours to stand in the gap for those who do not yet see. It's a commitment that mirrors the resolve of Daniel, who, understanding the importance of perseverance, knelt down three times a day and prayed, giving thanks before his God (Daniel 6:10).

Focusing on the unseen might seem daunting, like walking through a fog with only faith to guide you. Yet, this is where the sharpened tool of focus comes in, carving out the distractions of the world to reveal a clearer path for your prayers. "Set your minds on things above, not on earthly things" (Colossians 3:2). The act of focusing transforms intercessory prayer from a routine into a dedicated mission, seeking to touch hearts with divine precision.

And what of being sensitive to the Spirit's leading? It is the gentle nudge that urges you to pray for a stranger, the inexplicable pull to intercede for a friend at a specific moment, or the sudden burden for a nation in turmoil. It is the Holy Spirit who guides your prayers, as

Romans 8:26 states: "In the same way, the Spirit helps us in our weakness. We do not know what we ought to pray for, but the Spirit Himself intercedes for us through wordless groans."

By merging commitment, focus, and sensitivity to the Spirit's whispers, your intercessory prayers become more than words; they become vessels of hope and change. Each prayer is a thread in a larger tapestry, woven with the faith that, though we may not see the immediate fruits, the seeds are being planted in fertile ground, watered by our persistent and passionate intercession.

The Silent Revolution of Intercessory Prayer

Jean, a 34-year-old nurse with a heart as tender as the patients she tends to, carried a burden that shadowed her even in the brightest of her days. The weight wasn't from her job, though its stresses were man, but from a deeper concern for her brother, Alex, who had drifted far from faith and hope.

Each night, as the moon rose high, Jean would sit by the small, worn-out bedside lamp, her hands clasped, and her spirit reaching out for Alex's hardened heart. The darkness of the night seemed to mirror the problem he faced: the distance in her brother's eyes, the skepticism in his voice, the spiritual "dragon" that held him captive in a tower of disbelief.

One evening, as the clock's hands met at midnight, a tear slid down Jean's cheek—an authentic emotion, a mix of love and desperation, that no one but her silent room could witness. What kept her up wasn't just the thought of her brother's estrangement from faith; it was the fear of him walking through life without ever experiencing the profound peace and love she had found in her own faith.

It was in one of these moments of heartfelt supplication that something shifted. Jean felt a warmth, an embrace of comfort and clarity that she hadn't known before. It was as if the silent room had whispered, "Continue in prayer, and watch in the same with thanksgiving" (Colossians 4:2). It wasn't an audible explosion, but a silent revolution of her heart.

Her strategy for prayer began to change. She would pray during her breaks at the hospital, sometimes holding the hand of a sleeping patient as she interceded for her brother. She sought out specific Bible verses, scrawled them on post-it notes, and placed them around her mirror, her dashboard, her life. It was no longer just about nightly prayers; it was an all-day, every-moment commitment.

The details of her prayers grew more vivid. She imagined Alex's laughter ringing true and clear, free from the cynicism that had tainted it. She envisioned the light returning to his eyes, the kind of transformation only faith could bring. She prayed for conversations yet to be had, for moments of softening, for opportunities to share the hope that so filled her life.

Jean's story is our story—not because we all have an Alex in our lives, but because we all have dragons to slay, whether they are doubt, fear, or the despair we see in the eyes of those we love. Her strategy became her testimony, an illustration of the power that lies in persistent, faith-filled intercession.

Jean's tale whispers to each of us, "They get me. They know what it's like to care so deeply that it hurts. They understand the battle fought on one's knees." Her strategy for prayer is not just a set of steps; it's the sword she wields with unwavering hope, a beacon that guides us in our own journeys of intercession.

======

Overcoming Barriers in Intercession

When we engage in the solemn practice of intercessory prayer, we often confront a silent battlefield, one where the obstacles are as invisible as they are deeply felt. It is a place where hope meets the hard ground of reality, and our spiritual fortitude is tested. "Be joyful in hope, patient in affliction, faithful in prayer" (Romans 12:12).

Within this sacred endeavor, we encounter barriers that may seem insurmountable. Discouragement whispers insidiously in our ears, casting long shadows over our hearts. The adversary, too, wages a relentless campaign, sowing seeds of doubt and fear, striving to deter us from our divine path. "Put on the full armor of God, so that you can take your stand against the devil's schemes" (Ephesians 6:11).

And then there are the moments that weigh heaviest on our souls—the times when Heaven seems silent, and our fervent prayers appear to vanish into the ether without reply. In these trials, we are reminded of the psalmist's cry: "I waited patiently for the Lord; he turned to me and heard my cry" (Psalm 40:1).

Yet, it is precisely here, amid these struggles, that our faith is refined. Like gold in the fire, we are called not to shrink back but to press on with a perseverance born of a love that transcends the visible. For overcoming these barriers is not an act of sheer will but a testament to the power of a steadfast spirit. "Consider it pure joy, my brothers and sisters, whenever you face trials of many kinds, because you know that the testing of your faith produces perseverance" (James 12:2–3).

Therefore, let us not grow weary. Instead, let us arm ourselves with spiritual wisdom, clothe ourselves in the full armor of God, and hold fast to the promises of Scripture. For in due season, we shall reap a harvest if we do not give up, believing that our intercessory whispers, carried on the winds of faith, have the power to breach walls and transform hearts. "And let us not be wary in well doing: for in due season we shall reap, if we faint not" (Galatians 6:9).

As we traverse this path of persistent prayer, may we find solace in the Word, strength in our fellowship, and unwavering resolve in the assurance that each prayer is a seed planted, each word a ripple in the vastness of God's grace.

Whispers of Faith

In the heart of a bustling city lived Francis, a 42-year-old pharmacist with compassionate eyes and a locket she wore that never failed to catch the light—a gift from her grandmother, symbolizing faith that withstands all trials. Her profession was her calling, but her passion extended far beyond the walls of the hospital—to the spiritual well-being of those she encountered, especially those who had yet to embrace faith.

The dragon Francis faced was not made of scales and fire but of the silent cries of indifference and the shadowy veil of disbelief cast over the eye of her customers and friends. She wielded no sword, but her knees were worn from the countless hours spent in intercessory prayer, her weapon of unseen power.

The authentic emotion that stirred in Francis's heart each night was a blend of deep love and aching concern—a burden for the souls that lay in slumber, untouched by the transformative power of belief. She tossed and turned, wondering if her prayers for them were heard, questioning if her solitary vigil made a difference.

Then came the moment that changed everything. It was an overcast Tuesday when one of her long-time customers, a stern man known for his cynicism, asked her why she cared so much, why her eyes held a hope that his own had never known. It was in the silence of that pharmacy, where pills being filled played the background score to so many stories, that Francis shared her faith openly, explaining that her peace came from something—Someone—greater than herself.

Specific details of that day were etched into Francis's memory: the way the sunlight peeked through the clouds and danced on the locket at her chest, the softness that overcame the man's weathered face, and the single tear that escaped as he whispered, "I want to believe, too."

That day, the dragon of doubt lost its power, and the sword of Francis's relentless prayer was revealed not as a mere tool, but as a conduit of divine love. Her faith, her intercession, had been the balm to a soul she had cherished in prayer.

This was the moment Francis's purpose crystalized; the realization dawned that every whispered prayer was a seed sown into the hardened soil of the human heart, and in time, with patience and perseverance, it could blossom into a story of redemption.

And to those who heard Francis's testimony, who saw her locket and listened to her story, the message was clear: they were understood, they were not alone in their silent battles, and there was someone who had already paved the way through the darkness—the ultimate intercessor, whose love had conquered the greatest dragon of all.

The Role of Community in Intercessory Prayer

In the tapestry of faith, each thread weaves through the fabric of community, binding us together in a shared purpose and collective strength. When we gather with intention, our individual whispers ascend as a chorus, piercing through the heavens with the fervent power of intercessory prayer.

In the book of Matthew, Jesus tells us, "For where two or three gather in my name, there am I with them" (Matthew 18:20). This profound truth illuminates the exponential power that ignites when believers unite in prayer. It's not merely about the number of voices, but the unity of the Spirit that amplifies our petitions.

Imagine a scene by the Sea of Galilee, the early morning mist dancing over the waters as a community of believers encircles a friend. They are not bound by their needs but propelled by their faith. Their hands are joined, a symbol of their solidarity; their voices, though varied in tone, united in purpose. Each prayer, a beacon of hope for those yet to believe, shines brighter together than any could alone.

The Acts of the apostles gives us a glimpse into the early church, a community steadfast in prayer, a fortress for the fledgling faith of many (Acts 2:42). It was within this bastion of belief that miracles were birthed and hearts were transformed. When one stumbled, others were there to lift; when one faltered in faith, others shouldered the burden of belief.

As we walk through the avenues of our lives, let us not forget the immense strength found in the congregation of kindred souls. When the weight of the unseen battle grows heavy, when the silence of the unseen seems deafening, we are reminded of the words of Paul to the Galatians, "Carry each other's burdens, and in this way you will fulfill the law of Christ" (Galatians 6:2).

To pray in community is to build a fortress of faith, not with stones and mortar, but with trust and intercession. In unity, there is resilience; in togetherness, there is power. Our collective prayers act as a symphony, each note critical to the harmony, each pause as significant as the crescendo, rising to the heavens in a single, unbreakable strand of hope and intercession for those who have yet to see the light of truth.

Embrace the role of community in your prayer life, and witness how the union of many voices becomes the clarion call for divine intervention, echoing across the valleys of doubt and ushering in an era of spiritual awakening for those yet to believe.

United We Pray

In the heart of the bustling city, there lived a woman named Farah, a 42-year-old physical therapist with gentle eyes that spoke of the compassion she carried within her. She wore a small silver cross around her neck, not merely as an adornment, but as a testament to her faith and a reminder of her calling beyond the hospital wards. Despite the love she poured out daily, there was a weight she bore, a burden that no medical expertise could lift—the spiritual well-being of her brother, Dean, who had drifted far from faith.

Night after night, Farah lay awake, the moonlight casting shadows across her room, mirroring the shadows over her heart. She felt powerless against the great dragon of doubt and disbelief that held her brother in its clutches. Her prayers felt like whispers in a tempest, barely reaching the ceiling, let alone the heavens.

But then came the moment that changed everything.

One Sunday, after a particularly heartfelt service, a new realization dawned upon Farah. Her pastor spoke of the multiplied power of united prayer, referencing the book of Matthew, where Jesus promised His presence among those gathered in His name. In that moment, a profound silence enveloped her soul, and the truth resonated within her. She was not alone in this fight.

The following week, she hesitantly joined a small prayer group in her congregation, a circle of individuals who believed in the power of collective intercession. Farah introduced the dragon that was her concern for Dean, and together, they lifted their swords—their prayers—against it.

As weeks turned into months, the change was gradual but undeniable. Dean began to show subtle signs of openness, and Farah knew it was not her alone but the collective effort of her community that wielded the sword of intercession with her. The prayer group became her fortress, and each specific prayer, a stone in its walls.

Her story—one of unity, faith, and the power of communal prayer—echoes in the hearts of those who hear it. It serves as a reminder that while we may approach the throne of grace alone, we wage the greater wars shoulder to shoulder with our brothers and sisters in faith. Farah's transformation from solitary warrior to a member of a prayerful legion tells us, "They get me," and in her story, we find the courage to seek out our community in prayer, to slay our own dragons, and to change our worlds through the collective power of intercessory love.

———

Witnessing the Fruits of Intercession

As we draw near to the close of our journey through the labyrinth of intercession, we pause at a verdant oasis, a place of both reflection and celebration: Witnessing the Fruits of Intercession. Here, amid the laughter of those who have found faith and the tears of joy from those who have prayed tirelessly, we recount the stories that are the heartbeat of hope and the evidence of an active God.

"Delight yourself in the Lord, and He will give you the desires of your heart" (Psalm 37:4). This verse becomes the anthem for those who have sown in prayer and now reap with shouts of joy. Each answered prayer is a story, a miracle of its own, a testimony that weaves itself into the grand tapestry of faith.

The joy of seeing a friend's eyes light up with the spark of belief, the hush that falls over a room when the prodigal son or daughter steps back into the fold—these are moments that defy words, yet speak volumes of the Father's love. They are the fruits of labor, born from knees worn in supplication and hands lifted in surrender.

As Paul exhorts the believers in Galatians 6:9, "Let us not become weary in doing good, for at the proper time we will reap a harvest if we do not give up." We understand now, more than ever, the steadfastness required to see this harvest. Every story of transformation is a ripple that turns into a wave of change within communities, a testament to the promise that our labor in the Lord is not in vain (1 Corinthians 15:58).

The narratives of changed lives are not just for us to hold close but to share far and wide. A we speak of the quiet child who now sings praises, or the skeptic who now kneels in prayer, we echo the words of Revelation 12:11, "They triumphed over him by the blood of the Lamb and by the word of their testimony." Each story is a battle won, a victory in the spiritual realms, encouraging and edifying the body of Christ.

This closing topic is an invitation to remember and to rejoice, to gather the stones of remembrance so that when others ask, "What do these stones mean?" (Joshua 4:6), we will have stories to tell of the wonders He has done. It is a call to be mindful that the fruits we enjoy today are often the result of others' prayers yesterday, and our intercession now is laying the groundwork for tomorrow's miracles.

Let us then go forth, sharing the fruits of intercession, bearing witness to His faithfulness, and inspiring a new generation to pray fervently and without ceasing, for this is the legacy of intercession—a legacy of eternal impact and unending joy.

The Unseen Victory of Persistent Prayer

In the small, close-knit community of Elmwood, there lived a woman named Darcey, a 52-year-old schoolteacher with a soft smile and hands that had turned many a tear-stained page of prayer. Darcey's problem wasn't one you could touch or easily see—it was the heavy burden of a heart that ached for her students, her neighbors, and her town, as she witnessed the dragon of despair and disillusionment breathing its cold breath upon them.

By night, Darcey would intercede with a fervency that could shake the heavens, her voice a steady stream in the silent hours. But by day, she bore the quiet, persistent worry—how many of her prayers were reaching through the noise of the world? The emotion that held her in its grip wasn't fear; it was a profound compassion, a longing to see the lives around her touched and transformed by the same faith that kept her own heart beating with hope.

The moment of change came unexpectedly on a Tuesday afternoon. Darcey was walking through the park on her way home when she saw a former student, Clay, who had always been closed off, sitting alone. His face was different, though, softer somehow, and when he caught sight of her, he approached with an openness that was new. "Mrs. D," he said, "something's changed in me. I can't explain it all, but . . . I found something . . . someone. I found faith."

In that moment, the silence that fell between them was profound; it was as if a dam had broken. Darcey knew, without a word, that her prayers—those countless, fervent whispers in the dark—had played a part in Clay's transformation. This was the explosion of joy in her spirit, the real value of her steadfast intercession realized not just in Clay's words but in the light of his eyes.

The story of Clay's turnaround spread, touching hearts and igniting conversations throughout Elmwood. Darcey's quiet, faithful prayers became known as the roots that held the community together when winds of change swept through. Her specific prayer for each child, each neighbor, adorned with specific details of their lives and struggles, had built a fortress of hope that stood firm against despair.

And so, the tale of Darcey and Clay became a living testament in Elmwood, a narrative that said, "She gets me. She prayed for me." It was a narrative of authentic, lived-out faith, encouraging others to see that their stories, too, might find such a beautiful unfolding in the hands of a prayerful believer who never gave up on the promise of the fruits of intercession.

═══════

Voices of Hope:
The Call to Share Your Faith

"Therefore go and make disciples of all nations, baptizing them
in the name of the Father and of the Son and of the Holy Spirit,
and teaching them to obey everything I have commanded you.
And surely I am with you always, to the very end of the age."

—MATTHEW 28:19–20 NIV

In the quiet moments of reflection, beyond the hum of everyday life,
lies a stirring—a call that resonates through the corridors of the
believer's heart. It is a call as ancient as the hills yet as immediate as the
beating of your own heart. Welcome to chapter nine, where we embark
on an intimate journey from the whisper of divine instruction to the
crescendo of living it out with courage and conviction.

As you turn these pages, you will rediscover the biblical imperative that rings out with clarity and purpose, the Great Commission that beckons each of us to be ambassadors of hope. But how do we prepare for such a quest? Fear not, for this chapter is your map and your compass—guiding you through the valleys of personal readiness and up the mountains of spiritual maturity.

You will learn to weave the tapestry of your life's story into a living testimony, a beacon that illuminates the path for others. With each word and deed, you will become a builder of bridges, reaching out across the chasms that separate hearts and minds, connecting with those who have yet to hear the message that has transformed your life.

Yet, this journey is not without its challenges. You will be equipped to share your faith with compassion, threading your conversations with love and respect, even in the face of indifference or rejection. For every closed door you encounter, you will find the strength to knock on another, armed with resilience and the unwavering belief that hope must be shared.

This chapter is an invitation—a summons to rise and answer the call that echoes in the actions of the faithful through the ages. As you heed this call, you join a symphony of "Voices of Hope." Each unique but united in purpose, each a critical note in the harmonious melody that sings of salvation and grace.

So let us begin, not just with the intent to speak but with the readiness to act and live out the faith we proclaim. For in sharing our faith, we find the joy and purpose of our own journey magnified, reflecting the light of truth into the lives of others, and writing our own verses in the eternal song of hope.

Hearing the Call

In the quiet whispers of our daily routines and the loud chaos of the world's hustle, there is a persistent call that beckons the heart of every believer—a call to witness, to share the faith that anchors the soul. This call is not born of human origin or conjured by fleeting emotions; it is etched in the very fabric of Scripture, an echo of the divine that resounds through the ages.

The Great Commission, as entrusted by Jesus in Matthew 28:19–20, is the cornerstone of this sacred duty. "Go therefore and make disciples of all nations," He charged His followers, igniting a flame that has been passed down from generation to generation. It is an invitation that speaks of action—"go," "make," "baptize," "teach"—verbs of movement that compel us out of complacency and into the vibrant life of sharing the good news.

But why do we witness? Acts 1:8 offers a glimpse into the power behind the call: "But you will receive power when the Holy Spirit has come upon you; and you will be my witnesses in Jerusalem and in all Judea and Samaria, and to the end of the earth." It is not by our might or eloquence that we share our faith, but through the Spirit's empowerment. As vessels of this promise, we become the voices through which hope and salvation can be offered to a world in need.

Romans 10:14–15 paints a poignant picture of the urgency and beauty of witnessing: "How, then, can they call on the One they have not believed in? And how can they believe in the One of whom they have not heard? And how can they hear without someone preaching to them?" It is a divine sequence that starts with the messenger and culminates in belief—a divine domino effect set in motion by the simple act of sharing one's faith.

In the parable of the sower (Luke 8:4–15), we find a narrative filled with the truths about witnessing. The seed, which is the Word of God, is sown in various soils, representing the hearts of all. Some seeds flourish, others falter, but the sower's task is not to discriminate or predetermine the outcome but to faithfully scatter the seed. So too are we called to spread the word, trusting in the unseen work of the Holy Spirit to bring growth.

Finally, 1 Peter 3:15–16 admonishes us to be ready to give an answer to everyone who asks about the hope that we possess, yet with gentleness and respect. Witnessing is not a call to arms for debate or coercion but a gentle offering of the truth that has transformed our lives.

This section, Hearing the Call, is thus a journey into the heart of why we, as Christians, share our faith. It is an exploration of the biblical imperative that nudges us gently but firmly out of the doors of our churches and in the streets, into our workplaces, our schools, and our homes, bearing the light of the gospel—the unquenchable hope that we have in Jesus Christ.

The Silent Warrior's Awakening

Once upon a modern day, in the sprawling expanse of a bustling city, lived a woman named Christina. Christina, in her mid-thirties, was an unassuming figure with a warm smile that seldom dimmed. By day, she was a skilled software developer, a master of code and digital realms; by evening, a loving aunt who always had her door open for family and friends. Christina wore a simple silver diamond cross around her neck—a symbol of the faith that colored her life, yet one that quietly lay beneath her blouse, often unseen by the world.

The dragon Christina faced was not of scales and fire but of silence and missed opportunities. Every day, she heard the stories of her colleagues—their struggles, their searching—and her heart ached. She longed to share the hope that sustained her, but uncertainty shackled her tongue. What kept her up at night was not the fear of rejection but the weight of untold stories—the message of love and redemption that burned within her, yet remained unspoken.

One evening, amidst the soft hum of her computer and the glow of the city lights, Christina stumbled upon an online forum discussing the Great Commission. As she read the familiar verses, a moment transpired that shifted something deep within her. It was as if she heard the verses for the first time: "Go therefore and make disciples of all nations." The words were an explosion of clarity; it wasn't about eloquence or persuasive speeches, but about stepping out in faith, equipped by the Spirit.

In the stories that unfolded on the screen, Christina recognized the authentic emotions of others like her—believers who had found the courage to speak, to act, to share. They were not superheroes or famed evangelists, but everyday people who found strength in their vulnerability. Their stories were marked with specific details—the coffee shared with a questioning friend, the simple prayer offered in a moment of crisis, the gentle conversation about hope and faith that opened the door to transformation.

It was in these narratives that Christina found a mirror to her own life. She realized the power of her testimony, the significance of her journey with God, and the value of each moment she lived her faith out loud. Her silver cross was not just a piece of jewelry; it was a testament to a life changed, a promise kept, and a story to be shared.

Christina's awakening was quiet, but the ripples of her newfound boldness were felt by many. She began to weave her faith into her conversations with a gentleness that was disarming, with a passion that was infectious. And though she was but one, her voice joined the chorus of countless others, a symphony of witnesses that could bring walls down and build bridges to hearts seeking solace.

This was the moment Christina realized the true power of her faith—when the silent warrior within awoke, and the whisper of her testimony turned into a roar of hope in her corner of the world. She understood then, it was not about the sword but about the knight, not about the tool but the hand that wields it, and in the story of her life, she had become a beacon of the hope she once kept hidden.

And thus, Christina's story whispers to us all: You, too, have a voice, a story, a life that can echo the love of the One who called you out of darkness into His marvelous light. Let the silent warriors arise.

Preparation of the Heart

In the journey of faith, the heart is not just the seat of emotion; it is the starting ground of divine purpose and action. Before one can embark on the sacred call to share their faith, there is a crucial step often overlooked in the haste of enthusiasm—the Preparation of the Heart.

Imagine a garden. Before it flourishes with life and color, the soil must be tilled and nurtured. Similarly, our hearts require preparation to become fertile ground from which the seeds of the gospel can grow and spread. The process is intimate and personal, involving prayer that is as constant as the rhythm of a heartbeat, study that delves deeper than mere intellectual curiosity, and an ever-present reliance on the Holy Spirit.

Prayer is the whispered conversation that aligns our heart with God's. It's in the quiet dawn hours or the stillness of a night when we lay bare our thoughts and seek His wisdom. As we articulate our desires to witness to others, we might reflect on Colossians 4:3, "And pray for us, too, that God may open a door for our message, so that we may proclaim the mystery of Christ, for which I am in chains." In these chains, not of bondage but of boundless love, we find the courage to speak and live out the truth of the gospel.

Study is the lamp that illuminates our path, a vital aspect of spiritual readiness. It is through the living Word that we draw the strength and knowledge necessary to share our faith with confidence. "Your word is a lamp for my feet, a light on my path" (Psalm 119:105). The Scriptures are not just to be read but to be absorbed, to resonate with our daily lives, and to embolden our witness.

Lastly, the role of the Holy Spirit cannot be overstated. It is the Spirit who empowers, who transforms our feeble attempts into divine encounters. "But you will receive power when the Holy Spirit comes on you; and you will be my witnesses . . ." (Acts 1:8). The power is not of human origin; it is the divine enabler that guides our words and actions, ensuring that they bear fruit.

In this section, we delve into the depths of what it means to be spiritually ready to evangelize. It's a journey that might take us into valleys of introspection and mountaintops of revelation. Here, we do not rush; we prepare. We tend to our hearts, ensuring they are soft to God's promptings, rich in His Word, and receptive to His Spirit. It's a sacred process, for a heart well-prepared is a vessel through which the extraordinary love of God can be poured out into the world, one ready to share the good news with an authenticity and power that is undeniably Spirit-breathed.

Preparation of the Heart is about more than readiness; it is about becoming a conduit of God's love, a beacon of His truth, and a vessel of His Spirit—fully equipped and spiritually attuned to embark on the highest calling: to share the faith that sustains us, with the world that awaits us.

========

The Heart's Journey to Spiritual Readiness

Amelia was a seasoned medical doctor, a woman whose compassionate touch had eased countless pains and soothed many a troubled brow. At 52, her silver hair was a testament to years of service, and her hands, though lined with the roadmap of time, were steadier than ever. Yet, nightly, she was haunted by a different kind of restlessness—a yearning to share the deeper source of her strength, her faith, but unsure of how to begin.

Her uniform, pristine and white, was like armor; it gave her confidence in the hospital wards but offered little guidance in the spiritual battle she faced. Amelia's struggle wasn't with wielding the sword of truth, but in preparing her heart to become its worthy vessel. The problem wasn't the message she longed to share; it was the inner turmoil of feeling unprepared.

The emotion that kept her up at night was fear—fear of rejection, of inadequacy, of saying the wrong thing. How do you fix a heart trembling at the edge of divine calling? For Amelia, the answer came on a rainy Tuesday afternoon that disrupted the melody of her routine.

In the quiet corner of the hospital chapel, Amelia found herself alone, except for the whisper of rain against stained glass. As she bowed her head, there was a profound stillness, a moment of surrender. It was as if the heavens themselves paused to listen. It was in this silence that Amelia discovered the true essence of readiness—a heart aligned with God through sincere prayer, a spirit nurtured by the Scriptures, and a will surrendered to the Holy Spirit's leading.

In this moment, the realization dawned on her; the true value was not in the "sword"—the act of sharing her faith—but in the preparation of her heart, the "knight." The details of this epiphany were vivid: the feel of the worn Bible beneath her fingers, the scent of rain-soaked earth wafting through the chapel, and the soft whisper in her soul affirming her readiness. Her heart, once heavy with uncertainty, now danced with the promise of what was to come.

The change in Amelia was palpable; her colleagues noticed a new vibrancy in her step, a gentle confidence in her words. She became a living testimony, not in grand gestures, but in everyday acts of kindness infused with an unspoken depth. The dragon of doubt was slain, not by the sword, but by the knight whose heart had been quietly, powerfully transformed.

To those who witnessed Amelia's subtle transformation, the message was clear: they were understood. The fear of sharing one's faith was a familiar giant to many, but here was the evidence that the battle could be won from within. Amelia's story whispered of a path they, too, could walk—of hearts prepared, spirits empowered, and lives changed—not by the force of will, but by the grace of preparation.

Living Testimony

In this section, we discover the compelling force of a life transformed by faith. Imagine the early church, a community vibrant with stories of change and hope. Just as the apostle Paul shared his blinding encounter on the road to Damascus, saying, "I once was lost, but now am found" (Acts 9), so too does your personal narrative carry a unique resonance that can pierce the hearts of listeners.

Each believer is a walking epistle, a human document inscribed with the evidence of grace, as Paul reflects, "You yourselves are our letter, written on our hearts, known and read by everyone" (2 Corinthians 3:2). Your story is more than a sequence of events; it is a testament to the dynamic work of God in your life.

Crafting your testimony isn't about embellishing the drama; it's about authenticity and the honest revelation of where you've been and where God has brought you. "Therefore, if anyone is in Christ, the new creation has come: the old has gone, the new is here!" (2 Corinthians 5:17). Your narrative is about the "new" that has emerged from the "old."

But how do you articulate this change? Begin by reflecting on the landmarks of your faith journey—what were the moments of struggle, the instances of revelation, the times of turning? Weave these with the threads of Scripture, for it is the Word that quickens the soul (Hebrews 4:12).

In sharing your story, remember that it is not by might nor by power, but by the spirit says the Lord (Zechariah 4:6). Your testimony is not an argument to be won but an offering of the work God has done in you, extended with the gentle confidence that what He has begun, He will complete (Philippians 1:6).

Thus, in the sharing of our personal stories, we allow others to see the silhouette of God's love against the backdrop of human experience. It is in this revelation that hearts are stirred, and lives are altered—not by our eloquence, but by the Spirit's moving through the living testament of transformed lives.

Bridging Souls with Stories of Faith

Imagine Oprah, a 42-year-old physician assistant, whose life seemed as orderly and predictable as the medication she dispensed each day. With a soft smile and kind eyes that hinted at a depth of experience, Oprah's gold cross necklace was the only visible sign of the faith that quietly anchored her.

The dragon in Oprah's life wasn't breathing fire; it was the silent despair she saw in the eyes of her patients, the same despair she once knew before finding hope in her faith. Every night, as she removed her cross before sleep, she'd remember the weight of her own past struggles, the feeling of being utterly lost, and the solace she'd found in the words of a simple prayer.

One ordinary Tuesday, the air in room 402 felt heavier than usual, as if charged with a silent plea for help. Oprah was administering medication to Raphael, a middle-aged man with weary eyes, who muttered, "I wish I had your certainty." It was a moment, suspended in time, that felt like a direct challenge to Oprah's spirit.

She hesitated, then began sharing her own story, not with the intention of converting Raphael, but simply to offer comfort. She spoke of her turbulent past, of nights filled with tears, of the day she found solace in a church pew listening to a message that seemed meant just for her. She recalled the passage that had struck her heart, "Come to me, all who labor and are heavy laden, and I will give you rest" (Matthew 11:8).

The room was quiet, except for the soft beeping of the heart monitor, as Oprah finished her story. In Raphael's eyes, there was a shift, a glimmer of something that looked a bit like hope. In sharing her testimony, Oprah hadn't just administered another dose of medication; she had provided a balm for the soul.

This was the moment Oprah realized the true value of her personal story. It wasn't just a series of events; it was a lifeline she could throw to others adrift in the sea of despair. Her story, woven with authenticity and vulnerability, had become a bridge connecting her faith to someone else's need for hope.

And for those listening to Oprah's story, it's not the details of her faith that resonated—it's the universal search for meaning and the transformation that comes when one finds it. Her story is a testament to the power of personal narrative, and it serves as an inspiration for others to share their own.

Building Bridges

In the landscape of faith, believers often find themselves at a crossroads of connection with those who do not share their convictions. "Building Bridges—effective ways to connect with non-believers—is more than a mere instructional; it's a journey into the heart of empathetic engagement, where understanding is the cornerstone of every conversation.

The foundation of this connection is love—agape love—as demonstrated by Christ Himself. Scripture reminds us, "Let your conversation be always full of grace, seasoned with salt, so that you may know how to answer everyone" (Colossians 4:6 NIV). This is the blueprint for building bridges, where our words are not weapons but tools for building understanding.

This section would not merely lay out strategies but illuminate them through the prism of God's Word. It teaches that, before a word is spoken, the heart must be prepared. For it is from the abundance of the heart that the mouth speaks (Luke 6:45), and so, a heart aligned with God's compassion will reflect His love in every interaction.

Discussions would revolve around practical empathy—seeing through the eyes of another. It means stepping into the shoes of the non-believer and walking the path of their questions, their doubts, and their worldview. Believers are called to be all things to all people so that by all possible means some might be saved (1 Corinthians 9:22). This is the art of spiritual cartography, mapping the route to common ground where conversations can flourish.

Through real-life anecdotes and narratives, this section would illustrate how Jesus reached out to the outcast and the misunderstood. He asked questions to provoke thought, not to pass judgment. In following His example, believers learn to ask with genuine curiosity, to listen actively, and to respond with insight steeped in the Scriptures, always ready to give an answer to everyone who asks about the hope that they possess (1 Peter 3:15).

Building bridges also involves recognizing the cultural scaffolding that shapes viewpoints. The wisdom from Proverbs 14:12, "There is a way that appears to be right, but in the end it leads to death," encourages believers to engage with cultural narratives, not with condemnation, but with the compassionate truth of the gospel. By acknowledging and respecting cultural differences, believers can better illustrate how the gospel is a transcultural truth that resonates with the deepest human needs.

Finally, this section would emphasize that connection with non-believers is not a project but a process—a journey walked together. It's a call to long-term relationships over transient encounter, exemplifying the steadfastness of God's love, a love that believers are commissioned to share, one conversation, one bridge at a time.

―――――

The Bridge Builder

In the bustling city of diverse souls and clashing ideologies, Victoria, a 32-year-old community advocate, stands as a bacon of empathy and understanding. With her characteristic teal scarf, a bright spot in the concrete jungle, she embodies the spirit of connection in her daily mission: to forge understanding where there is division, to build bridges where there are chasms.

The problem is not in the message she carries; it is the chasm of disconnected that has widened in society. Victoria's restless nights are spent pondering over the city's skyline, thinking about the "dragons" of misunderstanding and prejudice that keep her community fragmented, her heart heavy with the burden of unspoken stories and unheard voices.

One autumn evening, as the amber leaves dance to the ground, Victoria encounters Jamison, a reclusive artist with a guarded heart, disillusioned by the dogmas of life. Their worlds collide at a local exhibit, amidst the stark portrayals of his search for meaning. In that moment of shared vulnerability, the air shifts, and Victoria realizes the profound power of authentic dialogue.

Every detail of Victoria's approach is considered, from her open posture to her inviting smile that disarms even the most defensive. She understand that in each story lies the seed of common humanity, and in each exchange, the potential for transformation. Victoria listens, not to respond, but to understand; she speaks, not to persuade, but to share truth wrapped in love.

The turning point comes when Jamison, once an impenetrable fortress of solitude, finds solace in Victoria's genuine curiosity about his journey. It is not a grand epiphany but a series of small, honest exchanges where Victoria's faith becomes less of an abstract concept and more of a tangible presence of hope and compassion in his life.

The value that Victoria brings into Jamison's life—and by extension, the lives of countless others—is immeasurable. It is not about converting on the spot; it is about planting seeds of consideration, watering them with sincere care, and ultimately watching as the once-barren landscape of division blossoms into a vibrant community of understanding.

In sharing her own story of faith, Victoria becomes more than just a bearer of good news; she becomes a living testament to the power of relationship. Through her, others see not a faceless advocate, but a friend, a fellow traveler, and a bridge builder. Her story whispers to the hearts of the audience, "I've been where you are. I see you. I understand. Let's walk this path together."

And thus, the story of Victoria, the community advocate with the teal scarf, becomes a parable of hope, a demonstration of the real value of building bridges—transforming not only her life but also empowering others to become architects of understanding in their own right.

Communication with Compassion

In the heart of every believer lies a profound story of hope, a narrative that is both personal and transformative. The art of sharing this story is not in the volume of one's voice but in the depth of one's compassion. The Bible speaks of this approach in Ephesians 4:15, "Instead, speaking the truth in love, we will grow to become in every respect the mature body of Him who is the head, that is, Christ."

The call to share one's faith is an invitation to walk in Jesus' footsteps, to embody the grace and truth that He lived out among those He encountered. Communication with Compassion explores this divine dance of dialogue, where words are not weapons but gentle seeds sown in the fertile soil of open hearts.

In the bustling marketplace of ideas, where beliefs clash and ideologies compete for allegiance, the Christian witness stands distinct—not in condemnation but in loving conversation. This approach does not compromise the message but enriches it, clothing the unchanging truths of the gospel in the tender fabric of human kindness.

As 1 Peter 3:15 advises, "But in your hearts revere Christ as Lord. Always be prepared to give an answer to everyone who asks you to give the reason for the hope that you have. But do this with gentleness and respect," we see a blueprint for engagement that honors the person while uplifting the truth.

PASSION FOR CHRIST: NEW BEGINNINGS

This section of our journey addresses the delicate art of conversation that bridges differences with dignity. It teaches us to listen—to truly hear the stories of those we speak with, for it is in understanding another's journey that we can share ours in a way that resonates. The Master Communicator, Jesus, exemplified this as He connected with people from all walks of life, from the Samaritan woman at the well to the inquisitive Nicodemus under the cover of night. Each encounter was steeped in respect and genuine care for the individual, beyond the cultural and religious barriers of the time.

Communication with Compassion unfolds the beauty of Christ-like communication, where the tone of love is not a strategy but a genuine reflection of the heart. It delves into the practicalities of empathy, the silent strength of active listening, and the profound impact of a respectful dialogue. It's about expressing the gospel in a manner that mirrors the heart of the message itself—a message that is as much about redemption as it is about relational restoration.

To share one's faith with love and respect is to recognize that every soul is on a journey, and every interaction is a sacred opportunity to reflect the love of God. It is to trust that the same Spirit who guides our words will also prepare the heart of the listener. For it is not our eloquence but the Spirit's power that transforms lives.

Through stories, anecdotes, and scriptural wisdom, this section invites us to engage in evangelism that doesn't just speak to the mind but also touches the heart, evangelism that is not about winning arguments but about winning souls, with the compassionate love of Christ as our guide.

Compassionate Conversations

Meet Olivia, a 34-year-old dietician with a warm smile and a gentle demeanor that calms her clients in their most vulnerable moments. Her brown hair is usually pulled back into a neat bun, and a small, gold cross necklace always rests against her scrubs—a symbol of the faith that anchors her life. Despite her compassionate nature, Olivia lies awake at night, wrestling with a gnawing feeling that she is not doing enough to share the hope that sustains her.

What troubles Olivia is not her demanding job or the challenges of life—it's the burning desire to communicate her faith to her friends and colleagues without coming across as intrusive or disrespectful. She yearns for her loved ones to experience the peace and joy she has found in her faith, but fear of damaging relationships leaves her silent, her story untold.

The pivotal moment arrives unexpectedly. One evening, while sharing a meal with a close colleague named Tom, who is grappling with life's hardships, Olivia listens intently, her heart heavy with empathy. Tom pauses, looks at her, and asks, "Olivia, how do you always stay so calm in the chaos?" There, in the soft ambiance of the little diner, amidst the clinking of dishes and the murmur of conversations, the silence that follows is profound. Olivia realizes that this is the moment—her opportunity not just to speak but to truly embody her faith through her words.

She takes a deep breath and, with a sincere and soft voice, shares her personal story. She speaks of her own struggles, her search for meaning, and how her faith has given her strength. There's no script, no rehearsed speech—just an honest heart speaking to a friend in need. She talks about her belief not as an abstract concept, but as a living, breathing reality that has changed her life.

As Olivia speaks, Tom's expression softens. The conversation that ensues doesn't immediately convert him, but it opens a door that was once closed. Olivia's story, shared with genuine compassion, becomes a bridge between two very different worldviews.

This moment marks the beginning of a new chapter in Olivia's life—one where fear is replaced by freedom, and silence by a story. It's a transformation that doesn't just change her life but has the potential to change Tom's as well, along with every other life she touches. The gold cross around her neck is no longer just a symbol of her faith, but a testament to the power of sharing that faith through love and genuine human connection.

Cultivating Resilience

In the sacred endeavor of sharing one's faith, not every seed sown will take root, not every heart will open at the first knock. Cultivating Resilience—facing rejection and staying the course—is a testament to the enduring spirit required to walk the often rocky path of evangelism. It is an exploration of the biblical truths that sustain and nourish the soul when met with the thorns of rejection and the brambles of apathy.

Consider the parable of the sower, where Jesus speaks of seeds falling on different types of soil—some rejected outright upon the rocky places, others sprouting quickly but withering under the sun (Matthew 13:1–23). This parable mirrors the experience of sharing the gospel; some messages are embraced, others are discarded, but the sower's role is not to dictate the soil's response but to continue the sowing faithfully.

Paul's words to the Galatians come to mind, "Let us not become weary in doing good, for at the proper time we will reap a harvest if we do not give up" (Galatians 6:9). This is the clarion call to resilience, the encouragement needed when faces turn away, and hearts seem closed. It is a divine reminder that our timeline is not God's and that perseverance is not in vain.

In the face of rejection, the disciple of Christ is called to reflect Christ's own resilience. When Jesus was rejected in His hometown of Nazareth (Mark 6:1–6), He did not despair; instead, He continued His mission, teaching and healing in other villages. His focus remained on the calling, not on the setback.

This section would delve into the spiritual practices that fortify the believer against the winds of rejection—prayer that anchors, Scripture that strengthens, and fellowship that supports. It would remind readers that rejection is not a reflection of the messenger but a step in the listener's journey to truth. "Blessed are those who are persecuted because of righteousness, for theirs is the kingdom of heaven" (Matthew 5:10). This beatitude gives perspective, framing rejection not as failure but as a part of the path to spiritual maturity and kingdom inheritance.

Cultivating resilience is also about cultivating hope. It's about trusting in the unseen work of the Holy Spirit, who can soften the hardest of soils and bring life to the driest of lands. "So neither the one who plants nor the one who waters is anything, but only God, who makes things grow" (1 Corinthians 3:7). The growth is God's domain; the believer's task is to plant and water with unwavering dedication.

This closing topic is not just an end but a beginning—a call to continue sowing with courage, to water with hope, and to trust in the harvest that is yet to come. It is a charge to stand firm, to press on, and to embody the resilience that marks the journey of every believer who has chosen to share the precious gift of the gospel.

The Resilient Messenger

In the quaint town of Eldersfield, where every cobblestone seems to whisper ancient tales, lives a 34-year-old man named Stephen. By day, Stephen is a well-loved teacher, his sleeves often chalk-dusted, a gentle smile his trademark. He is known not just for his keen intellect but for the unusual pendant that always rests against his shirt—a small silver cross, polished by the touch of his fingers.

But Stephen has another role, one that stirs his heart as much as it challenges it. He is a modern-day knight, not clad in armor, but armed with a message of hope and salvation. His dragon? Indifference. The cold, steely gaze of rejection that greets him as he shares his deepest convictions. His sword is his faith, a mere tool, for it is the conviction in his spirit that truly wrestles with the apathy of the age.

The problem that keeps Stephen awake at night isn't the apathy itself but the thought of a single soul walking through life without the light of hope that has so radically changed his own existence. It's the possibility that he could have spoken a word that might have kindled a flame in someone's heart but remained silent instead.

Then comes the moment—etched in the hush of an evening's conversation. Stephen sits across from a longtime friend, Judah, whose heart had seemed as impenetrable as the ancient oak in the town square. They've had countless debates, shared numerous meals, but this night is different. As the golden glow of the hearth flickers across Judah's face, Stephen sees it—a softening, a questioning in his eyes. This is the moment he has prayed for, the pivot upon which his tireless efforts turn.

The specific detail, the soft crackling of the fire, the dimming light, the quieting of the day, they all build to this crescendo. In this hushed moment, Stephen shares his own story of transformation—a tale not of grandeur, but of grace. And in the eyes of the townsfolk, the teacher, the neighbor, the messenger, they see something familiar—a longing, a search for truth, a desire for meaning.

The value of Stephen's perseverance is realized not in a thunderous victory but in the silent acknowledgment of his friend's need for hope. And to those hearing this story, it's clear—they get it. The struggle against indifference, the need for resilience, the power of a persistent, loving witness.

Stephen's story becomes a beacon—a call to all who have known the bitter taste of rejection, to remember that the worth of the message they carry is not diminished by a hundred dismissive glances. It's a reminder that in the heart of every resilient messenger, there beats the promise of a dawn where every effort counts, and every steadfast step is a victory in its own right.

CHAPTER TEN

Designed for Forever:
Living with Eternity in Mind

"Set your minds on things above, not on earthly things."

—COLOSSIANS 3:2 NIV

As you turn the pages to the final chapter of this journey, "Designed for Forever: Living with Eternity in Mind," you stand at the threshold of a profound revelation—the call to view every breath, every moment, every heartbeat through the lens of eternity. This is not just a chapter; it's a gateway to a transformed life, where the temporal fog lifts to reveal the shimmering horizon of the everlasting.

Imagine living each day infused with purpose, every decision anchored in the promise of a horizon that stretches beyond the here and now. This is the essence of an eternal perspective—a way of life that echoes through the ages, a song whose melody lingers long after the notes have been played.

As you embark on this final voyage, you will be invited to recalibrate your compass to true north—the eternal kingdom of God. Here, the fleeting shadows of worldly pursuits are illuminated by the radiant dawn of divine truth. You will explore the promises etched in Scripture, promises that are as steadfast as the stars in the celestial tapestry, guiding you to anchor your hopes not in the sands of time but in the solid rock of Christ's enduring presence.

With each topic, we will weave through the fabric of what it means to truly live for forever. From the personal to the profound, from the practical to the spiritual, we will journey together through the choices that shape not just our earthly walk but our eternal destiny.

So, take a moment. Breathe deeply the air of potential that this perspective brings. Let your eyes rise above the horizon of mortality and glimpse the boundless expanse of eternity. Herein lies the path to a life of significance, a life designed not just for the transient tick of a clock but for the unending glory of forever.

Welcome to the chapter that never ends, where the final word is not "The End," but "To Be Continued . . ." in the presence of the One who calls us to an eternal hope, an everlasting joy, and an unfading inheritance. Welcome to living with eternity in mind.

Eternal Perspective: The Starting Point

Embarking on the voyage of faith with an eternal perspective is akin to setting sail on a vast ocean, guided by the stars of divine promise. As you hoist the sails of your life, the wind of the Spirit urges you forward, whispering truths that echo through eternity.

To live with the end in mind is to recognize that our days are not mere drops in an endless sea, but precious moments crafted by the hands of an eternal Artist. The apostle Paul captures this sentiment when he writes to the church in Corinth, "So we fix our eyes not on what is seen, but on what is unseen, since what is seen is temporary, but what is unseen is eternal" (2 Corinthians 4:18). In these words lies the call to an eternal perspective, to look beyond the horizon of our finite existence and anchor our hope in the eternal.

What does it mean to live with the end in mind? It is to understand that every choice, every action, and every word is a thread woven into the tapestry of eternity. It's to grasp that our lives are but a brief prelude to a never-ending symphony, where the choices we make resonate far beyond the confines of time.

Jesus Himself spoke of this when He said, "Do not store up for yourselves treasures on earth, where moths and vermin destroy, and where thieves break in and steal. But store up for yourselves treasures in heaven, where moths and vermin do not destroy, and where thieves do not break in and steal" (Matthew 6:19–20). Here, Christ is not dismissing the importance of our earthly journey but is inviting us to invest in the eternal, to collect treasures that time cannot erode, nor circumstance diminish.

An eternal perspective infuses our daily walk with significance. It means that the mundane can become majestic, and the ordinary can become extraordinary. It transforms our worldview, prompting us to live not as passengers on a temporal train to oblivion but as pilgrims on a journey towards a celestial city with foundations, whose architect and builder is God (Hebrews 11:10).

As you ponder the notion of eternity, let it shape your understanding of purpose. May it guide you in wisdom, enrich you in love, and ground you in the peace that surpasses all understanding— the peace of knowing that the story of your life extends far beyond the final chapter of your earthly existence.

So begin this journey by setting your sights not on the fleeting shadows of the present but on the enduring substance of the future. Let an eternal perspective be the compass that guides your path, the lens through which you view every sunrise and sunset, every joy and challenge, every beginning and end. For in doing so, you will find that living with the end in mind is truly the only way to begin.

Blueprints of Eternity

In the quiet suburb of a bustling city lived Randal, a 42-year-old architect, known among his peers for his practical, down-to-earth designs. His life was like the structures he created: functional, predictable, and safe. Randal wore the same style of crisp, blue shirts and had a routine that rarely saw a shift. But beneath the surface, he wrestled with a nagging sense of restlessness, a question that kept him up at night: "Is this all there is?"

One unremarkable Tuesday, which began like any other, became the fulcrum upon which Randal's life would pivot. It was at the funeral of a colleague, a man who, like Randal, had dedicated his life to erecting edifices that scraped the sky. But in the eulogies, Randal heard not of the man's accomplishments but of the lives he had touched, the laughter he shared, the family he cherished. In that moment, the air seemed to still, the drone of the eulogy became a distant echo, and Randal felt a stirring within. The realization dawned upon him that life was not about the buildings he designed but the memories created within them.

As the days passed, this moment refused to fade into the tapestry of routine. Randal saw his blueprints not as mere plans for structures but as the groundwork for spaces where people would live out their stories. He understood that his legacy wouldn't be in the glass and steel that bore his name but in the unseen moments of life that his buildings would host. It was as if he had traded his steel sword for a plowshare, turning from battling the dragons of deadlines and prestige to cultivating a field ripe with the potential for eternal impact.

With this new perspective, Randal's approach to architecture underwent a metamorphosis. He began integrating communal spaces that encouraged interaction, designing homes that were not just houses but potential havens for love and growth. His conversations with clients shifted from focusing solely on aesthetics and function to discussing the legacy they wanted to leave through the spaces they built.

Years later, when Randal would walk through the neighborhoods he helped design, he saw children playing in the courtyards he had envisioned and communities flourishing in the common areas he had prioritized. Specific details like the laughter ringing from open windows and the sight of old friends chatting on benches under the shade of trees he had deliberately preserved told him that his work had transcended the physical.

Those who knew Randal felt understood by him. He had become more than an architect; he was a weaver of stories, a craftsman of legacies, and a gardener of human connections. His story—once punctuated by questions in the stillness of the night—now echoed with the answer that what we build in this life can resonate into eternity, not through the stone and mortar, but through the lives we touch and the love we foster.

———

Scriptural Promises of Eternity

As we weave through the tapestry of time, it's the golden thread of eternity that pulls us forward, past the fleeting moments into the profound depths of God's promises. The Scripture, a timeless guide, brims with these promises, illuminating the path to eternal life—a beacon for those yearning to grasp their place in God's endless kingdom.

Let's embark on a journey through the Scripture, where the whispers of eternity echo in every verse, drawing us closer to the heart of divine assurance. We discover in the Gospel of John, a declaration that resonates with the soul's deepest longing: "For God so loved the world, that He gave His only Son, that whoever believes in Him should not perish but have eternal life" (John 3:16). Here lies the cornerstone of our hope, the unfathomable love of a Creator who calls us into an everlasting embrace.

In the vaults of the Psalms, we find a hymn of eternal refuge, "The Lord is King forever and ever; the nations will perish from His land" (Psalm 10:16). Amidst the transience of earthly kingdoms, this Psalm sings of the unshakable reign of God, a sovereign rule where decay and demise hold no power.

The prophet Isaiah, with eyes set beyond the horizons of time, speaks of a future unfurled in the promise of renewal, "The wolf and the lamb shall graze together; the lion shall eat straw like the ox, and the dust shall be the serpent's food. They shall not hurt or destroy in all my holy mountain," says the Lord (Isaiah 65:25). Here, in the serenity of God's mountain, the scriptural vision of peace and restoration unfolds like a divine masterpiece, calling us to glimpse our everlasting inheritance.

As we traverse further, the apostle Paul in his letter to the Corinthians reveals the victory over the grave, "Behold! I tell you a mystery. We shall not all sleep, but we shall all be changed, in a moment, in the twinkling of an eye, at the last trumpet. For the trumpet will sound, and the dead will be raised imperishable, and we shall be changed" (1 Corinthians 15:51–52). The sting of death is conquered, not by our might, but through the triumph of Christ, gifting us the keys to an eternal kingdom.

In the intimacy of Christ's words in the book of Revelation, a final promise is tenderly laid before us, "He will wipe away every tear from their eyes, and death shall be no more, neither shall there be mourning, nor crying, nor pain anymore, for the former things have passed away" (Revelation 21:4). A new heaven and a new earth await, where sorrows are as distant as the shadows at dawn, and joy is as enduring as the stars.

These scriptural promises of eternity are not mere words, but the living breath of God, infusing us with hope, strengthening our faith, and anchoring our souls to the eternal. They invite us to look beyond the temporal veil and to live in the profound certainty that our story, intertwined with the divine, does not end at the last chapter of this life, but continues into the glorious narrative of eternity.

―――――――――

Embracing the Promises of Everlasting Life

In the midst of a bustling cityscape, we find Cliff, a 42-year-old building designer. His life, a blueprint of success by worldly standards, yet within, Cliff grapples with a dragon—his fear of insignificance, the dread of his existence being a mere footnote in the annals of time. With each project he completes, the dragon's breath scorches closer, whispering of oblivion.

Age has bent Cliff's once towering confidence into a question mark that looms over him, casting a shadow even in the noonday sun. He wears his father's watch, a timepiece that ticks away moments with a precision that Cliff wishes he could apply to understanding the meaning of his own life.

Then, at his daughter's insistence, Cliff finds himself at a small group meeting, an unlikely place for an building designer who built his life on concrete realities. Here, he's introduced to a "product" unlike any other: the promises of Scripture, an assurance of eternal significance, an answer to the dragon that's been threatening to consume his peace.

One evening, a passage from 1 Peter 1:4 about an inheritance that is imperishable, undefiled, and unfading catches his breath. It's the moment the world around him goes silent—the whir of thoughts, the ticking of his father's watch, the relentless pace of the city. It's as if he's standing at the edge of eternity, gazing into a forever that could hold his name, his story, not just in memory, but in a tangible, living reality.

This revelation brings an authentic emotion to Cliff, stirring what has long been dormant beneath his structured facade. The fears that keep him up at night—the dragon's roar—are met with a resounding battle cry from Scripture, echoing the promise of eternal life, a life of meaning, purpose, and a legacy that extends beyond the steel and glass of his creations.

Specific details of his life begin to realign; the watch becomes not a countdown to his end but a reminder of timeless promises. His blueprints start to represent more than temporary structures; they become metaphors for building a life that lasts. The conversations with his daughter gain depth, infused with talks of a legacy beyond the tangible.

Cliff's encounter with the enteral promise of Scripture doesn't just slay his dragon—it changes the course of his life. The fear of insignificance is replaced with a role in an eternal story, and this newfound perspective is not just for him. It's a beacon for anyone who wears a watch, not as a reminder of time slipping away, but as an emblem of the eternal moments gifted by faith.

And thus, Cliff's story unfolds, showing us that when the dragons of our deepest fears breathe down our necks, the sword we need isn't made of steel or might, but of the enduring promises found in the eternal Word, a truth that carries us beyond the final tick of the clock into the vast expanse of forever.

The Temporal vs. The Eternal

In The Temporal vs. The Eternal, we wade into the delicate balance of living fully in the present moment while keeping our compass set on eternity. This world, with its shimmering allure and instant gratifications, often masquerades as the ultimate destination. But as pilgrims passing through, we're reminded that our true treasure lies beyond the visible horizon.

Jesus' words in Matthew 6:19–21 echo through the ages, urging us to store up treasures in heaven, "where moths and vermin do not destroy, and where thieves do not break in and steal." This profound statement illuminates the heart's position as the ultimate treasure chest, one that should be filled with eternal riches.

The early believers, like us, grappled with this contrast. The apostle Paul, in his letter to the Philippians (3:20), reminds them, "But our citizenship is in heaven. And we eagerly await a Savior from there, the Lord Jesus Christ." Here lies the dichotomy; our feet may tread the earth, but our citizenship is signed with the ink of the eternal.

How then do we revel in the beauty and joy of the here and now while longing for our eternal home? It's akin to enjoying the warm glow of a campfire, recognizing that, though it wards off the night's chill, it is not the earth we gather around in our lasting abode. 1 John 2:17 provides this wisdom: "The world and its desires pass away, but whoever does the will of God lives forever." This is the compass that helps us navigate the temporal without getting lost in it.

As we consider the laughter of our children, the embrace of a loved one, or the satisfaction of a job well done, let us do so with a heart of gratitude, knowing these are mere foretastes of the joy that awaits. Let us engage in our earthly responsibilities with integrity and passion, yet hold loosely to the accolades and achievements, as we would souvenirs from lands through which we only journey.

The writer of Ecclesiastes wrestled with this tension, ultimately finding peace in fearing God and keeping His commandments (Ecclesiastes 12:13–14), for this is the essence of living with eternity in mind. The temporal offers shadows and shapes; the eternal holds the substance and reality.

Eternal Echoes in Temporal Halls

Elliot, a seasoned design engineer in his late fifties, has always been the embodiment of success. His designs punctuate city skylines, and his reputation precedes him in concrete and glass. Despite his accolades, Elliot finds himself wrestling with a gnawing question as the twilight of his career looms: "What does it all mean in the light of eternity?"

His nights are threaded with restlessness, the soft glow of his drafting table often the only light in the darkness. The question of legacy haunts him—what keeps him up is the fear that his life's work, these temporary structures, might not withstand the winds of time, much less touch the edge of eternity.

The moment came during the quiet dedicating of a small community center he had designed pro bono in a neglected neighborhood. As he watched children's laughter echo through a space made with love, not profit in mind, a silence fell over his heart. It was an architectural whisper of eternity. The value of his work was not in the steel beams or the awards on his wall but in the spaces that fostered human connection and community. This simple structure, possibly overlooked by critics, was a monument in the making for its eternal impact on souls.

Elliot's signature piece, always present on his worksite, is a worn leather wristband, inscribed with the phrase "Ad astra per aspera" (To the stars through difficulties). It was a gift from his late mentor, a reminder that the true worth of his work was not just in reaching toward the sky, but in uplifting others.

Elliot's story resonates with us as we navigate our own temporal achievements and longings. It's a poignant reminder that our truest impact is not measured by time but by the eternal ripples we create through acts of kindness, love, and selfless giving. Elliot's journey redirects our gaze to an eternal horizon, encouraging us to build our lives with eternity in mind, laying bricks of fleeting time into the everlasting.

Living Out Eternity Today

In the midst of our fast-paced lives, where the urgent often bulldozes the important, the concept of Living Out Eternity Today emerges as a beckoning oasis of perspective. This isn't about withdrawing from the world to meditate on mountaintops; it's about infusing our everyday with the kind of significance that transcends our ticking clocks. "So whether you eat or drink or whatever you do, do it all for the glory of God" (1 Corinthians 10:31).

Picture Colleen, a young school teacher, who has learned that living for eternity doesn't start at life's finish line; it begins now, in her classroom, with a heart full of purpose. She sees beyond the lesson plans and grading papers to the souls in her care, knowing that each word of encouragement is a seed planted for an eternal harvest. "And let us not grow weary of doing good, for in due season we will reap, if we do not give up" (Galatians 6:9).

Every decision Colleen makes, from spending extra time with a struggling student to integrating values of kindness and integrity into her lessons, is a conscious effort to mirror the eternal into the temporal. It's in the way she chooses patience over frustration, love over indifference, and faith our cynicism. "Set your minds on things above, not on earthly things" (Colossians 3:2).

For Colleen and for us, Living Out Eternity Today is about seeing each day as a fresh canvas on which is painted with eternal colors. It's making the daily choice to pursue what is noble, pure, and of good report. In our workplaces, our homes, and in our communities, every interaction is a chance to reflect a larger story, a grander narrative written by the hand of the Divine. "Therefore, whether you eat or drink, or whatever you do, do all to the glory of God" (1 Corinthians 10:31).

It's about priorities—choosing relationship over convenience, stewardship over consumption, service over self-interest. These are the markers of a life painted with the brushstrokes of eternity. "For where your treasure is, there your heart will be also" (Matthew 6:21).

Engaging with Living Out Eternity Today doesn't require a change of circumstances but a change of heart. It's not a matter of adding more to our to-do lists but of aligning our actions with timeless truth. It's a reminder that our smallest deeds are threads woven into an eternal tapestry, and that in the mundane can be found the profound.

Let's walk with Colleen in the truth that while our time on earth is brief, the echoes of our choices carry on into eternity.

Luke's Awakening to Lasting Foundations

Meet Luke, a 35-year-old building planner, skilled in crafting structures that reach defiantly towards the sky. A silver cross dangles quietly around his neck—a gift from his grandmother that's more a memento than a testament of faith. He's the modern-day knight, armed not with a sword, but with blueprints and ambition, wrestling not with dragons but with deadlines and client demands. His daily dragon is the existential monotony, a whispering threat of life's fleeting purpose.

Luke's armor is his impeccable reputation, and the battlefield is his office, strewn with the spoils of success. Yet, as the twilight hours stretch and the city's heartbeat fades into the quiet, a gnawing emptiness often keeps him company. Authentic emotion haunts his solitary moments—the fear that perhaps the buildings he's so proud of are as transient as the time he trades for them.

Then comes the moment—the pivot upon which Jacob's story hinges. It happens on a routine Sunday as he visits his grandmother. The television is playing a sermon, something about "building foundations on things unseen." The preacher's words detonate in the silence of the living room, disrupting Luke's world not with an explosion but with an arresting whisper of truth.

As his grandmother speaks fondly of her faith, describing it not as an antique relic but the very essence of her strength, Luke sees a lifetime of perseverance and love built on an invisible yet unshakable foundation. Here is the real value, not in the structures he erects but in the legacy he will leave.

Specific details in his grandmother's house start to stand out—the worn Bible on the coffee table, the family photos filled with decades of laughter and trials, the simple yet contented life that seemed richer than any of his affluent creations.

In this scene, familiar as Sunday visits and as profound as eternity itself, Luke finds resonance. He starts to see his cross not just as a symbol of tradition, but as a compass pointing towards true north. It isn't about discarding his work but about redefining the why behind it. As he now sketches and designs, Jacob infuses his projects with community spaces, with green areas where children can play—a legacy of his time, an investment in eternity.

The value story of Luke's transformation is less about a dramatic change in his daily routine and more about the profound shift in his understanding of worth. The cross around his neck, once a mere accessory, becomes the lens through which he views his world. It reminds the audience that even in a secular vocation, the eternal can be sown into the temporal, turning every moment into a step towards an everlasting legacy.

Impact and Influence: Leaving a Legacy

In a world obsessed with the fleeting, where today's headline is tomorrow's forgotten tweet, the notion of legacy can seem like an ancient tapestry in a digital age. Yet, within the heart of every believer stirs the desire to leave an imprint that outlives the tick of a clock or the closing of an app. Impact and Influence: Leaving a Legacy is a call to that timeless yearning, an invitation to weave threads of eternal significance into the fabric of daily existence.

For the follower of Christ, legacy is not constructed of bricks and mortar, nor is it etched in the annals of human accolades. Instead, it is inscribed in the lives touched by divine love and the moments seized for heavenly cause. "Do not store up for yourselves treasures on earth, where moths and vermin destroy, and where thieves break in and steal. But store up for yourselves treasures in heaven, where moths and vermin do not destroy, and where thieves do not break in and steal" (Matthew 6:19–20). Here lies the believer's blueprint for a legacy that endures beyond the dust—treasures woven in the tapestry of eternity.

What does it mean to impact and influence with an eternal lens? It is to walk in the footsteps of the Master, who "went about doing good and healing all who were oppressed by the devil, for God was with Him" (Acts 10:38). It's a journey marked by acts of kindness that ripple through time, words of hope that echo beyond the whisper of the present, and a life lived as a testament to the transforming power of the gospel.

As Paul reminded the Corinthians, "So we fix our eyes not on what is seen, but on what is unseen. For what is seen is temporary, but what is unseen is eternal" (2 Corinthians 4:18). To leave a legacy is to fix our gaze on the invisible, to anchor our actions in the unshakeable, and to measure success not by the scale of now but by the weight of forever.

Envision a life where every decision is filtered through the sieve of perpetuity, where the mundane becomes a mission field, and the ordinary becomes an opportunity for the extraordinary grace of God to manifest. This is the heart of legacy—not a monument of self, but a living, breathing testimony to the One who called us out of darkness into His marvelous light.

In crafting such a legacy, the believer becomes a beacon of influence, not by the volume of their voice but by the virtue of their life. For "by this everyone will know that you are my disciples, if you love one another" (John 13:35). Love, then, becomes the indelible ink with which our stories are written in the annals of eternity, a love that speaks louder than time and echoes into the everlasting.

Impact and Influence: Leaving a Legacy is an echo of the divine, a chorus of lives harmonizing with the eternal, and a testament to the fact that the true measure of a life is not its span, but its depth in the waters of eternal purpose.

———

Echoes of Eternity: The Carpenter's Tale

Anthony, a 57-year-old carpenter, is known for the sturdy homes he builds and his commitment to his craft. He wears a leather tool belt, each pouch weathered by time and each tool telling a story of structures raised and lives sheltered. But as his hands work the wood, his mind wrestles with a nagging thought: "What am I truly building that will last?"

His days begin before sunrise and end when the stars claim the sky. Yet, in the quiet moments, Anthony's heart is restless. He longs for assurance that his life's work extends beyond the temporal frames of houses. The dragon he faces is the fear of insignificance, the dread that his years might vanish like sawdust in the wind.

One evening, as Anthony sands down the rough edges of a wooden beam, his granddaughter, Lisa, sits nearby, her eyes wise with wonder at the tale of Noah's Ark she hears from her grandfather. "Noah built something that saved lives, Lisa. It wasn't just wood and nails; it was a promise of survival, of a future," Anthony muses aloud, not realizing the impact of his own words.

That night, Anthony wrestles with his thoughts. He considers the homes he's built, the families that will live in them, the memories that will be created, and the generations that will find shelter and comfort within those walls. The realization dawns on him—the houses are his ark, his contribution to the future, his echo in eternity.

The revelation is his moment of explosion, the quiet breakthrough that comes not with fanfare but with the profound silence of truth settling deep within his soul. From that moment, Anthony sees his work differently. Each nail driven is a commitment to durability, not just in structure but in legacy. Each home is a testament to love, security, and warmth. The authentic emotion that fuels his renewed passion is the realization that his hands, though roughened and lined with time, are instruments in crafting legacies.

Details of his story resonate with those who understand that the true worth of their work isn't in its immediate utility but in the intangible values it upholds. Anthony's narrative resonates with people who see themselves not just as workers or professionals but as crafters of legacy, stewards of the future.

And so, Anthony's story spreads, inspiring others to look beyond their daily toil and see the eternal echoes of their work. Each of us, in our way, is invited to join Anthony, to take up the tools we've been given, and build—not for today or tomorrow, but for forever.

The Hope of Glory: Focusing on Jesus

In the final exploration of our journey towards eternity, we anchor our souls in the greatest example of eternal perspective: Jesus Christ Himself. He, who "for the joy that was set before Him endured the cross, despising the shame, and is seated at the right hand of the throne of God" (Hebrews 12:2). This profound verse encapsulates the heart of an eternity-focused life—it's about vision, endurance, and ultimate glory.

Jesus' life on earth was a masterclass in living with eternity in mind. From the wilderness to Gethsemane, His actions were not just for the moment but for the everlasting impact they would have on humanity. He was never swayed by the transient, never seduced by the temporal power or pleasures that so often divert our gaze. Instead, His eyes were fixed on something beyond—on the hope of glory.

Let's delve into how we, too, can draw on His strength and example as we navigate our paths:

1. **Vision Beyond the Visible**. Jesus saw beyond the immediate. He looked at the broken, the sick, the sinful, and saw what they could become in the light of eternity. As His followers, we are called to do the same—to look beyond the present troubles and see the potential for eternal transformation in ourselves and

others. "So we fix our eyes not on what is seen, but on what is unseen, since what is seen is temporary, but what is unseen is eternal" (2 Corinthians 4:18).

2. **Endurance in Suffering**. In the garden and on the cross, Jesus faced suffering that is beyond our comprehension. Yet, He endured. His example teaches us that the sufferings of this present time are not worth comparing with the glory that is to be revealed to us (Romans 8:18). Our trials are not the end of the story; they are the refining fire that shapes us for our eternal home.

3. **Joy in Sacrifice**. It was "for the joy set before Him" that Jesus endured the cross. This joy was not rooted in present circumstances but in the knowledge of the redemption and eternal joy that would come through His sacrifice. When we sacrifice, when we give of ourselves for others, we share in a tiny fragment of that joy, glimpsing the eternal weight of glory that our actions carry (2 Corinthians 4:17).

4. **Glory as the Goal**. Our ultimate goal is not the fleeting accolades of this life but the eternal glory of the next. Jesus did not seek His own glory but the glory of the One who sent Him (John 7:18). As we follow in His steps, we seek not our own glory but to glorify God, knowing that our greatest reward is in His eternal presence.

5. **Christ in Us, the Hope of Glory**. Finally, it is Christ in us that is the hope of glory (Colossians 1:27). He is our strength, our guide, and our example. In every act of love, every moment of faithfulness, every sacrifice, we see the reflection of His eternal work. And as we set our hearts on things above, where Christ

is (Colossians 3:1), we find that our lives begin to mirror the eternal hope we have in Him.

As we close this chapter, let's carry with us the image of Christ—our pioneer and perfecter of faith—as the blueprint for our lives. In focusing on Jesus, we find the courage to live lives that are "Designed for Forever," threading the hope of glory into every moment we are given.

<hr />

Blueprints Beyond Time

In the dim light of early dawn, Mauricio, a seasoned architect in his late forties, stands before a vast construction site. He's the kind of man whose deep-set eyes reflect decades of seeing structures rise from mere sketches. But today, there's an unusual tremor in his hands that hold the blueprint, a tremor that's not from the chill of the morning air.

The blueprint? That's the sword—a mere tool. The building? It's impressive, sure, but it's not the dragon. The dragon is a haunting question that breathes fire into his restless nights: "What am I leaving behind?"

Mauricio's career is a tapestry of accolades, yet the thread of purpose seems to unravel more with each passing year. His heart longs to design something that lasts, something that transcends the limits of time—his legacy.

One evening, in the quiet sanctuary of his study, an old leather-bound Bible catches his eye—a relic from his grandmother. The spine creaks as he opens it, and a verse stands out, hitting him with the force of a revelation, "So we fix our eyes not on what is seen, but on what is unseen, since what is seen is temporary, but what is unseen is eternal" (2 Corinthians 4:18).

That's the moment. The quiet explosion of realization that eternity can be woven into his life's work. In that hush, Mauricio's purpose pivots. He begins to see his work through a new lens, considering how his structures can serve communities for generations, how they can be spaces where memories are made, where beauty is celebrated, and where people find shelter not just from the elements but from the storms of life.

With a renewed spirit, Mauricio returns to his drafting table. He pours not just his skill, but his soul into his designs. He volunteers to teach young architects, imparting wisdom that will outlast his own career. He begins to build not just for today, but with an eye for tomorrow, fostering sustainability and community.

The familiar weight of the blueprint in Mauricio's hand now feels different. It's not just a set of lines and measurements; it's a map to a treasure that rust cannot corrupt. The buildings will one day age, but the lives they touch will carry on the legacy of his values.

In this new chapter, Mauricio sleeps soundly. The dragon of doubt has been slain, not by the sword, but by the hand that wields it with an eternal perspective. His legacy is now built on the foundation of eternity, each blueprint a testament to a hope that outshines the glimmer of any prestigious award.

To the onlookers who pass by his creations, it's just architecture. But to those who hear his story, Mauricio's work is a canvas where the unseen is painted with the stroke of the eternal—a whisper that says, "They get me." And perhaps, in their own quests, they'll find the courage to weave the eternal into the tapestry of their everyday lives, just as Mauricio did.

Afterword

Where Do We Go from Here?

As we close the pages of "Passion for Christ: New Beginnings," we find ourselves at a crossroads of reflection and anticipation. We've traversed through ten transformative chapters, each a stepping stone on the journey to understand what it truly means to embody a life in Christ. The road ahead beckons us to deeper discovery—one that promises not just knowledge, but the profound embrace of a living faith that reshapes every horizon.

In this voyage of the heart, we began with the seed of faith, understanding that our journey with Christ is a canvas of ongoing beginnings, each brushstroke marked by grace and growth. We've looked back to discern where we've come from and gazed forward to where we are being led. Our contemplations have taken us from the stirrings of new birth to the steady pace of maturing belief, with the Word of God as our map and the Holy Spirit as our compass.

The path ahead is one of purpose and promise. The forthcoming books in The Living Waters series will not merely expand upon the foundations laid here but will seek to delve into the depths of each chapter's theme, enriching our understanding and challenging us to grow. Each book will be a devoted exploration into the heart of living as a real Christian—fleshing out the skeletal framework we've constructed with the muscle of deeper insight and the breath of practical application.

As real Christians, our narrative is etched in eternity. The books to come will guide us in adopting an eternal perspective, inviting us to measure our moments not by the tick of a clock but by the impact they have on the eternal tapestry we're a part of. We will learn to see beyond the temporal, to set our hearts on things above, and to live in such a way that our lives echo into forever.

Knowledge, while powerful, calls for action. The subsequent volumes will empower us to live out the truths we profess, to practice the passion we preach, and to pursue Christ with a fervor that is contagious. We will explore what it means to embody the love of Jesus, to serve as He served, to give as He gave, and to love as He loved.

Our pilgrimage is not solitary. The church, the body of Christ, is where our individual stories intertwine to create a narrative of collective faith. In the books to follow, we will examine the power of fellowship, the strength found in unity, and the beauty of diversity within the body of believers.

Being a real Christian is as much about our inner transformation as it is about our external influence. We will discover how to translate our faith into action that touches lives, shapes communities, and leaves an inedible mark on the world for the glory of God.

AFTERWORD

The essence of our walk with Christ is not in the sprint but in the steadfast marathon, with eyes fixed on the prize that awaits. We will seek wisdom on persevering with joy, on nurturing a faith that lasts, and on passing the torch to future generations who will run the race set before them.

"Passion for Christ: New Beginnings" is but the prelude to a grander symphony of faith. As we look to the future, let us do so with hearts ablaze, minds renewed, and spirits willing. May we embark on each new book with the anticipation of adventurers and the wisdom of wayfarers, for in Christ, we are both.

Where do we go from here? Forward, dear reader, ever forward—into the depths of His love, the heights of His grace, and the breadth of His mission. The journey continues, and you are an integral part of this divine adventure.

"May the God of hope fill you with all joy and peace as you trust in Him, so that you may overflow with hope by the power of the Holy Spirit" (Romans 15:13).

Onward, in His name and for His glory.

God bless . . .

Lori Ann Moeszinger

Bibliography

The Living Waters Series

In the quest to explore the depths of what it truly means to be a follower of Christ, the journey often leads us to the wisdom of many who have walked the path before us. "Passion for Christ: New Beginnings," along with its ten resulting volumes in The Living Waters series, stands as a beacon, illuminating the manifold facets of Christian living.

The bibliography presented herein is not merely a list; it is a tapestry woven from the threads of countless believers, theologians, historians, and spiritual leaders whose insights and experiences have been invaluable in shaping the discourse within these pages. It serves as an atlas, guiding the earnest seeker through the landscapes of thought that have been traversed to bring these works to fruition.

Each book has been carefully selected to enrich understanding, to challenge preconceptions, and to offer solace and strength on this pilgrimage we embark upon in our daily lives. They are not just citations but conversations with the past, dialogues with the divine, and intersections with ideas that compel us towards a deeper, more profound faith.

As you peruse this bibliography, may it be more than a reference. May it become a repository of knowledge, a companion in study, and gateway to an ever-expanding world of theological richness and spiritual depth. Here lies the foundation upon which The Living Waters series is built—each book contributing to the symphony of voices that call us to live out faith with vigor and sincerity.

May this bibliography serve you as your guide and inspiration, beckoning you to further exploration, deeper understanding, and a more passionate pursuit of the One who calls us to new beginnings.

The Living Waters Series

The Living Waters Series is a beacon for all those navigating the depths of Christian faith. Encompassing a collection of eleven transformative works, including the cornerstone overview, "Passion for Christ: New Beginnings," this series is a comprehensive journey through the core tenets of Christianity. From the awakening of the soul to the embrace of eternity, each book delves into critical aspects of belief, practice, and divine experience. Readers are offered a wellspring of wisdom on salvation, baptism, the Holy Spirit, Scripture, church community, giving, evangelism, and living a life that echoes beyond time. Crafted for both new believers and seasoned disciples, The Living Water Series stands as a testament to the enduring power of faith and the relentless love of God that flows through every page.

Passion for Christ: New Beginning

In the pages of "Passion for Christ: New Beginnings," we embark on a spiritual odyssey that redefines the contours of faith and discipleship. The bibliography you hold is not just a scholarly foundation of this endeavor; it is a vibrant collection of milestones and signposts that have illuminated our path to profound truths and deeper understanding.

With each chapter, you are invited to explore the rich tapestry of theological discourse, spiritual wisdom, and transformative narratives that have influenced this work. From the early church fathers to contemporary Christian thought leaders, this curated selection represents a dialogue with history, a conversation with the divine, and a bridge to the heart of what it means to live a Christ-centered life.

Dive into this wellspring of knowledge and let it be a starting point for your own journey of discovery and passion for Christ.

Faith on Trial:
The Startling Reality of Genuine Belief

In this compelling narrative, Lori Ann Moeszinger presents a thought-provoking examination of the Christian faith's authenticity. "Faith on Trial" takes the reader on an introspective journey through the complexities of belief, challenging them to test the genuineness of their convictions against the bedrock of biblical truth. It offers an unvarnished look at the principles of salvation, the intricacies of grace, and the life-altering implications of living a faith that transcends mere intellectual assent. With its rich scriptural references and poignant personal insights, this book is an invaluable addition to the libraries of theologians, pastors, and believers seeking a deeper understanding of what it means to truly live by faith.

Drenched in Faith:
The Transformative Act of Water Baptism

In "Drenched in Faith: The Transformative Act of Water Baptism," Lori Ann Moeszinger delves into the sacred waters of Christian tradition to explore the enduring significance of baptism. With a tapestry woven from scriptural exegesis, historical context, and contemporary application, this seminal work invites believers to revisit the ancient rite and rediscover its profound impact on the individual spirit and the collective soul of the church. A pivotal addition to any theology collection, this book offers an immersive experience into the heart of baptism's transformative power.

Spirit-Filled Life:
The Unseen Force of Divine Power

"Spirit-Filled Life: The Unseen Force of Divine Power" offers a vibrant journey into the heart of the Holy Spirit's transformative power. This bibliography is a curated collection of profound works and sacred texts that inspired Moeszinger's insights, serving as a guide for those who seek to delve deeper into the mystery and majesty of the Spirit's presence in our lives. Each source is a stepping stone further into faith's river, beckoning believers to wade deeper into understanding and personal revelation.

The Bible Unbound:
Trust, Translation, and Transformation

In the compelling volume "The Bible Unbound: Trust, Translation, and Transformation," readers are invited to traverse the rich tapestry of Scripture with fresh eyes. This pivotal work by Lori Ann Moeszinger serves as both a lantern and a compass, guiding believers and seekers alike through the labyrinth of biblical translations and interpretations. With scholarly precision and a pastor's heart, Moeszinger unlocks the profound truths of Scripture, from the nuanced beauty of its languages to the transformative power of its prophecies. Each page turns with revelations that are as timeless as they are timely, offering a beacon of understanding in the quest for spiritual depth and authenticity. A truly indispensable addition to any theological library, this book is a wellspring of wisdom for those who yearn to ground their faith in the bedrock of God's Word.

BIBLIOGRAPHY

Prophets and Pulpits:
Discerning Truth in the House of God

In "Prophets and Pulpits: Discerning Truth in the House of God," delve into the vital task of discerning genuine spiritual leadership in a world brimming with voices. This essential tome not only equips believers with the tools to recognize authentic biblical teaching but also serves as a beacon, guiding through the often-turbulent waters of spiritual guidance. Grounded in scripture and imbued with practical wisdom, it's a compass for those seeking to navigate the complexities of church teachings and prophetic claims with a discerning heart and an anchored faith.

Beyond the Tithe:
The Transformative Power of Generous Faith

In the compelling read "Beyond the Tithe: The Transformative Power of Generous Faith," delve into the profound narratives and theological insights that ignite a passion for generosity. This book weaves a tapestry of biblical wisdom, historical anecdotes, and practical advice, offering a rich resource for anyone seeking to deepen their understanding of tithing and Christian giving. Each chapter is a testament to the boundless potential of a heart aligned with God's spirit of abundance. A quintessential addition to your spiritual library, this work is not merely a reference but a transformative journey through the landscape of faithful stewardship.

Heart of Abundance:
The Journey to Radical Giving and Receiving

In "Heart of Abundance: The Journey to Radical Giving and Receiving," Moeszinger delves into the transformative experience of philanthropy. This seminal work examines the essence of generosity, exploring its impact not just on the recipients but on the giver's soul. Through a compelling blend of biblical wisdom, personal anecdotes, and practical guidance, the author navigates the reader through the art of giving with a full heart. With each chapter, Moeszinger invites us to reconsider our relationship with material wealth and challenges us to open our hands and hearts in ways that ripple through eternity. This book isn't just a resource; it's a treasure map to the kind of wealth that truly enriches.

Heaven's Reach:
Drawing the Unbelieving into the Fold

In "Heaven's Reach," delve into the art of spiritual conversation and discover the transformative power of prayerful intercession. This pivotal work guides believers through the nuanced journey of engaging with non-believers, armed with compassion, wisdom, and an unshakeable faith. Each chapter unfolds rich, biblically grounded insights, equipping you to extend Heaven's touch to the those around you. A quintessential addition to any believer's library, this book not only reinforces the call to witness but empowers you to become a beacon of hope in a world searching for the divine.

Breaking Silence:
The Charge to Uphold the Faith Out Loud

In the stirring pages of "Breaking Silence: The Charge to Uphold the Faith Out Loud," readers are invited to explore the vibrant call to discipleship and witness. This pivotal work serves as a beacon, guiding the faithful through the nuanced journey of sharing their spiritual convictions with courage and love. Each chapter is a testament to the power of voice in the Christian walk, challenging believers to step out of the shadows and into the light of vocal faith. As a part of The Living Waters series, this book is an essential resource, illuminating the path for those ready to embrace their calling and transform their world through the gospel.

BIBLIOGRAPHY

Beyond the Final Breath:
The Christian's Voyage into Eternity

In "Beyond the Final Breath: The Christian's Voyage into Eternity," readers are invited on a profound exploration of life's ultimate journey—into the heart of eternity. This pivotal work navigates through the most pressing questions of the soul's destiny, the Bible's promises on eternal life, and the indelible impact of living with an everlasting perspective. Each chapter serves as a beacon, guiding through the complexities of spiritual growth, divine will, and the anticipation of what lies beyond our final earthly breath. For anyone seeking to understand the intersection of earthly existence and heavenly calling, this book is an essential addition to their spiritual library.

Author Photo © 2023 Edwin Wolfe

LORI ANN MOESZINGER, affectionately known as "L," stands at the creative helm of The Ridge Publishing Group and its diverse imprints. A prolific American author, insightful blogger, and dynamic publisher, she crafts words that resonate and narratives that captivate. Now, nestled in the scenic tranquility of Coeur d'Alene, Idaho, Lori finds inspiration in the lakeside whispers and the companionship of her husband and their two beloved dogs.

Her writing journey traverses various pseudonyms, each a distinct facet of her expansive expertise. As Ann Patterson, she delves into the intricacies of business law, distilling complex concepts into clear, actionable advice. Under the byline L. A. Moeszinger, she navigates the nuanced realms of writing, marketing, and publishing, guiding aspiring authors toward their dreams. In her biblical and personal writings, she embraces her full name, Lori Ann Moeszinger, offering reflections steeped in faith and introspection.

Yet, it's through the New Youniversity Chronicles, The Manhattan Diaries series that Lori's versatility truly shines, showcasing her storytelling prowess across a spectrum of voices, each as engaging and unique as the last. Her foundational belief in faith's power, the virtue of blessings, and the virtues of industrious dedication pulses through every line she writes.

Transcending her former life as a lawyer, Lori now revels in the freedom of expression that authorship and publishing afford—a stark contrast to the rigid confines of law. Her new chapter is one marked by a fervent passion for empowering others, a commitment to hard work, and the joy of sharing her literary gifts.

Discover the multifaced worlds Lori has woven at her websites and blog sites, or connect with her on her social media platforms where she continues to inspire, educate, and transform the written word into a shared experience of growth and discovery.

Parent Website: https://www.RidgePublishingGroup.com and

blog site https://www.PublisherAndHerWorld.com

Publisher Website: https://www.GuardiansofBiblicalTruth.com and

blog site https://www.Jesus-Says.com

Author website: https://www.LAMoeszinger.com and New Youniversity sites:

https://www.NewYouniversity.com, https://www.ManhattanChronicles.com

Bridge Website: https://www.AuthorsDoor.com and

blog site https://www.AuthorsRedDoor.com

Entertainment website: https://www.EthanFoxBooks.com and

blog site https://www.KidsStagram.com

Want More?

Welcome to Coffee with God! Jesus-Says! Dive into our blog for inspiring insights and biblical truths that deepen your faith and enrich your spiritual journey. Explore thought-provoking articles, personal testimonies, and practical guidance rooted in Scripture. Whether you're new to the faith or a lifelong believer, Jesus-Says offers wisdom and encouragement for your walk with Christ. Join our community and grow in your relationship with God!

Guardians of Biblical Truth Hub

Welcome to our Guardians of Biblical Truth Facebook page! Join our community to deepen your understanding of the Bible and live out its principles. Engage in enriching Bible studies, share faith testimonies, and connect with like-minded believers. Whether you're new to the faith or a seasoned believer, you'll find support and inspiration here. Join us today and grow in your walk with Christ.

Guardians of Biblical Truth Forum

Welcome to our Guardians of Biblical Truth Forum! Join our closed Facebook group to deepen your understanding of the Bible and strengthen your faith. Engage in enriching discussions, share personal testimonies, and connect with a supportive community of believers. Whether you're new to the faith or a seasoned believer, you'll find inspiration and encouragement here. Join us today and grow in your walk with Christ!

www.ingramcontent.com/pod-product-compliance
Lightning Source LLC
Chambersburg PA
CBHW021614120626
46545CB00001B/227